INVENTING A SCHOOL:

EXPANDING THE BOUNDARIES OF LEARNING

JANE KERN

Neapolitan Books
INVENTING A SCHOOL: Expanding the Boundaries of Learning.
Copyright © 1999 by Jane Kern

For information contact Jane Kern, Neapolitan Books, 2001 Unity Way, Naples, Florida 34112. E-mail: janerkern@aol.com

ISBN 0-9676416-1-6
LC Number 99-091510

Grateful acknowledgment is made to the following:
Stephen Tenenbaum & Company, Inc. for permission to reprint excerpt from lyrics, "Castle on a Cloud," © 1986 Alain Boublil Music Ltd. ASCAP.
Foreword by Robert David Ward.
Penny Taylor Photography.
Photoworks Photography.

Includes bibliographical references and index.

To Jack

TABLE OF CONTENTS

ACKNOWLEDGMENTS

From the first days of the planning of Seacrest School to the present, I have felt enormously supported by all the people who participated in its development. I wish to express my thanks to the following:

Lloyd and Norma Sheehan, the Founders of Seacrest, who envisioned a new school and made it possible to bring it into reality.

The children of Seacrest who are living the dream. With the exception of *Tanya* and Danny, (*The Prodigy*), the names of the children have been changed, though they will recognize themselves in their stories.

The original members of the Seacrest Board, who served for a decade with loyalty and unwavering faith, each supplying what was theirs to give—The Sheehans, Daniel Conley, Vera Lindabury, Jerry Shellabarger, and Dr. Joseph Spano.

Succeeding board members who brought new energy and talent when they were needed the most, led by the incomparable leader of leaders, Miriam "Mim" Clark, along with her wise and perceptive husband, Kenneth Clark. The Clarks rescued Seacrest when it was in danger of going under, reviving it to health and new strength. Our work could never have been accomplished without their bold and professional skill and vision in charting a new course.

The list of those who led the way is long: the teachers, whose devotion and creative genius are unsurpassed; the parents, who continue to give their time, talents, energies and resources to all the activities of Seacrest; the administrative staff, who tend the center of communications with patience, good humor, diplomacy and expertise; Pat Handwerk, our Business and Development Officer, who is as skillful under a "hard hat" as she is with the budget; and her successor, Helen Ruisi, who stepped in without missing a beat; Jennifer Amico, Assistant Head of Seacrest, who tops the list for getting things done; Caroline Randall, the Admissions Officer, who was one of the first select group of parents to take a chance with a new school.

And especially, with heartfelt gratitude, Lynne Powell, the person who worked beside me as partner and best friend, who finally inherited my job as Head of Seacrest, continuing to fashion the dream.

The tutors for extraordinary service.

Eleanor Toledo and her custodial staff for bringing order out of chaos. The grounds-keepers who know the importance of a safe and beautiful outdoor environment.

The spouses, who were railroaded into service to accomplish all the things we could not manage.

The many people in the surrounding community of Naples, who donated their resources and opened their doors to help teach the students. Although some of the names in the book have been changed in the interest of professional ethics, I wish to thank Frank Gazzola, Pat Warren, the late David Thoburn, and James Elkins, who helped and supported through times of crisis.

My colleagues in the public schools, who gave me experience and friendship, and who lent me support in the planning of Seacrest.

All my friends in the Florida Kindergarten Council and the Florida Council of Independent Schools, for their support of Seacrest and for all the meetings, retreats, and visits to other schools we shared.

The person who acted as my editor during the initial draft, Eleanor Sommer, for good-natured guidance in managing to tap into the way I wanted the story told, always patient with awkward phrases and wordy paragraphs, seeing me through to the end despite numerous and lengthy interruptions. Barbara Barton, for her generosity in lending me her time and expertise in technical assistance. Ann Seltz, Steven Alm, and Raymond Fowler for their thorough attention to both detail and substance in reading my manuscript, and for their valuable advice.

Dr. Brugh Joy, the one I think of as my Master Teacher. I cannot imagine moving through the patterns and rhythms of my life without his wise counsel. Sometimes I think he knows me better than I know myself.

Suzanne Timken, my friend and kindred spirit, for extraordinary support and encouragement during the best and worst of times.

All my teachers, through all time, with special thanks to Clara Pederson, Bill Martin, Jr., Roy Fairfield, Eric Jensen, and Susan Dietz. Bud Gardner, Dan Poynter, Kenneth Davis, Jack Canfield, and other renowned professionals at the Maui Writer's Retreat, for the ultimate experience in "learning by doing."

My kinfolks who gave me the rich heritage of my Southern roots. My childhood friends and contemporary cronies, Ed Givhan and David Ward, for shared stories and e-mail musing.

Bill Rogers, historian, editor, and perfect person for helping me prepare the manuscript for publishing.

Jack's and my combined family of nine, their spouses, and our children's children, with all my love and appreciation.

Most of all, my husband, Jack. There are no words to express my love and gratitude for all that he does and for all that he is. He knows, without my telling him.

FOREWORD

This is a book about a school in Naples, Florida, called Seacrest. It is the story of how that school was conceived and slowly built, grade added upon grade like the rings that mark the growth cycles of trees, varying in size with the benefits or hardships of the seasons. Since it is a story about the building of a school it is equally the story of an adventure in education and thus, irreducible, it is the story of teachers. It is the tritest of truisms that good schools demand good teachers. Short of far more than we presently know, that is a useless statement. No one has yet invented "The Good Teacher Test" where a passing score guarantees not simply the transference of knowledge but the excitement in learning that changes individual lives and may in fact change both society and civilization.

So what qualities, what quirks of personality, what mental configurations produce good and often great teachers? The answers to such questions come from our own experience which suggests that we are looking less for universal standards than for some qualities of at least broad applicability.

My answer to Jane's questions (and she is a indefatigable questioner) was to describe the best teacher that I ever had. When I was a raw and half-formed student at Auburn many years ago I took a course in history entitled "The New South." And that is where I first met Jack Kendrick. Oh boy! This was not the same old stuff! Here was the most sophisticated, cosmopolitan, urbane, brilliant teacher that I had ever imagined. Oh, yes, I learned the sad content and strange events of Southern history, but I heard it illuminated with meaning, I saw connections I had never dreamed of — I saw the form, the shape and the substance of social forms and relationships. With the "hard items" we received a fitted box to hold everything. Jack taught a "world view," a picture of life in its beauty and its utter squalor. It did not matter what the content of the course was. He was teaching reality, he was teaching us the present by showing us the past. He was trying to explain how life works, how logic and illogic operate — the endless opera of ignorance and intellect locked in ceaseless battle.

It was Jack Kendrick who urged me and my great friend Bill Rogers to go to Chapel Hill — I suppose he saw some possible hope for the two of us. We would have headed for Mars if he had recommended it. He was the greatest teacher that I ever had. He changed my life because he showed me a way to think, the value of doubting, the supreme delight in finding connections that made sense out of the senseless piles of data. I do not think that Jack ever considered himself a great success as a teacher. He never seemed to realize what extraordinary powers that he possessed, abilities given to all too few of us.

Teachers come in two broad groups: there are the reciters and explainers of information and they have their place and their utility. And there are the ones who can make your brain sing with the wonder of its power and its endless abilities. How nice it would be to go back and tell such people what they really meant to us — to tell them how rare and precious they really were, to explain that what they saw as a career of mediocrity hid the greatest triumphs they and others ever could have wished for.

Could we have Seacrests everywhere? Perhaps we never can. Can we have the ideas and the creativity and the joy of learning that it represents? It's worth our deepest concern — and it's getting later every day.

Robert David Ward
Professor Emeritus of History
Georgia Southern University

PREFACE

This is a book for people who have a passion for learning—for those who have a compelling need to find better ways of managing their lives for themselves and for their children. The book examines learning, teaching, and leading through first-hand experiences in building a new school from the ground up. Moving beyond the fragmented compartments of a typical school setting, the best of tradition is synthesized with cutting edge research and common sense to develop a workable, balanced approach to learning. For people who wonder if there are authentic formats for schools to provide a comprehensive program that fosters the excitement of learning, this book shows how teachers, parents, students, and leaders used their particular strengths in forming a community of learners.

The results of this collective achievement came from leaders, teachers, and parents who worked together. They were unhampered by bureaucracy in using the best of who and what we are—to stay in the "beginner's mind" in continuing to grow and learn in an open-ended journey. The book is not a technical study. The methods described in initiating and developing a new school are not presented as a blueprint for education. Yet, it provides a road map for the processes we used to plan and chart our course of action as we undertook the challenge of opening to a larger view of learning.

For leaders who are interested in a collaborative approach for organizations, the book offers ideas that worked for us as the school evolved. For teachers who are looking for more personally satisfying practices to challenge the minds of students, there are many examples of how we used a variety of approaches. For parents who want their children to become skilled in the fundamentals and at the same time experience the joy of expanded, meaningful learning, I hope the story of Seacrest will serve as a useful reference.

The initiation and development of a new independent school grew out of a broad spectrum of experiences gained in many different public schools. It pulled together years of learning the craft of teaching, studying the research, trying to make sense out of all that I learned about teaching, learning, and leading. An avid student of learning theory, I am always excited by new ideas for educational improvement, ready to put them into action.

Initially, I had no purpose in mind other than to write down the true story of Seacrest School. When an editor and professionals outside the field of education read the first draft for critical review, they believed the book held potential value not only for educators but for a wider audience as well. Although the story takes place in an independent school, most of the things that happen in the classroom are outgrowths of ideas from teachers, most of whom worked in public schools. Prior to my work at Seacrest, my background, training, and professional career were accrued in the public sector. My belief in public schools remains steadfast—not because of the way they are typically run, but because of the teachers. As with any organization, the end result depends on the people within it who do the work. A great teacher is able to bring out the best in students regardless of external factors. So, the book is about the courage, commitment, and unique gifts of people who find ways to use their own ingenuity and power to inspire, encourage, and communicate.

Today, more than ever before, everyone seems to have an idea about how to best educate our young; yet there is considerable confusion about how to make it happen. Certainly, parents want their children to receive the best education possible, but parents hold widely different views about what a good education means. Information in textbooks reflects the pressures wielded by special interest groups. Political agencies call for reforms and national standards, with higher test scores as the objective. Business corporations have entered the educational arena, promising better results. Reforms, national agendas, and mandates from the top come and go with little substantive change.

For most of the twentieth century, people have searched for one best way to structure schools. An astonishing array of organizational designs and techniques have made their way into selected schools across the nation. Even though many innovative ideas through the past decades are based on solid, well-defined research, even the best new programs are not around long enough to make a lasting change. Despite all the research on how people learn best, the "back-to-basics" movement prevails. An obsolete educational system is left in the wake of a drastically altered society.

Our best hope for positive, lasting change in education may well come from small grassroots efforts—one school at a time. Building a community of learners with a common vision implies that each member of the community has a special attribute or insight to contribute. Rather than trying to create a model in which teachers and students become clones of each other, why not acknowledge our *differences* as a source of strength and balance?

Early in the development of my career as an educator, I began to notice the contrasts among my colleagues. We were all using the identical curriculum, under the same conditions, trained to use an equivalent set of techniques for similar goals; yet the differences among us were distinct and observable. Everyone, including the children, knew that Mr. Johnson lectured for twenty minutes, assigned pages from the text and end of chapter questions for homework. Mrs. Davis held spirited discussions, leading her students to probe beneath the surface for divergent possibilities. Miss Edward's class did projects. The kids in Mr. Peterson's class got away with murder.

We are trained to believe that every child is unique with distinct differences and talents. Are those differences educated out of us by the time we reach adulthood? In my opinion, no. No matter how hard we try to model ourselves to be like those we admire, our uniqueness is with us forever. We become apprentices to learn the craft of our profession, integrating the skills that serve to strengthen and complement our authentic individuality.

Several years after I accepted the challenge to plan and develop Seacrest School, I came to know, beyond a shadow of doubt, that over and above all the methods, approaches, theories, and new programs we used in designing a school from the ground up, it was the *people* who made the critical difference in forming this venture into a community of learners.

One of the predominant themes of the book is the way my own perceptions and attitudes changed as Seacrest evolved. Nothing in my years of experience or training prepared me for all the unfamiliar circumstances I would face on a daily basis as the new school materialized. I was continually awed by the way teachers came up with ingenious solutions for obstacles that seemed insurmountable. I have learned much about the power of shared leadership and the diversity of talents that each person can bring to the collective when the freedom to act is set into motion.

Deborah Meier, the founder of successful small public schools in East Harlem, insists that there cannot be just one system of learning and teaching that works for all. She writes, "Every school must have the power and the responsibility to select and design its own particulars and thus to surround all young people with powerful adults who are in a position to act on their behalf in open and publicly responsible ways." [Deborah Meier, "Can the Odds Be Changed?", *Phi Delta Kappan*, January, 1998, p. 359.] She believes, as I do, that balance comes from diversity with the freedom to make responsible decisions. Common sense tells us that teachers are more likely to be responsive to self-growth when they are enabled to be who they are and to do what they do best.

As the first outline of the book evolved, it became obvious that this would not be another how-to cookbook with recipes for educating children. It is not about new remedies or reforms or new systems of learning. The market is filled with self-help books designed with steps, keys, and secrets for success, and many of them sit on my shelves, dog-eared and underlined. In contrast, the book here is not prescriptive in nature. It could have been entitled after one of the talismans I keep in my work space that says, *Nothing Here is Written in Stone*, because of my resistance to fixed boundaries and labels. I have lived long enough to cast a skeptical eye on any one system that claims to have *the* answer to education.

When people ask me what kind of school Seacrest is, I cannot give them a pat answer. It is not an alternative school. To me, it is just an independent school, and I choose not to attach labels to it. The story of Seacrest School is not intended to portray one big happy family, with never a word of dissent. There were times when I wondered if the school and everyone in it were plummeting toward disaster. Positive communication was not always the rule of the day. If some of the descriptions of individuals sound too good to be believable, it is because I have focused on the best that they have demonstrated and proved through time. All too often, the accomplishments of the people within the organization go unrecognized.

Recently, I had the opportunity to hear Frank McCourt, whose book, *Angela's Ashes* has won international acclaim. He said his breakthrough to success as a teacher came only after he learned to teach in his own voice.

I hope this book will encourage people to acknowledge their truest strengths, and to use their own voice, to find in themselves their own power to be their best. The person who says, "My boss won't let me" needs to think again. There are countless ways to follow the rules and still work in the way that is true to your nature. *Inventing a School* points to some of the ways that worked for us. But then, you need to look within to find your own way.

As the story unfolds, I suggest that you look back on your journey as a learner. What events changed your life? Who were your best teachers, and why? What were your greatest challenges, and how did you overcome them? What prevented you from exercising your natural talents? How would you change your work environment? What is your vision for the future? Use the stories in *Inventing a School* to help you question, imagine, and consider a larger, broader range of learning and leading. Expand the concept of "school" as a building that occupies a space in a particular location containing a specific number of students. Think of school as a timeless journey, beyond the reach of current trends, interweaving the events and relationships of your life as a whole.

Use the examples of leadership, parent participation, and learning as a channel to provoke questions about your perceptions, beliefs, and values as an individual and as a member of a group. Whether you are a parent who is concerned about your child's education, a teacher who works in a public or private school, a community leader in an urban or rural setting, or a principal in a large school district, I hope you will find ideas that are worth thinking about. There are many examples that can be adapted to your particular circumstances if you so choose.

Like a family, each school has its own distinct personality, molded by the people within it. The ways in which children learn are more effective when teachers are supported in making decisions and choices. If this support is not available, there are other avenues and options that can be used by the teacher with initiative and resourcefulness.

This belief is borne out by the hundreds of leaders, teachers, and parents I have known from all types of schools—inner city, urban and country, public, private, parochial. Great learning can come in a multiplicity of ways, and it is often found outside the confines of schools. Just as it is rare to find abrupt limits in nature, true learning is indifferent to boundaries.

The signals of excellence can be recognized by the reciprocal relationship between teacher, student, and the landscape of discovery. We recognize excellence by the exquisite artistry of the teacher who knows how to captivate the imagination and stimulate inquiry. For those who can accept the idea of learning and teaching as continual, active change, *Inventing a School* pays tribute to the men and women who are totally involved with what they do. They are fully immersed in the present, creating new pathways to successful, joyful learning, meeting each challenge with total commitment.

Think of the story of Seacrest as an invitation to look behind the scenes of a new school, as if I am walking with you, sharing our adventures. Look for the uniquely human qualities that defy strict definitions. Look beyond the boundaries and between the lines to the faces of children who learn by invention and imagination, in a place where learning is celebrated.

I find the great thing in this world is not so much where we stand, as in what direction we are moving: To reach the port of heaven, we must sail sometimes with the wind and sometimes against it but we must sail, and not drift, nor lie at anchor.

Oliver Wendell Holmes

INTRODUCTION

On a crisp December day, in a Minnesota hospital room, an incredibly tiny baby girl, born four- and-a-half hours earlier, locked her dark eyes with mine. We stared at each other as if peering into mirrors of our own souls. I was entrained in a timeless, motionless moment in which nothing existed outside the smells and feel of the little ball of new skin wrapped in the softness of a blanket and held in the crook of my left arm. I gazed at her head, framed with downy wisps of dark hair, as her perfectly formed miniature hand clutched my finger with surprising strength.

I was spellbound by the depth of wonderment induced by this initial communication with my first grandchild, who would later that day be named Hannah Jane. Hannah Jane, the first born of my first born. I wondered what she would be like, who she would become. What adventures would she have? What sorrows and joys and challenges? What talents would she develop? Would she find this planet to be a friendly place? Would she learn the values of kindness, honesty, integrity, and service to others?

I wondered what her school would be like—if it would be a place where she could experience the excitement of learning and creating with the freedom to grow and explore in a safe, nurturing environment; a place where she would learn the importance of responsibility and self-discipline.

The birth of my first grandchild took place in 1990, seven years after the birth of Seacrest School. Becoming a grandmother gave new meaning to my work that was underway in developing a new school; a system of learning and growing that provides the very ideas that I aspired for my new granddaughter that cold Minnesota day in 1990.

Told here is the story of that school, Seacrest School, conceived, born, and cultivated as a place where children experience the excitement and joy of learning; where each day offers fresh new possibilities to be tried, touched, tasted, and tested. It is an honest story, told without the use of educational jargon. The story is based on my own experiences and perceptions, so it naturally contains my own biases and beliefs.

Because I am an eternal student, much of my writing has been carefully documented with the research studies, books, articles, and opinions of others. The opportunity to tell the story of Seacrest from my personal perspective is both exciting and intimidating. The process of letting go of the need for acceptance and to write from my own insight is for me a considerable departure and a significant leap in acknowledging what I truly believe. Taking the time to pull together my experiences and knowledge and to synthesize them into an interconnected whole has been much like weaving a tapestry of multiple strands of color and textures. The journey of a new school was set into motion when a few small strands of a dream were woven into reality.

I

FOUNDATIONS

The Journey Begins

CHAPTER I

The Journey Begins

On September 3, 1983, the morning dawned bright and beautiful in Naples, Florida. A small group of anxious young parents brought their three-and four-year-old children to a new school. This was more than the first day of school. This was truly *the first day of a school*. It was the birth of Seacrest, a school that promised the collected ideas and aspirations for a new vision of education and learning.

On that day, Seacrest was charged with the care, nurturing, and education of eighteen children who comprised its first students. New grades would be added each year, and prekindergarten was phase one in the sequence. At that time there were only two teachers: an innovative educator named Becky Herrman and I. It was our task to initiate these eager learners into the world of "school."

Whether or not they knew it, the adventuresome explorers and their parents were part of the cast that was gathered that day to launch a dream into reality. That dream continues to this day to unfold and expand. The school currently has a student enrollment of 350, from preschool through eighth-grade middle school.

The idea for Seacrest emerged from earlier conversations with Lloyd and Norma Sheehan. Lloyd was a real estate developer, a visionary and philanthropist who had an abiding interest in helping children and teenagers. For a number of years the Sheehans had thought of starting a school where young people would discover how to tap their own potential and inner resources, a school in which students would progress through the years experiencing the joy of successful learning. They were interested in creating a school that was independent, one that was not tied to restraining external influences. As we talked, the seed of an idea began to form.

After several months of conversations, the ideas began to take shape. Our plan was to begin with preschool, adding grades each year up through eighth-grade, with the possibility of a high school in the distant future. We brought in a consultant, Dr. Clint Van Nagel, who helped us develop the framework of a curriculum. I was formally offered the challenge to plan, implement, and develop a new school in the fall of 1982. This is the story of the making of that school—from the bricks and mortar to the gathering of the children, parents, teachers, a small board of advisors, and people from the community to help make it happen. It is about what it takes to give birth to a school.

Searching for the best ways to teach and learn has been a lifelong goal for me. Most of my experiences had been within the context of already existing systems and, despite my capacity and love for creating new programs, any changes still had to take place within the existing parameters. The opportunity to create my own school with total freedom seemed like the dream of a lifetime.

The couple who became the founders of Seacrest held a dream as well. The Sheehans had envisioned a school where children would be encouraged to "go inside and look for their own answers within." They believed that each child has a deep inner wisdom, a part that *knows,* and they also believed that children can be taught to access this *knower.* Their notion that learning takes place by drawing out from within is the same concept taught by many of the world's great teachers and philosophers since ancient times.

The Sheehans also believed that school should be a happy place where learning should be a joyful process. This seems like such an inherent right of children, and yet, there are too many examples where learning is a dull and cheerless daily grind.

One Sunday afternoon in 1982, Lloyd and Norma Sheehan met with my husband Jack and me in our living room to give the school a name and to select our board members. After a period of animated discussion, someone came up with "Seacrest," which triggered an instant agreement. Our choices of candidates for the Seacrest Board were settled just as easily.

The first priority was to select people who would be attuned to our goals. We also wanted a small group of people with expertise in specific areas who would be easy to work with. Dan Conley was selected because he was an attorney who worked closely with Mr. Sheehan. Vera Lindabury was a mutual friend, appreciated and admired by everyone who knew her. The Sheehans had talked with Vera and her husband, Bob, for a number of years about their dream of beginning a school, and we knew that she would be fully committed to the idea.

Joseph Spano, a highly regarded physician, was also a friend who we felt would share the ideals of Seacrest. Jerry Shellabarger was well known and a respected business leader in the community, and we hoped he would join our group. When we presented our plans to the prospective members, they seemed enthusiastic about the project, and they all agreed to serve on the board.

Our informal and infrequent meetings were held in each other's homes. Decisions were made through a consensus from discussions, with no Robert's Rules of Order or voting. Usually, the meetings consisted of a summary of my progress, after which I would ask for whatever help I needed from individual members.

Mr. Sheehan had generously offered his financial backing for Seacrest, and I met with him frequently to discuss the budgetary needs as they developed. The meetings were marked by an easy, always amiable spirit of cooperation and good humor. Our talks always concluded with a discussion about the philosophy of the school.

Seacrest was incorporated as an independent, nonprofit school. The word "independent" held a special meaning for me, because it signified freedom to act and make decisions, and to move beyond traditional limits, unhampered by rules dictated by external sources. I believe all our board members felt the same sense of satisfaction in the way we worked and bonded together.

As the seeds of building a new school grew, questions that had plagued me throughout my career as an educator began to surface. New knowledge is generated and doubled every few years, so I wondered what educators could do to cope. Why should there continue to be such a wide gap between what we know about learning and what actually happens in the classroom?

I often hear over dinner conversations that the world would be better off if people would just return to the "good old days." The truth is, education has not changed all that much in the last fifty or sixty years. Despite the addition of the latest technology into the schools, including a host of audio visual aids, electronic gadgets, and beautifully bound textbooks, the things teachers teach and how they teach is pretty much the same as decades ago.

Deborah Meier, in an article entitled, "Drop the False Image of Education's Golden Past," reminds us that until World War II the average American did not graduate from high school but instead left school to work. Even students bound for college rarely took more than two years of high school math, history, or science. In the same article, Meier reported on a recent study that compared seventeen-year-olds from the 1930s with those of today in answering questions about the names of presidents, dates of wars, laws of science, and other basic information. The study showed virtually no change in the past fifty years, despite the fact that the students tested in those earlier years were overall a far more elite group than today's general student body.

A friend of mine in his sixties, a college graduate who had achieved great success in business, was known for his scathing attacks on the current state of schools. His answer to education was to go back to the way he was taught. Yet, every letter I received from him was peppered with dozens of grammatical and spelling errors—more than could be attributed to typographical slips. It is even more depressing to receive applications from *teachers* with errors in spelling or grammar. No less surprising is to hear flagrantly ungrammatical phrases spoken by professionals, or to observe adults of any age who are unable to make change when the computerized cash register goes down.

Despite all the rhetoric, research, and reforms through the years, the old systems are still in place. Reforms have not worked. Education seems stuck in a time warp. Meanwhile, major changes in the rest of the world are escalating, all too often in a chaotic and turbulent fashion. With the third millennium drawing near, it is time for schools to move from outmoded reforms to a new form—to transform and transcend in ways that prepare future generations to create a better, healthier society.

Thinking about these issues, I looked backwards over my own journey, where I came from, where I am, and reflected on what I have learned.

CHAPTER 2

First Lessons

My own schooling took place in Montevallo, a small college town in central Alabama, in a public school that was also the laboratory school for what was then a state college for women. My particular school came under the influence of Dewey's Progressive Education era, when everything had to be discovered, experienced, and integrated.

I "progressed" through the years from nursery school through high school with no grades, no final exams, no isolated drills, and no rules or facts to be learned in phonics, spelling, handwriting, history, geography, or math. Because rote memorization was considered "low level learning," we were never required to memorize anything.

We had great experiences puttering around in the college chemistry lab, creating wonderful images out of clay, taking nature walks, playing musical instruments, acting, dancing, swimming, and discussing world events and problems. The major goal was for us to be well adjusted and to learn to work together democratically as a group. We did a lot of voting to decide things.

Somehow most of us learned to read and develop a love for books, and we were able to express our ideas verbally or in writing. We developed a lifelong appreciation for physical activities, the arts, sciences, and humanities. And we most definitely experienced the joy of learning.

Imagine the shock when this group entered college. Our well-adjusted and well-rounded lives were abruptly and forever changed. We were thrust into a confusing maze of competition, grade-point averages, examinations, and lengthy assignments from obscure textbooks. We heard lectures delivered by professors from notes yellowed with age. They could have cared less about individualized differences or interrelated learning.

Memorizing facts was a major challenge, since we had never learned to memorize and we did not know any facts. The lecture—delivered in stuffy halls filled with hundreds of students who seemed to understand what was being presented—was the standard means of imparting information. The information seemed to change little from year to year. Most of the students I knew had easy access to antiquated final exams that were used over and over through the years and filed away for future use in sorority and fraternity houses.

Although I learned to play the game of college and its "real world" of learning, I emerged with a clear conviction that a more balanced approach between my earlier education and college experiences was needed. The conviction was stored away in my brain for use in the future along with other bits and pieces of information mentally filed under the heading of "What not to do when I'm a teacher."

During my junior year of college, I married and found myself on the way to my new husband's home in North Dakota. My limited knowledge of geography was further restricted by my lack of travel. Never having been north of Aunt Winnie's house in Beechgrove, Tennessee, I had no real notion of where I was headed.

After driving north through endless stretches of Iowa corn fields, and observing the color of the earth turn from the familiar red clay of Alabama to deep, chocolate brown, we finally arrived in North Dakota. There I encountered mile after mile of flat, golden, windswept rows of wheat fields that stretched ahead to the horizon. Looming up from the distance like a skyscraper, the vast landscape was broken by a narrow, tall metal structure, which my husband said was a grain elevator. Crystalline clear skies above appeared immense and foreign, unlike the low hanging clouds of southern skies that usually sat on the horizon, heavy with un-spilled rain.

Driving into the outskirts of my husband's hometown, a small hard pit of homesickness formed in my stomach as the stark reality of my new existence registered. The hundred-year-old oak trees that arched over the shady streets of my childhood seemed of another world. The familiar roads winding through lush green hills covered over with kudzu were replaced by flat terrain, squared off by straight roads. At a glance I recognized that there were no run-down shacks with rusted tin roofs here; no chickens scratching through haphazard patches of gardens overgrown with Johnson grass; no graceful residences of brick or colonial structures. There were no magnolia trees or hedges gone wild. The familiar thick, musky smells of damp vegetation were replaced by the scent of dry, acrid dust.

A cloud of black dust swept before us with swirling gusts of wind as we drove into this tiny prairie community of two-hundred people, all of Norwegian ancestry except for one lone Swede. A few sparse trees and sturdy frame houses led to the unpaved main street consisting of one grocery store, two restaurants, a bank, a Lutheran church, a filling station operated by the Swede, and several bars and pool halls. I saw no multicolored faces among the small groups of people gathered in front of the small, neat storefronts. Everyone had names like Peterson or Torgeson or Bjornson or Swenson.

My new Norwegian family took me in with good humor. Before long I was immersed in a culture of meat and potatoes, a strong work ethic, and fiercely guarded family values. No one there seemed to know about black-eyed peas, butter beans, collard greens, or biscuits and gravy. I spent the summer learning to bake Scandinavian pastries and teaching swimming in an icy cold lake in temperatures that rarely rose above sixty-five degrees.

The following fall, I joined my husband in Augsberg, Germany, where he was stationed as an army officer. After a brief stay in Augsberg, we returned to civilian life in North Dakota where I enrolled in the university to complete a major in music. The summer winds had turned to icy harsh blusters, cutting into my face like sharp crystals. Snow drifts piled as high as telephone wires. Staying on my feet while walking across the frozen grounds of the campus was a major accomplishment and learning to drive on ice-glazed roads was even more of a challenge.

Life in the Dakotas demands ruggedness. I gradually became accustomed to the forty-below-zero weather and learned to appreciate the unique qualities of the people who live there. I had caught the spirit of the land and its people. Shoveling snow, cleaning and scrubbing, baking and socializing held a down-to-earth, genuinely satisfying sense of accomplishment for me.

The following year, I began my career as a fledgling teacher and as any beginning teacher can testify, that was when my *real* initiation began.

CHAPTER 3

Surviving the System

At age twenty-two, I had my first classroom teaching experience: a junior high school music teacher. My tenure began and ended in the small town of Sisseton on a Sioux Indian reservation in South Dakota. There was no question that I was a failure that first year. I knew it and the kids knew it. The principal did not seem to realize he had hired someone with no earthly idea how to control seventy pubescent teenagers, much less teach them any music. His lack of awareness of my floundering was because he never entered the music room, and never experienced the total bedlam and chaos created by my students and me. I went to school each morning with a stomachache, wondering how I would get through the day. That was the year I decided to start my family, and my first child was born in the spring. The labor pains were nothing compared to the pain of my daily failure as a teacher, and I was happy that motherhood provided me with an honorable means of escape.

A few years and two children later I went back to school, enrolling in the University of North Dakota at Grand Forks, to get a degree in elementary education. By that time I had gained a little maturity, and I was privileged to have a professor, Clara Pederson, who gave me both inspiration and a solid background in teaching methods and classroom management.

Following graduation, I was offered a job teaching third-grade at Nathan Twining School at Grand Forks Air Force Base. The school was set in the midst of frozen tundra fourteen miles from town. As I prepared the first lessons, my memory flashed back to third-grade and Miss Jones. I remembered sitting at her feet, listening with rapt attention to *The Wizard of Oz*. Miss Jones wore brown alligator pumps that squeaked with a certain elegance and authority when she walked. Her dark hair was brushed into a chignon, which emphasized her Romanesque nose and features.

Miss Jones was no pushover, but she never raised her voice. I remember thinking to myself at age eight that when I grew up I would teach third grade and wear brown alligator shoes and read *The Wizard of Oz* to my class. Eighteen years later, I confidently strode into my very own third-grade classroom wearing a brand-new pair of fake alligator pumps with my own copy of *The Wizard of Oz* tucked under my arm.

This time I was armed for success with lesson plans so detailed and creative that they could have been framed in the halls of any college of education as examples of excellence. My intention was to become the best teacher the world had ever known. My preparations extended to taking the advice of one of my professors to eradicate my Alabama drawl, so that "my words would be understood." Through painstaking practice, I learned to put endings on all my spoken words and to eliminate phrases like "Shoowa nuff?" and to add or drop vowels and consonants in what I hoped were the correct places.

Because it was an air force base school, when my thirty-seven third-graders filed into my classroom, most of them came from somewhere else and over half from southern states. About a third of the children were black and, having grown up surrounded with the customs and culture of the Deep South, I could not help noticing the absence of racial prejudice among them. Still, I soon discovered that rank mattered, especially among the children of military families, and my young students lost no time in letting me know which ones were the sons and daughters of the highest ranking officers.

As I set about organizing the children into the three prescribed reading and math groups, I discovered they did not fit into the three prescribed groups, or even four or five groups. Even though my university professors had emphasized the importance of attending to individual differences, no one had taught me exactly how I was supposed to do that with thirty-seven children.

The difficulty may have been based in part by a nagging resistance to sorting children into "slow," "average," or "fast" categories. Even though the groups might have been named "Bluebirds" or "Dolphins," children quickly see through such thinly disguised labels. Besides, they already knew who were the fastest readers or who needed more help with math, and who were the artists, the scientists, or the athletes among them. Surely there were better ways to serve children's needs.

My decision to try something new was approved by my principal. Luckily, he believed I was a capable and talented teacher since my transcripts showed all A's in education courses, and he was not privy to my previous failure as a music teacher. He agreed that I could initiate a new type of instruction, more on the order of a quasi-individualized plan that included the whole class, short-term grouping patterns, and individualized instruction based on specific purposes. I spent several weeks poring over books, hoping to gain insight about how to organize my classroom. The search yielded meager results. Most of the books either contained the cut and dried basic skills approach or stressed the other extreme, similar to my childhood schooling.

It was important to me that these young students learn the basics, and further, to stretch themselves and become independent thinkers with interests in the arts, science, and literature. They also needed a teacher who was able to manage a peaceful and calm learning environment. My dilemma? How to keep the kids from going berserk in the process of initiating a new style of classroom management. Slowly, I pieced together my own eclectic system, and together my class and I began an astonishing journey of learning.

Throughout that year, at least six hours each evening were spent in planning for the next day, and the entire weekend seemed concentrated on getting ready for the week to come. The preparations not only included all the subject matter of what was to be taught but endless details and checklists of specific skills each student needed. Then, there were the tasks of deciding how it would be accomplished—who did what and how did they do it? Intricate schedules were devised for individuals and small, short term groups for specific purposes. Large blocks of time were mapped out for dozens of activities while I worked with groups or individuals. Like all elementary teachers, I had to plan, create, and arrange the materials for instant action.

It was time consuming, but it worked. My students and I experienced the thrill of a cooperative adventure. They progressed and achieved at a higher rate than I had expected. Best of all, they learned to be independent little people who knew how to move into their next task or project without my standing over them.

Other teachers in the school system, and subsequently, from around the state, began to come and observe and to try out their own adaptations of the program. Teachers seemed eager to try something created and implemented by a fellow colleague, a person who knew first-hand the daily challenges in the classroom.

In those days, the luxury of aids or specialists or built-in planning periods did not exist. As elementary school teachers, we were expected to teach all the academics plus physical education, art, and music. In addition, we each took our turn with hall duty, bus duty, and lunch duty.

These early years strengthened my notion that perhaps there were not any proven, surefire ways to teach children. They also strengthened my conviction that while small classes, a period of planning time during the school day, and specialists to teach certain subjects are of great benefit to a teacher, they do not guarantee the creation of great schools, higher achievement scores, or a better learning environment for students. Rather, it is what takes place *within* the space—what happens between teacher and student— that is important.

CHAPTER 4

Moving On

Over the next decade, rich and varied experiences as an educator and learner opened up still more questions than answers for me. In 1968, a move to Mankato, Minnesota, felt like stepping into an oasis, with its profusion of crystal clear lakes banked by evergreens and timberland. There were hills, and lush green valleys, and ravines thick with tangled vines and vegetation.

My inclination for change and new discoveries led the way for a wide range of teaching experiences, with children from varied backgrounds and requirements, one being a federally funded program for children with severe learning difficulties. Most had emotional problems as well. My team teacher and I used every ounce of our combined energy and ingenuity in helping these children catch on, catch up, unblock, and unlock hidden potentiality. We celebrated the tiniest victories and took every setback personally. It was during this period when I learned that humor is a prerequisite to maintaining sanity. Time and again, Diane, my zany, talented team teacher, rescued me from near despair by her hilarious antics.

Other Minnesota assignments included new approaches and innovations in classroom management. My teammates, Jean and Beth and I devised a new system for using time, space, materials, and groups.

When we decided to revamp our fourth-grade program, the three of us spent a weekend in retreat. We began our task with a question: How could we use our time, space, materials, and strengths to the best possible advantage?

Large blocks of time were mapped out in the mornings for teaching small groups and individuals, with multiple activities planned for independent student work. After the fourth-graders completed specific required assignments, they had a number of choices for follow-up practice and independent activities. Children could work alone or in groups from any of the three classes, provided they could work together responsibly.

We turned our small teacher planning space into an audiovisual lab where children could use various machines for viewing, listening, or creating a project. Jean, Beth, and I planned our teaching schedules to reflect our particular strengths and interests. For example, Jean was the resource person for social studies. She transformed her classroom into a workshop for hands-on activities that related to history, geography, government, and culture. Beth supervised the math program, interweaving music, learning games and apparatus connected to units in mathematics. I was the resource teacher for language arts and science, with centers for reading, writing, basic skills, and science activities.

There were times when all three groups came together for specific presentations. Part of the day, we worked alone with our own classes. This arrangement was not departmentalized in the usual sense. It was more of an expanded version of the self-contained classroom, with each of us retaining responsibility for our classes. We simply worked together to create a broader range of resources, using our time, space, materials, and strengths in a more efficient way.

The plan could not have worked without the commitment, respect, and flexibility of our team; nor could it have taken place without the full support of Mary Lou, our principal. I was fortunate throughout my teaching experience to work with principals who allowed me to develop new ways of managing my classroom—to take risks, to make mistakes, and to try different approaches. It is especially satisfying when a team of compatible minds use each others' abilities and ideas in creating an original course of action.

In 1976, I began a whole new life, one which would be filled with high adventure. I had been divorced and a single parent of three children for several years. When the two older ones, Mary Jane and Steven, entered college, my youngest son, Kevin, was nine. It seemed to be a good time to move to the best place in the world. Having no idea where that place was, a picture in a travel magazine of a beautiful white stretch of beach, located on the Gulf of Mexico in Southwest Florida captured my attention. In a flash of insight, I thought, "That's where we'll live." Several months later, I packed up Kevin, my golf clubs, and summer clothes and moved to Naples.

As a supervisor in the Collier County Public Schools, I worked with the federally funded program for children of migrant farm workers. I traveled around the county to schools in Naples and Marco Island, working at least three days a week in the predominantly migrant community of Immokalee.

I loved it all—the teachers, tutors and administrators, and most of all, the migrant kids, from the three-year-olds to the high school seniors. The older students especially seemed to appreciate whatever we did for them, and they always addressed their teachers with great respect.

The mixtures and contrasting cultures of my new community were intriguing: the affluent elite society and the pride and poverty of the migrant families; the multimillion dollar mansions and dilapidated shacks; the non-English-speaking working alongside blacks and Caucasians. The Catholic nuns and the Baptist preacher became my friends. I learned where to find diesel fuel for my Volkswagen Rabbit anywhere in the county and where to go for the best southern or Hispanic or "soul-food" lunches.

My new condominium and my palm trees and the beaches and wearing summer clothes in March all sent me into a state of ecstasy. Walking outdoors with no boots or jacket or gloves made me feel as free and light as a newly emerged butterfly.

A year and a half later, in 1978, I met and married Jack Kern, who was a bachelor father of six children. Needless to say, the merging of two families in a household overflowing with teenagers extended my capacities to phenomenal dimensions. Taking on the role of step-mother was an awesome, often frightening, and humbling experience. All six were (and are) beautiful, brilliant, and wise beyond their years, and all had distinct personalities. Ranging in age from ten to nineteen, there was Annie, the artist; Joy, the dancer/singer; James, the magician/ inventor; David, the peacemaker; Laura, the care-giver; and Kim, the young mother/wise business person.

Driving home from work each afternoon, I began a daily ritual in which I would make a conscious shift from *supervisor* to *servant*. Although the work at home required different tasks, the two roles became almost synonymous to me, and have remained so ever since. I view the work of a supervisor or administrator as one who is in service to others. My task for both roles is to enable children or teachers or others to grow and learn and become the best they can be.

The confusing part in taking on the roles of parent/step-parent/ supervisor is in figuring out who is responsible for what. Especially when things go wrong. If someone gets into trouble, how much of the blame is mine and how much is theirs? Did I try hard enough? What should I have done differently? When teachers or students or my children fall flat on their faces, should I rescue them or not? How much help is too much or not enough?

These are the dilemmas that every parent or teacher or anyone who is in a position of leadership faces. During that period I began the gradual process of shedding the images of "SuperMom," or "Super Teacher," or "Super" anything else, and simply did each day's work as it came, whether in the schools or at home, with little or no time to analyze mistakes or successes, right or wrong. There were celebrations, camp-outs, giant birthday parties, and trips to Disney World on a regular basis. Life overflowed with small and large crises, good and bad moments, hard and smooth times. We laughed and cried, rejoiced and mourned. If we had it all to do over again, maybe we would have done it better, or maybe not. All I know for sure is that it's *much* easier to be a grandmother!

CHAPTER 5

Breaking the Mold

Early in 1982, I was ready for a change in jobs. Throughout my career, after about five years, I would begin to get the urge to do something different. The internal need for change opened up many opportunities for new growth and learning in a wide range of arenas. My experiences prior to the planning and developing of Seacrest were in the public sector where I tried out, and sometimes invented, an endless array of methods, models, and materials.

In my quest to develop my own potential as an educator, I experienced "open" and "closed" schools, team teaching, various individualized programs and grouping patterns, programmed and computerized instruction, diagnostic and prescriptive teaching, behavioral objectives, assertive discipline, interdisciplinary instruction, "whole-brained" learning, "cooperative learning" and smatterings of many other educational concoctions.

My conclusion from this first-hand experience is that the process of learning is not so much an *either-or process* as it is an *and-also* process, one that is never finished. I have come to accept that most educators and researchers have yet to determine what learning should take place, how it should be taught, or what materials should be used. This is especially true today in the information age with all the exciting new technology. We are like pioneers, exploring uncharted territories that were unimaginable a few years ago. I believe it is even more important today than ever before that we pay close attention to the development of our human qualities and values as we continue to gain new knowledge in the sciences and technology. How we use the knowledge is crucial.

In the frighteningly fast-paced world of technological achievements and remarkable discoveries of how the brain works, we have the potential to unravel many of the mysteries of the mind. Those of us receptive to our own growth are being seduced by the latest educational models, technology and techniques, some of which may prove to be useful for many children.

Although I am as interested in putting the latest research into action as I was in earlier years, my zeal has been tempered by the realization that any tool, method, or technique is only as good as the person who uses it. Educational literature abounds with many wonderful ideas of great potential. Ideas are tried and tested for a time and then fall by the wayside. As with most new ideas, the key lies in how they are used or misused. We often have abandoned potentially valuable information because teachers and administrators are not able or willing to adjust or change their thinking in order to implement them.

Many useful concepts are never implemented, I believe, because of society's reluctance to make changes. We all know the most famous examples of this: the initial rejection of the telephone and electricity being two. My own experience tells me the same attitude of suspicion and rejection continues to be society's reaction to the innovative.

I recall a conversation at a dinner party with a renowned neuroimmunologist who was to speak to local physicians and mental health practitioners the following day. The topic concerned scientific advances made in the field of brain chemistry and the relationships between brain chemicals and emotions. Questions tumbled out of my mouth, prompted by my interest in the field, especially as it related to children, mental health, and the learning process. At first, the responses were conservative and cautious.

As I continued to probe, it became obvious the researcher possessed a wealth of fascinating theories and was knowledgeable about many scientific studies. When asked if he would be elaborating on these topics the next day, he made it clear that these topics were too controversial for the mainstream medical and health care community. In order to receive approval for the limited research funds, the proposals need to conform to narrowly defined parameters. How disheartening, I thought. It seems scientists as well as educators find themselves pressed into the mold of conformity and rigidity by the structure of the system.

Many teachers and administrators who bring fresh ideas to their jobs find themselves frustrated and exasperated by the lack of freedom and support from the bureaucratic structure. Our educational system has become so cumbersome and controlled that even superintendents who desire to encourage growth and positive change find it impossible to cut through the maze of red tape and political pressure.

Over time, numerous teachers have shared with me their frustrations of having creative ideas squelched, of being forced to teach in lockstep progression with every other teacher, and of students who are required to learn at the same pace. After more than twenty years of hard evidence that it does not work, children are still labeled and lumped into slow, average, and high ability groups, or put into tracks from which they can never emerge.

Even in the more innovative schools, the sense of helplessness among teachers persists. A young high school math teacher from a northern state once visited me on her spring break. Her school had received substantial funding for four years to create an experimental school within the school. Smaller classes, integrated curriculum, a team approach, and more challenging projects and work for students were the goals.

As described by the teacher, it sounded like a wonderfully creative plan. I am encouraged by the recent effort in some of the larger schools to create "schools within schools." More and more people are discovering that bigger is not better; that when the student population rises above four-hundred, everything becomes more complex. Dealing with violence in the schools, the quality of learning, and the sense of community is more difficult to manage when the school is too large for personal knowledge and involvement among teachers, students, and parents.

But as the teacher described it, the plan for an interdisciplinary, collaborative, small school concept was not working. Some of the teachers within the project were not interested in the process, but had been arbitrarily placed there without being asked. The teachers rarely met for joint planning. There was pressure to cover the material in the book by the end of the year and to make sure the students made higher test scores to provide the proof needed to continue the funding. It was obvious from her description that nothing innovative was going on in the experimental program.

Although it was an experimental school with additional funds, few up-to-date resources such as computer programs and individualized instruction were in use. According to my young friend, there was little or no integration of classes or interdisciplinary learning. The students inside the experimental school were just as bored as those in the shell school, where students and teachers resented the extra money, smaller classes, and recognition given to the inner school.

"I was counting on getting together with the other teachers to plan more interesting and meaningful projects, but they don't seem to have the time or interest," the visiting teacher lamented. Little wonder she was discouraged.

In the book, *Learning Organizations,* John H. Wood, a founder and president of the Center for Developmental Organizations, described the current state of educational change:

> The characteristic ongoing turmoil of change in education, the frenzy to enact the latest theory, is a re-application of . . . deeply held tenets in different forms. The process drains energy and recreates what has always been.
>
> Change in education is like a thin layer of stratus clouds, ever changing with the wind but always the same. What is needed is a bank of air-cleansing thunder clouds—fresh leadership with new concepts from outside the educational community.

In recognizing the truth of Wood's statement, I disagree that fresh leadership must come from outside the educational community. In order for change to have a lasting and meaningful effect, I believe it must come from people within the schools; people who believe in a new vision and will do whatever it takes to make it happen. Mandates forced from the outside, or from the top down, with no sense of ownership from within have seldom, if ever, been successful in producing lasting change.

Armed with these and other discouraging yet challenging issues, I was determined that our new school would be a place where the freedom to explore and test new ideas would be afforded to teachers and students. Teachers would know their opinions mattered, and their work as professionals would be honored and respected. I envisioned a learning environment in which everyone would be a learner and a teacher; a place where students, their parents and teachers were all involved in creating a community of learning.

II

BEGINNINGS

CHAPTER 6

Setting the Stage

The planning of a new school, built on the backdrop of experience, study, and observation, developed from a deep resolve to do something better. Specific purposes and goals began to take shape as I visited other schools, gathered advice, studied, read, and contemplated the many aspects of building a school from the ground up.

I knew it must be a school in which children would explore, experiment, create, and discover; where children would learn to respect and to help each other; where minds would be stretched and strengthened; where information would be experienced, touched, smelled, tasted, and then practiced. Emotions, feelings, and a strong sense of self awareness would be developed in positive ways. Children would know they are an important part of their environment, and they would develop the responsibility to care for themselves, others, and their world. They would experience the joy of artistic expression and physical movement with sound, color, texture, and motion.

During 1982, I created the conceptual framework of Seacrest, spending much of my time analyzing research, visiting schools, and gathering advice from consultants I knew and trusted. I synthesized what I believed to be the best of traditional approaches with the best of the most innovative educational and psychological theories and models.

In that same year, the National Commission on Excellence in Education was formed. Thinking that the new body was a fortuitous event in timing, I gathered each piece of information from the commission as quickly as it was released.

On April 26, 1983, the Commission presented *A Nation at Risk: The Imperative for Educational Reform*, a report that generated a wave of additional reports and studies defining the problems and offering solutions for educational reform. By the beginning of 1984, almost every state had formed its own commission or task force to reform education.

Though much was written about the need for major changes in the national educational system, most of the recommendations had more to do with longer hours, longer semesters, additional credits, or harder tests than with quality, creativity, or innovation. Once again the nation was doing a repeat performance of the "back to basics" drama. Timed tests, tens of thousands of work sheets, drills and no frills were in vogue. The results were dismal. Test scores fell and students dropped out.

Predictably, a few years later, the next new wave of reform came into being: the pendulum of change swung to the opposite extreme. Out went the work sheets, timed math tests, phonics, basic readers, and drills. In came what was termed a brand-new inception—"Whole Language." Integration was in, tracking students into ability groups was out. Why did all this sound so familiar? It seemed to me that the circles and cycles are no different from the fashion industry where the latest vogue appears remarkably similar to dresses my mother wore in her twenties.

Previews of current educational conferences still promise exciting breakthroughs in schooling. We are tantalized by titles such as *The Age of Multimedia, Using Total Quality Management, A Transdisciplinary Team Approach, Robotics for Everyone,* and *A Transformational Outcome-Based Education Model*—all designed to encourage new approaches that are unfortunately often built upon the existing paradigm. I will most likely attend these conferences and bring back new ideas. I will probably never stop searching for something better.

My plea is for balance. I also want to stress that real change is not going to happen without a change in the whole value system of what constitutes a good education and a good school. Longer school hours, a lengthened school year, and added credits are not the answer if they only repeat the past. And swinging back and forth from one extreme to the other is counterproductive and a waste of resources.

As the plans for Seacrest progressed, I came to trust my own experience and intuition. As founders, the Sheehans and I agreed that the best way to begin was small, with four-year-old prekindergartners.

So in the winter and spring of 1983, the school philosophy was written, the first curriculum was developed, and the first teacher was hired.

CHAPTER 7

First Teacher

Becky Herrman was ecstatic over the idea of being a part of our new venture, especially about the freedom and responsibility of becoming a vital member of a new creation. She and I had been friends since my move to Southwest Florida, and over the years we had shared ideas and philosophies about kids and teaching.

As we sat around my kitchen table one day talking about the concept for the school, I could see her eyes lighting up as if she recognized a long cherished friend who had appeared out of nowhere. She listened intently to the philosophy and my visions, interrogating and examining my ideas and trying them on for size.

Her face suddenly lit up with a large smile as she exclaimed, "Jane! This has been my dream for as long as I can remember—to start a prekindergarten where I have the freedom to do the things I've always wanted. I want to be the teacher." Becky is immensely dedicated. Once committed, she spends whatever time it takes to develop ideas into practical plans and to put details in place before she begins. The instant we reached an agreement, months before she would receive her first paycheck, she put into motion the myriad details and preparations for the first Seacrest prekindergarten class.

Becky was the first of many conscientious—even perfectionist—teachers who would be a part of Seacrest. The formidable forces of the perfectionists, while often too hard on themselves, bring a definite advantage to the creation of a new organization. These are people who take action without being asked. They have an inborn single-mindedness to do a better job than anyone else has ever done and, more often than not, their instincts are correct.

Together, Becky and I plunged into preparations. We pored over books, materials, and catalogues. There were endless discussions, questions, and debates as we made decisions and plans. We agreed on ten children in the morning and ten in the afternoon. We planned multisensory activities; physical development; creative movement, artistic and dramatic expression; whole group, small group, and individualized activities. Field trips and a multitude of people from the community were an important part of the plan. We scoured the town and hundreds of catalogues for the most creative, best quality and most economical equipment, instructional materials and furniture.

Our initial budget was $90,000 for the year, which included salaries for Becky, a tutor, a custodian, and myself; all the furniture, materials, books, and equipment, marketing, and supplies.

Along with the fun of planning programs, choosing furniture, and finding supplies came the administrative tasks of dealing with rules and regulations, creating the budget, designing the marketing, and finding the first students.

Earlier in the year, in fact on the first day I began planning the new school, I called the head of non-public schools at the State Department of Education in Tallahassee. I asked for copies of the standards, rules, and regulations for private, independent schools.

"There aren't any," said the woman who had taken my call. Thinking I had misunderstood her, I asked again. She clearly informed me that there were no state standards for private schools in Florida, and that the only rules that applied were those of the local county governing safety and health.

My first reaction was, *Wow! No Rules!* Even so, I quickly realized that the lack of regulations might be the reason so many of the private schools and day care centers I had visited were poorly conceived and managed. I was stunned that anyone anywhere could be picked off the street and hired as a teacher, with no degree, no experience, and no qualifications. In my search for ideas and models, I had stumbled upon some abysmal situations, and wondered how such schools could be allowed to exist. After the phone call to Tallahassee, I knew.

First Teacher

The next step was to contact the accrediting agencies for non-public schools in Florida. Here there were definite standards to be met, although back then, in 1982, they were loose in terms of curriculum requirements, and at that time, early childhood teachers were not required to have a college degree. There were no particular certification requirements. Although the major accrediting agencies now require a teaching degree, there are still some agencies in Florida that do not require a teacher to be certified.

Building credibility for the school was important to me, and of much greater importance was ensuring that our school had teachers who were not only qualified, but who were truly masterful in teaching children. While certification, years of experience, and degrees may not carry the guarantee of a great teacher, such credentials seemed a minimum base from which to start. From that baseline, I added the required standards of the public schools, and then, expanded them to develop our own philosophy and requirements.

Finding a Home

With the program planned and the practices and standards under control, we were faced with the challenge of finding space to house the first class. We needed a space large enough for movement with a variety of learning centers and space for spreading out and constructing projects. We needed storage for books, equipment, and materials. We needed sinks, bathrooms, sturdy and flexible furniture, and of course we needed a wonderful playground, fenced in, with imaginative apparatus.

The element of beauty was also important to me. A comfortable, spacious, appealing setting for learning helps create the tangible message that we want the learner to enjoy a sense of well-being. We tracked down every lead in town and on the outskirts of town for possible space, with dismal results.

As it happened, my husband Jack was the minister of the Unity church in Naples, which he had established thirteen years earlier. The church had just completed constructing two large classrooms for Sunday school. The church's property is located a few miles from town, encompassing twenty acres of pine forests, landscaped with lush palms, native trees, and luxuriant flower gardens. This seemed the ideal setting for the initial stages of school, although I had some concerns that parents would think Seacrest was a church-affiliated school. Seacrest was designed as an independent, nonsectarian school, and I hoped our firm convictions would become apparent as we got underway. Jack was in total support of the project, and he agreed to rent the space to us for a token annual fee.

There were many advantages to the school's situation. For instance, Jack gave his consent for us to screen in the porch for art and other projects and to install a sink for cleaning up the paint, mud, and other gooey substances associated with the prekindergarten set. We also made full use of Jack's collection of technological equipment and gadgets. George, the grounds keeper, designed and built the playground equipment in a large fenced-in, shaded playground. Mr. Sheehan, our founder and benefactor, took care of the cost of the fencing, the playground, and remodeling the porch. For the next decade, he continued to donate the shortfalls in our operating budget. Each year he funded children for scholarships, and he held the responsibility for the purchase of land and construction of buildings.

Behind the classrooms, subtropical ferns, mosses, and bromeliads flourished under the slash pines, live oaks, and cabbage palms. Saw grass and palmettos gently sloped down to marshy, swampy mud, sand, debris, and large boulders overlooking the lake. This was one of our first challenges. As with most contained bodies of water in the South Florida subtropics, the lake had its own resident alligator, along with a few water moccasins and rattlesnakes. Florida residents know that if you leave them alone they will leave you alone.

Jack and I had purchased and built a home on five acres adjoining the church property, and although our teenage children were not allowed to swim in the lake, our dog, Guido, an unlikely mixture of white Lab and great Dane, would occasionally take a cool dip in the lake on still, sultry midsummer days. Whenever he failed to appear promptly after a call or whistle, I began to worry that the alligator had decided to vary his diet with Guido as a substitute. It is well known that an alligator will eat most anything.

The deceptively calm surface of the mirrored silver lake induced a lingering image in my mind. With visions of students wandering off to climb on the slippery moss-covered boulders, slipping into the lake where the alligator lay hidden, I established the first rule of Seacrest: No child would ever, under any circumstances, be unsupervised for any reason at any time. The rule still stands today, especially when classes of older students frequently take trips to the nearby Everglades and squish around barefooted in the muddy swamps amidst the cypress knees and floating water weeds to observe the egret, great blue herons, and other exotic Florida wildlife. I always breathe a silent prayer of thanks and relief when every student returns with fingers and toes intact.

Finding a Home

PreKindergarten Morning Class, 1983-'84
Photo Credit: PhotoWorks

PreKindergarten Afternoon Classs, 1983-'84
Photo Credit: Photoworks

Chapter 8

First Learners

With plans and preparations under way, I turned to the most important aspect of any school: the students and their parents. Who were the parents of our first class of preschoolers and what would convince them to entrust their four-year-olds to an unknown, untested place of learning? How would I find these parents?

We began by creating and distributing brochures, submitting newspaper articles, sending letters, and appearing on radio talk shows. We placed an ad in the local daily paper and invited interested parents to attend an informational talk about Seacrest. It was our first attempt at marketing and could scarcely be called a roaring success. Hardly anyone came except my friends, who were only there to support me. After this trial run, we realized that I would have to go to the people—to their clubs and organizations. Luckily, education is always a timely subject among young parents, and they were just curious enough to agree to hear about a new school.

I made arrangements to speak before a variety of local organizations, including the Junior Women's Club, Rotary Clubs, and other places where bright young parents gathered to take their positions as emerging custodians of the community.

Speaking to large groups of total strangers required, for me, a tremendous leap in courage. Planning and implementing curriculums and instructional programs were tasks I had dealt with throughout my career. But advertising and marketing, along with a host of other business aspects, including sales pitches, were foreign to me. Any talks or speeches I had given were, for the most part, to other educators, and certainly the stakes were not nearly so high. The thought of going before large groups of business men and women to sell my new school had me hovering between mild discomfort and stark terror. After coming so far in our plans, everything hinged on the success of the public relations campaign. I labored endless hours over speeches, tailoring them to the special interests and characteristics of each group. I rehearsed and over-rehearsed, hoping to appear calm and confident with the delivery of my message.

Soon after my club circuit, parents came trickling in, one by one, to question and interview me, to talk with Becky, and to see the new classroom. Through the parents, I learned about the children who would be part of the first class. Our first class of learners who set the stage and flavor of Seacrest was a diverse mix of personalities.

There was three-year-old Jay. His Chinese father and Canadian-born mother said Jay was fascinated by the world around him and even more fascinated with outer space. He had an astounding amount of information about rockets and how they worked. Jay's father and I talked for several hours about our philosophies of education while Jay played in and around the fountain in the foyer of my living room, returning again and again for pennies to pitch into the pool of water, asking each time why there were no fish in the fountain.

Jay and his family found the concepts of Seacrest to their liking and in addition to being one of the first families at the school, Jay's father, a graphic artist, helped create the Seacrest logo. He incorporated the symbols for Seacrest— vivid shades of blue and green for sea and sky—with an 'S' tipped slightly on its side, creating the suggestion of the crest of a wave. Some people have interpreted this as the Oriental yin and yang, a symbol of harmony and balance, although at the time, that was not my intention. But perhaps the symbol of the balance in the universe has proven to be the underlying message of Seacrest. Through the years, this same artist created beautiful cards and prints for fund-raisers and was instrumental in designing the first brochures. In the early years of the school, Jay's mother, also an artist, used her talents innumerous ways for Seacrest bazaars, festivals, and scenery for plays.

Laura and her mother also were two of our first visitors. Shy, with blond pigtails and a perpetual smile, Laura was to become the prime example of loyalty and friendship to all who knew her throughout her years at Seacrest. She was the listener, the sympathizer, the protector of all who came under her guard. Always one to avoid conflict, Laura expected and received the approval of the group.

There were two Kim's, both incredibly bright and otherwise totally distinctive from each other in their personalities. One Kim had a round expressive face with a smile that invited others to participate in her fun. Persuasive, confident, poised and cordial, Kim would quickly establish herself as the leader. Whether she was dancing, writing a story, creating an art project or performing in a dramatization, she was happiest when expressing herself.

The other Kim, equally brilliant, was a methodical, logical, and deliberate thinker. Her dark, naturally curly ringlets framed a sunny, dimpled face. She loved life, people, and learning, and her smile radiated vibrancy and joy. We were to discover that the second Kim needed an unlimited amount of time in an unhurried atmosphere to pursue her projects and interests. She had a vast vocabulary, and Becky and I were entertained and amazed at her sensitivity and depth of understanding.

The mothers of both Kims became our first kindergarten teachers the following year. The two daughters are now in high school, and their mothers *still* teach at Seacrest. Both mothers have played a significant role in developing and preserving the Seacrest philosophy and in representing teaching and learning at its highest level.

Jim was a precocious and expressive four-year-old who appeared to have an unlimited wealth of knowledge ready to share with us at all times. His penetrating large brown eyes seemed to take in the world around him with insatiable curiosity. His analytical and inquisitive mind thrived on figuring out how things worked. A student of Suzuki violin, he reveled in performing. A verbal encyclopedia in perpetual motion, Jim was happiest when teaching the rest of us the intricate details of scientific phenomena.

Chris, who entered Seacrest at age three, was later known as the one who read everything in sight. A lover of history and biographies, he was bored to distraction with practice, repetition, and homework. During any kind of structured assignments, he usually had a secret stash of books ready to amuse himself when boredom set in.

Sean was the boy who personified kindness and good sportsmanship. Self-contained, handsome, and modest, he was adored equally by both boys and girls. Nan, with her long, dark, curly hair and leisurely, languid movements and speech patterns, was the 'beauty' of the bunch. She valued comfort and kinesthetic activities. Fascinated by the extraordinary and unusual, she often allowed her intuition to lead her into a free-spirited world of imagination.

Brian, a child with a visual disorder and one of the youngest of the group, captured my heart from the first moment. He had a droll sense of humor and an uncanny ability to comprehend and demonstrate volumes of sophisticated concepts. I was determined that he would receive the best that we had to offer, and that he would never be treated or labeled as handicapped. Brian's parents had given him a wonderful beginning in his first three years of life. He had a healthy self-esteem despite his visual impairment, and he had been offered all the resources needed for success. His parents made it clear that they wanted their son to do everything that the others did and to be able to progress through school with as little special attention as possible. My promise to the parents to honor their terms was followed by the teachers for over a decade at Seacrest. From prekindergarten through the eighth grade, Brian more than held his own with his classmates—in academics, in sports and, best of all, in his social and emotional development.

It goes without saying that children typically have their own sets of personality traits that are less than sterling. Our first class was no exception, and it would be misleading to suggest otherwise. The emotional development of children includes a complex and broad spectrum of physiological and psychological patterns that must be recognized and attended to with utmost care. It was clear from the beginning that the children of Seacrest shared many of the imperfections and foibles as well as the strengths and virtues that are commonly found in most settings.

There were the strong-willed achievers and sore losers; the hot-tempered with short fuses; the restless and easily distracted; the overly shy and easily hurt; the teaser; the fighter; and the disrupter. There were those who showed early signs of learning difficulties of various types.

These characteristics were no more nor less remarkable than what we expected. We did not set out to select only the brightest and best-behaved. An important goal in developing the Seacrest program was to weave the lessons of emotional well-being into all aspects of learning. Children would be taught to recognize and face their emotions and to learn that they could choose appropriate responses in managing conflict.

Throughout the spring and summer of 1983, prior to the September opening of Seacrest, Becky and I became acquainted with

38

the parents who had enrolled their children in Seacrest. As I got to know the unique qualities, hopes, fears, and dreams of each mother and father, common qualities emerged from the group. Just as each class has its own built-in collective personality, the same seems to be true with each group of parents. First and foremost, the parents all wanted their children to be challenged in a nurturing, sensory-rich atmosphere. They were open to a holistic program that provided active experiences. They appeared to value the arts, including the performing and physical arts. They wanted their children to be excited about learning and to become good readers, writers, mathematicians, and scientists. They expected the highest standards, and it became obvious that every decision concerning the school would be discussed, critiqued, and analyzed. Authentic in their desire to help in every way possible, the parents immediately became involved in the projects and preparations for the opening of Seacrest.

Becky and I soon discovered that the talented group of parents had among them many skills: there were artists; carpenters; typists; and people who had connections for finding the best deals on equipment, materials, and supplies. Since all my previous experience was with public schools, I had never foraged and bargained for furniture, sinks, cabinets, carpet and paint, not to mention the instructional materials, equipment, and supplies—right down to the pencils needed to start a new classroom. But everyone seemed eager to pitch in, including my husband who, with one of the parents, provided master cabinetmaking skills and adequate, if not expert, plumbing talents.

Preparing the Space

Everything was a new, and sometimes frustrating, experience for me mainly because beginning a school has little to do with teaching. Take for example the day the furniture was delivered. An enormous truck arrived, driven by a proportionately enormous truck driver. Just as he pulled up, the afternoon Florida rains moved out of the Everglades and poured mercilessly down on Naples. In an instant, the area was turned into pools of water and puddles of mud. The trucker, anxious to be on his way, announced that he would unload twenty large cartons at the tailgate of his truck.

I looked at the surrounding mud, estimated the distance from the tailgate to the classroom and posed what I had thought to be a rational question: Can you bring the cartons to the classroom? With a withering glare of disbelief and a surly tone of superiority, he retorted, "No Ma'am, I can't do that."

My next tactic—that of portraying the helpless female completely unable to drag all those heavy cartons up that long walk in the mud and rain also proved to be futile. It seems I had not paid for *inside delivery* (a term now indelibly imprinted on my brain), and according to the driver, there was absolutely nothing he could do. As we were both stranded at the tailgate of his truck getting drenched to the bone, I decided to try logic and assertiveness. I asked him his name and told him he would have to wait until I phoned the manager of the trucking company to tell him that twenty cartons of furniture were about to be unloaded and left in the mud and pouring rain, and that the school would be holding the driver and the company responsible for any damages. I also let him know that I would be happy to pay the cost of *inside delivery* directly to him if he should decide to change his mind. My final suggestion was met with agreement, and soon we were both out of the rain and the furniture was safely stored inside our new classrooms.

This was my first adventure with the trucking industry, one that continued as we added grades each year. I soon learned the ropes and determined which companies were the most reliable, which drivers the most accommodating, and what to do when shipments arrived damaged. I also became adept at slicing open huge cardboard cartons and stamping them down into flat pieces so that they would fit into the garbage dumpster. That talent, I discovered, was all part of the endless tasks of running a new school with only a single administrator and no office staff.

Of course, getting the boxes inside was only half the battle. Once the tables, chairs, and shelves were removed from the cartons, the legs, clamps, hinges, and screws needed to be unpacked, assembled, and attached to their rightful places. Viewing the mysterious maze with bewildered wonder at my own ineptness, my husband once again came to the rescue by performing his magic with assorted hammers, screwdrivers, and impressive motorized tools.

I realized with each passing day that much of what had to be accomplished had little to do with curriculum planning or the development of creative learning activities for young children. Countless weeks were spent dealing with water treatment, trash disposal, bookkeeping systems, fencing, lighting, electrical outlets, and tasks that required hard physical labor and trips to obscure industrial and county complexes. I became good friends with the county nurses, water management personnel, and fire inspectors.

And finally we turned our attention to filling one of the most critical positions at a school: qualified and responsible cleaning people. The prerequisites include: conscientiousness, honesty, thoroughness, high energy, strength, reliability, flexibility, and patience in the face of the special messes created by children. Cleaning a school is not like cleaning a business office, or even a home. Challenging and mysterious messes are generated each day—everything from clumps of mud to colorful hand prints and splashes of tempera paint on the floor, walls, sometimes even the ceilings. Tables are sticky with films of paste and debris, possibly mixed with some lunch. And, of course, the bathrooms are a special case because very often little ones miss the mark. And all that is *after* the children and teachers have cleaned and picked up and put away. I often think there must be an exalted place in heaven for the extraordinary custodian who provides such selfless service.

We were fortunate to find the right person for the task, and once school began, we made sure that we did everything possible to keep her happy as we went about the daily ritual of "cleaning for the cleaning lady."

These preparations and the small cast of characters laid the groundwork for what became some of my most valuable lessons in leadership; more specifically, who to call if you do not have the foggiest notion of how to do something. Another important piece of learning was centered around my daily lessons in humility and awe at how little I knew about so many things. It is said that the recognition that you know nothing is the beginning of wisdom, and if so, I must have been on the right track.

I quickly formed a support group, made up of unlikely partners in education, any of whom could make or break the entire flow of progress. For instance, when the plumbing fails, you had better know whom to call: a person who arrives on a moment's notice, who knows exactly what to do, and how to do it at lightning speed. Preschoolers without bathroom facilities can quickly turn into a recipe for disaster. You also need to know someone who can repair any number of malfunctioning, broken and necessary objects, such as playground apparatus, air conditioning, or power systems. One never knows when a crisis can lead to unsuspected sources of talent and even genius from those generally considered to be outside the business of school.

Honey bees brought us one such unlikely compatriot. One midday, several years into Seacrest's history, it was close to lunch time, when the classes emptied into the multipurpose room and onto the playground. Summoned by a tutor, I gaped at an enormous swarm of bees surrounding the door of a classroom in a cloud of furious frenzy. First, I commanded our secretary to find someone who could do something. Then, donning a mask of confident intention, I eased my way to the side door of the classroom, leaving several feet of space between the bees and me. I entered the classroom and informed the children that they were not to open the doors or leave the classroom until I gave the signal. Lunch would have to wait.

Our secretary located the one and only beekeeper in Naples. The ingenious man, assisted by his wife, carefully nabbed the queen bee who had settled into her new nest beside the classroom, and carried her gently and safely to a newer, more acceptable spot in the nearby woods. Her loyal subjects followed obediently behind. Thus, a new partnership was formed in our growing file of improbable and invaluable bedfellows in education. The beekeeper was summoned on several more occasions, not only to deal with bees, but also to share with students and faculty a wealth of fascinating stories about the tribal practices of bees and their ruling queen.

Countdown to the First Day

As the time grew near for the long awaited opening day of our brand-new school, the level of activity swelled to a burst of boundless energy. All the regulations for health and safety had been met, and we proudly displayed our license for operating the school. The furniture and fixtures were assembled and in place. Freshly painted walls held colorful charts and works of art. Every corner beckoned eager children to touch, manipulate, taste, smell, and explore various centers of learning. Nutritious snacks for the month were planned and posted. Miniature carpet squares reserved individual seats in a semicircle for sharing whole group activities.

Shelves with cubbies were marked for each child's projects, and hooks were ready to be adorned with paint smocks, sweaters, and book bags. New screening on the porch protected the science and art equipment from mosquitoes and other south Florida creepy crawlers. Easels, paint brushes, and clotheslines waited for budding young artists. Rhythm instruments, tape recorders, and earphones were set for music, stories, poems, dancing, marching, playing, singing, listening, and acting.

On the afternoon before the children were to arrive, Becky and I stood in silent reverence and appreciation as we surveyed the results of our labor of love, sweat, and perseverance. Our senses were filled to overflowing. Like the moment when a tiny ripple is set in motion from the still, calm ocean floor, undefined and fluid, swelling and shifting toward the light, the journey is begun and a wave begins to take shape. A new school was being born with new children, new possibilities and new hope. The dream had started to manifest, and tomorrow, a new wave of learning would reach breakpoint.

CHAPTER 9

First Day

Like explorers venturing into uncharted territory, the first parents made their way up the boardwalk, holding the hands of their shy and tentative children. Leaving children on the first day of school is always an emotional milestone and leaving them at a brand-new school without any track record must be especially difficult.

Looking back, I am struck by the courage, confidence, and openness of the first parents. Courage, because we would be exploring and expressing a new and untested vision, breaking out of accepted norms. Confidence, because these parents were entrusting the lives of their children to our care. And openness, because we would be creating and developing new ideas and re-forming old ideas.

We had carefully prepared the parents for this moment of separation, encouraging them to come in often beforehand to familiarize the children with their surroundings. Still, that first separation is not easy, and with rare exceptions, much harder on the parents than the children.

While Becky ushered the first learners into their new world, I tried to reassure the parents. During subsequent years, it was not unusual for me to lead a tearful mom, or even a dad into my office on the first day of school, supplying tissues and expressions of sympathy. On several occasions, parents and children from foreign countries arrived speaking little or no English. It was during those times that I witnessed the remarkable moments when the language of feelings cuts through barriers to connect with meaning and understanding.

On this special September morning in 1983, excitement won over apprehension, and the rites of passage were initiated with a peaceful promise of a good day. Beginning with a song, Becky moved into motion with masterful certainty, weaving her magic through the minds, bodies, and spirits of four-year-olds.

In a kaleidoscope world of sound, color, movement, and rhythm, the children became artists and storytellers, actors, dancers, musicians, scientists, and inventors. They played hard, ate with gusto, and rested peacefully. They giggled at each other's tall tales. They shared toys and tools, produced original creations with concentrated deliberation, picked up, took apart, and put away.

As I slipped silently in and out of the classroom, following Becky's lead, I was moved by the flow of creative expression, the relaxed and peaceful atmosphere, and the beauty of the scenes before me. Each child was intensely absorbed and engaged with the work of prekindergarten. Some worked with partners, others alone. There was a sense of entrainment, like a symphony when the conductor and musicians are transported into a larger unified whole of time and space, becoming the music itself.

Would any other day ever hold the magic of this first one? Aware of the fact that there would be good days, days bordering on disaster, and days with conflict, I mused: *If we can have one day like this, there will be another, and maybe there would be many such days. It's possible.*

Perhaps that first day can never be relived, but in the years that followed, a similar excitement has been expressed in many ways by hundreds of parents and visitors as they took the first journey through the classrooms. And the teachers who followed Becky's opening number brought their unique energy and ingenuity to our school. That first day was a forecast of the future: over the years when visitors come to Seacrest they invariably make comments such as: "It feels so good here"; or "All the children are working on different projects, but it's still so calm and peaceful"; or "The students all seem so happy"; or "The children seem to love learning here." Words such as these made the effort worthwhile on the days when nothing seemed to go right.

The weeks following that first day were filled with trips and adventures. The community opened its doors for our young explorers to discover how their food was grown, harvested, and marketed; how their carefully composed letters were processed at the post office; how their clothes were manufactured; and how their homes were constructed. They experienced the excitement of sitting in the driver's seat of fire engines and the awe of talking to policemen. There were regular trips to the Collier County Nature Center and the public library. The beaches and nearby woods became scientific laboratories, teeming with life to observe, collect, and study. Musicians and gymnasts came to visit and instruct on a regular basis. Local artists, authors, doctors, and nutritionists came to share their trades and talents.

Jo Ruhl, an eighty-year-old artist, woodworker, and maker of museum-quality doll houses and toys worked with the children once a week, helping them to carve, paint, and sculpt. Jack and I held classical concerts, selecting the music of famous composers. The children danced, clapped, conducted, and acted with the music in natural, uninhibited abandon. One of the parents taught elementary French, and all the parents took turns sharing their considerable talents, driving on field trips, or helping with projects.

It was not long before we hired part time tutorial assistants, Janine for the morning class and Patty for the afternoon, to help Becky with the preparation of materials and projects, snacks, and cleanup. Janine and Patty, carefully trained by Becky, also worked with individuals and small groups, guiding and helping. We were all given definite instructions by Becky not to do for children what they must learn to do for themselves. Whenever Becky noticed me picking up a child's blocks or completing a learning task for them, she would admonish, "Jane, let them do it for themselves."

Holidays were celebrated with flair. Our first Thanksgiving began a ritual that has become a Seacrest tradition. The children participated in roasting a turkey, rolling out dough for pumpkin pies, and making their own cranberry relish. All the families gathered together at a long table set up outside, where we sang, gave thanks for Seacrest and each other, stuffed ourselves, and played games. Nancy, one of the original Seacrest parents, recently reminded me of these feasts, when the school was new and small, and how special these ceremonies were. Nancy's daughter, now in high school, is still as good natured, kind and academically successful as she was in earlier years, virtues her mother attributes to Seacrest.

The values of kindness and respect for others were firmly entrenched in the hearts, minds, and actions of the preschoolers by using a concept called "The Love Light." Becky discovered this phrase in a little book entitled, *Something Special Within*, by Betts Richter and Alice Jacobsen. In the story, the Love Light comes shining through with a warm glow inside when you cuddle a pet, love yourself for helping others, or feel love from friends and family. If feelings of sadness or anger come, the Love Light dims. When that happens, you take deep breaths, imagine and say, "In comes the good fresh air and out goes the sadness and anger." As children would complete their tasks well and share with others, you would hear Becky exclaim, "Oh, I can see that Love Light shining now! Do you see it, everybody?" And the children would always nod their heads and glow with pride.

The Love Light has withstood the test of time and is one of the mainstays of early childhood learning at Seacrest today, despite the occasional scoffing of an older student who considers himself too worldly for such imaginings.

The first Halloween parade also became a yearly affair when young performers, transformed into pumpkins, astronauts, fairies, ballerinas, angels, and animals, paraded before our small audience of parents, grandparents, and siblings. Years later, with the addition of the Seacrest Middle School, I was informed that these older students would think it too babyish to participate in the Halloween parade, and that I should not expect them to do so. I readily agreed that it was entirely possible that they had outgrown this childhood ritual. A few days after my decision, the middle school students entered my office with banners and posters in their first peaceful protest. They politely requested that they be allowed to participate in the upcoming parade, and they hoped that we would not discriminate against them because of their advanced age. Bursting into laughter, I thanked them for their courteous request and granted them their wish. The Halloween parade prevails for all ages at Seacrest.

So, too, does the annual Christmas/Hanukkah program, although we have grown too large now for every class to perform on the same evening. The premier program was staged in our one classroom, with families and friends squeezing in together. During the performance, one of the children's baby brother crawled into the middle of the scene and into the lap of his older brother where he happily joined in with the scheduled musicians and actors.

In preparation for one of our celebrations, the following poem was composed by two thankful five-year-olds who entered Seacrest several years later.

Thanksgiving Dinner

Thanksgiving you will eat a lot
people do not let food rot
Turkey, drinks, mashed potatoes
In your salad there are tomatoes
Cranberries, corn, and gravy with biscuits
Saltine crackers also Triscuits

Turkey, corn, pies and beans
Eat a lot by all means
Eating different kinds of foods
Gives you very happy moods
Once your belly begins to hurt
Watch out it's time for dessert

By Meggen and Sarah

First December Program

Building Muscles

Dr. Spano says Our Hearts Are Strong!

CHAPTER 10

Kindergarten

The fall of 1983 passed swiftly into the cool, dry sunny days of winter. The families of that first year fused into a tightly knit group, and parents often lingered at the school after they dropped off children; clusters of moms and dads formed little knots around the boardwalk. The easy camaraderie sprang from common interests and extended into outings at the beach, picnics, dinners, or boat trips together.

The visits around the boardwalk became a ritual similar to the way neighbors chat across the back fence in amiable and relaxed exchanges of daily happenings. Parents seemed eager to tell me their innermost secrets, trials, and troubles. Current financial problems or marriage crises were revealed openly with the hope that I could provide some answers, possibly because I was older than most of the parents and already had been through the struggles and ordeals they presented. I was able to connect with their feelings and sometimes offer small bits of practical advice. Mostly though, I think it was the simple act of listening and the sense of mutual trust and understanding that helped more than the words of advice I might have offered.

I have learned over the years that for the most part, people have to work through their challenges and patterns of behavior in their own way and in their own time, regardless of how obvious the solutions may appear to others. It is the same with children. Mistakes have to be made and personal challenges overcome, and then children can grow into finding their own solutions.

A wise person once told me that the only one we can really change is oneself. We can and should use all our resources in teaching and raising children, or in helping other people in need. But if children (or adults for that matter) are to develop an authentic inner core of strength that is theirs to rely upon, it ultimately must come from each individual, regardless of our well-intentioned urge to rush in to shield and rescue them.

That first year was a golden year, a happy and uncomplicated time when even unexpected upsets and stresses were greeted with good-natured determination. Endless hours of work, meetings, debates, conversations, and planning sessions blurred with shared meals, games, parties and field trips, laughter and music. Whenever I watched the children perform a puppet show or listened in on a conversation in the "Housekeeping Center" between two four-year-olds enacting a family scene, I always felt a sense of astonishment at the innate awareness and perceptiveness contained within these young bodies.

In February, visitors began to arrive: prospective parents of next year's preschool and kindergarten. It was time to think seriously about plans to add kindergarten and the attendant tasks: new enrollees, more space, additional materials, furniture, equipment, budget, and books.

More important, my thoughts turned to finding another teacher. For me, the teachers are the critical factor that can determine the success or failure of a student or a school. The most exemplary curriculum in the world or the most lavishly constructed building is of no value in the hands of a poor or mediocre teacher. My goal at Seacrest always has been to seek out the best teachers on the planet.

If teachers are to inspire and empower learners, they must themselves be inspired and aware of their own greatness. As new grades were added throughout the years, I selected teachers who were confident in their abilities to facilitate learning, those who understood the processes involved in creating a dynamic, inspiring, and encouraging environment. I looked for teachers who believed they could make a difference. Commitment; a sense of humor; flexibility; the desire to explore, grow, and change were prerequisites. The selection process included those who were open to new ideas and had the capacity to do whatever was required to sustain a joyful and successful learning experience.

Applicants who had an attitude of knowing it all were rejected. Candidates who appeared to be low in self-confidence or who believed they had been victimized by the world were quickly passed over.

Before offering positions to teachers, I frequently asked them to prepare and teach a demonstration lesson at Seacrest. This practice emerged from the treacherous discrepancies that sometimes exist between excellent resumes, good recommendations, brilliantly executed interviews, and the ability to "walk the talk." For example, I visited another school to observe an applicant teach her own class. From our prior conversations and interviews, I was certain this teacher had all the qualities I could hope for, and she verbalized an impressive amount of knowledge about the latest educational models.

Within the first five minutes of her lesson, though, there were clear signs of chaos. Determined to withhold judgment, I steeled myself at the outset, but it soon became apparent that the first five minutes had been the best. Three of the fifteen children went to sleep, two crawled around the room on top of the desks, and several others were engrossed in their own conversations throughout the lesson. Two quiet, obviously shy children patiently waiting with raised hands to respond to the teacher's questions were totally ignored and unnoticed throughout the lesson. The remaining children had a sensational time embarrassing the teacher with obscene or outrageous comments and gestures. The teacher and her lesson were lacking in energy, interest, content, and creativity, and there was little evidence of any preparation. Since this was an arranged visit, I assumed this was her best effort.

Desiring to find the ideal teacher for our first kindergarten class, I lay awake one night as the images of two faces flashed to the forefront of my mind. The answer was so obvious. Marcia and Ann, both parents of two of our preschool children, were also experienced teachers. Perhaps one of them would be interested?

I was so excited by the thought of two teachers who understood and believed in our philosophy and goals that I slept little that night. In my mind it was already a *fait accompli* and all I had to do was to introduce them to their new position . . . tomorrow. Early the following morning, I arranged a meeting with Ann and Marcia after school. We sat on Marcia's porch with glasses of ice tea while my proposal was discussed and questioned. I watched their tentative reactions grow into enthusiasm. Within the week they decided that Marcia would take the morning class and Ann the afternoon.

These two spent most of summer engrossed in designing the first Seacrest kindergarten. They interviewed and tested new students, recorded the progress of the existing preschoolers, and ordered instructional materials. Together we formed the curriculum and expanded the brochure. New furniture was selected, purchased, and delivered—this time by an accommodating trucker contracted for the imperative "inside delivery." The new classroom was set up next to the preschool.

The new kindergarten room, identical in size to the preschool classroom, had been my office. I moved across the patio into the church's fellowship hall, a large, open space where we frequently met for concerts, dance and creative movement, or physical education on rainy days.

Since Becky had a screened-in porch with a sink and overhead fans, Marcia and Ann also expected and acquired their own newly constructed and installed screening, sink, and fans. They shared the playground and devised schedules for outdoor activities.

Our founder and benefactor, Mr. Sheehan, understood the importance of matching the salary schedule to that of the district public schools, and salaries for the coming year were satisfactorily negotiated. In those days none of us had written contracts, and, of course, in private schools tenure and bargaining unions are nonexistent. We were well aware that positions in an independent organization greatly depended on enrollment and satisfied parents.

Our approved budget allowed us the additional benefit of hiring a tutor for each teacher. These assistants, trained by the teachers, have proven to be of infinite value, and they continue to be part of the staff and are shared among grade levels. They typically contribute much beyond their required tasks, and so we reap additional benefits while trying not to take them for granted. Some have eventually acquired education degrees and have become teachers at Seacrest.

Taking Turns

The additional funds needed to employ tutors are justified by the fact that they alternately help with the After School Program. Parents seem more than willing to bear the additional cost for the convenience of having their children in a safe, organized, and fun environment for the hours after school.

When the Seacrest preschool class moved up into kindergarten in 1984, they took their legacy for success and fun for granted, as a natural and inherent right. Seacrest's premier kindergartners appeared to have a wonderful time, and they thrived in a bright and secure world of stimulating adventure.

Each age has its own unique characteristics, and five-turning-six year-olds are in a delightful age of independent, carefree, spontaneous, and uninhibited stages of growth. Kindergartners are friendly and accepting of others' differences. They love to help each other. Above all, they are eager to express themselves with abandon. They often operate on impulse. They love to talk and tell their stories, sing and laugh and play. They can listen with rapt attention to someone else's story, but not for too long, for they are bursting to tell their own stories and experiences.

They can decipher and transpose strange, squiggle marks into letters, sounds, and words. They can guide a pencil into shapes and stories that make sense to them and then read it back to you. They can stand before an easel ready with large crisp white sheets of newsprint and propel brushes dripping with bold and beautiful primary colors into rabbits, fish and ducks; flowers and people; houses and space ships. They can erect the most intricate bridges and towers and mold lumps of clay into dinosaurs or lions. They can hang by their legs upside down and cross the monkey bars with facility hand over hand. Kindergarten is the age of communicating in multi-leveled layers of whole-bodied, all-out, and undiluted animation.

The unique styles of our three teachers blended together in a concurrent and congruent program. The original kindergarten curriculum was transposed into sequential, but more sophisticated levels of learning, as the students began to show the unmistakable signs, some even in preschool, that they were ready, eager, and even impatient to read and write their own stories and books.

There was a time when it was considered wrong to teach children to read before they reached first, or even second grade. On the other end of the scale, there were the groups who daily flashed dozens of words to babies, thinking they were getting a head start on reading.

There were the "pushers" and the "don't do anything till they are ready" advocates, with both extremes vehemently attacking the other.

Using our trusted instincts for common sense and balance, we gave the children a stimulating environment and watched to see what they did. It was obvious that some children were not only ready to read, but you could not keep them from it . . . so we helped them along. There were others who needed more time with auditory and visual development, and they were provided with a wealth of activities for listening and looking, eye-hand coordination, and visual memory. There were the kinesthetic learners who needed to build, mold, pick apart, and put back together. And there were the ones who simply needed to play and mature . . . the ones who cannot be pushed, no matter how tempted you may be.

The importance of reading to children every day by parents and teachers is ancient advice, and it still seems to be the best predictor of success in learning to read. Writing down children's own stories as they talk is another tried and true method that has been packaged and labeled under a variety of names through the years. Where is the child who does not love to see his or her name written in big bright letters displayed on a large chart for all to see? It is a pretty simple matter for a child to see his own name in print and to see that the *D* in *Danny* looks the same as the *D* in *Dinosaur* and *Daddy*. The transition from speaking and listening to writing and reading can be a joyful, natural process, providing the groundwork is laid. But it takes parents who form the foundation and teachers who build in hours, months and weeks of time and ingenuity in setting the stage for the emerging readers and writers.

Becky summed up our objective for a balanced program in a rich environment in a newspaper interview when she said, "I discovered that many of the four-year-olds were ready to begin reading at about midpoint through the preschool program. We're not interested in pressuring children to read before they're ready, but neither will we hold them back. We want to take them as far as they can comfortably go."

No Tiptoeing Allowed Here

The new kindergarten classroom was designed to ensure a well-planned, successful school year. Learning centers with dozens of modules for science, math, geography, and language arts were designed by Ann and Marcia and packaged into large envelopes or colorful bins.

Tables were set up with earphones and tapes, musical instruments, science and math materials and placed among computer games, easels, book racks, and cozy corners designed to lead the learners to explore, question, discover, and to always want to come back for more.

In helping to design the kindergarten program, I relied on my memories of my oldest son's first experience in school. Steven was born with a low pitched, lusty cry, which, from babyhood on, developed into a powerful, prominent voice. Unlike my first born daughter, Mary Jane, whose main concern was to please the teacher by sitting quietly, always working with neat precision, Steven was a mover and a shaker. He loved to talk and to perform. To this day he lives life boldly and plays it to the hilt. I would often notice him at an early age, wildly conducting imaginary symphonies or rushing pell-mell on a sled down a steep snow-filled ravine.

When Steven entered kindergarten, his teacher announced with earnest gravity that she had two primary goals for kindergarten. The first was to teach the children to speak in whispering voices. My heart sank. Steven had never whispered in his life. Her second goal was to teach children always to tiptoe. I knew then we were in trouble. Steven spent most of the first half of kindergarten sitting behind the piano, which is where you were sent if you failed to whisper or tiptoe. As the year progressed, he learned to conform. With each passing week, he became quieter and more subdued, even at home. I watched and worried as he withdrew into himself. His teacher had accomplished her two goals with Steven, but I began to question the method as I observed my vibrant and happy child turn into a silent stranger.

At the time, I was completing a degree in elementary education, and I spoke with my professors, asking if tiptoeing and whispering were indeed the primary tasks to be learned in kindergarten. They were both astonished and outraged at the idea and emphatically declared that the role of the kindergarten teacher is and always has been to teach children to express themselves, to extend their vocabulary, and to encourage them with activities and experiences that engage the large muscles.

Because I was in my early twenties, I felt too inexperienced and reticent to challenge or question the teacher or even to talk to the principal. Yet, I desperately wanted my son back. I wanted him to reclaim his singularly exuberant identity. I carefully observed the first-grade teachers in his school and insisted that Steven be assigned the teacher of my choosing. Over the summer and into the next year, he gradually recovered his voice, his personality, his confidence and his zest for life.

From that time on, I continued to handpick my children's teachers throughout all their elementary years.

Such seemingly obsessive behavior holds true for many parents who are actively involved with their children's education, especially for parents who are teachers themselves, and it may explain why so many public school teachers enroll their own children in Seacrest for the first few critical years. Because of the experience, I was especially resolute in establishing a Seacrest kindergarten program that offered an environment in which young children could flourish and expand, speak in their own voices, and avoid tiptoeing at all costs.

Moving Toward Accreditation

Once kindergarten was in place and in full swing, we were ready for our first evaluation for accreditation. On a prearranged date, two members from the Florida Kindergarten Council came to review every aspect of our program. The job of the evaluation team is to make sure that the standards for accreditation are met and that the school is following its written philosophy and program.

We first met with our evaluators over dinner, which is designed to put us at ease for the next day's inspection. I am not sure they succeeded with me. The chairperson of the two-member team, Natalie Jordan, was formidable in stature and character. Having organized the first Florida Kindergarten Council, she was without question the Grand Dame of early childhood. As Natalie quizzed Mr. Sheehan throughout the dinner, I tried to attend to Jeannette, the other member of the team, and at the same time, listen in to the interrogation going on across the table. Apparently, Mr. Sheehan's responses must have satisfied Natalie, because she became quite jovial as the meal progressed.

When the two arrived early the next morning for their initial tour, they were obviously struck by the beauty of the surroundings. As they studied the lesson plans and observed the teachers and children in action, their expressions registered unmistakable signs of approval. They appeared to like the organized manner in which we prepared our classes. They were visibly impressed by the learning centers, materials, and equipment. As they watched the children in action and interviewed them, their whole demeanor seemed to take on an aura of *endorsement.*

At a much later date, after we had been approved for accreditation, Natalie revealed to me that after reading our philosophy and our self-study, she had decided personally to make the initial visit to Seacrest because she was skeptical about the program's ability to reach the high standards we had set forth in the curriculum and philosophy—but that we had met the test. And I heard from another board member that when giving the narrative about Seacrest at the board meeting, Natalie reportedly said she thought she had died and gone to heaven.

Passing the first crucial step to becoming an accredited school was one of our first big milestones. Almost immediately, I was invited to serve as a board member of the Florida Kindergarten Council, and I spent the next ten years as an active member and officer.

With each change in program, facilities or administration, a school must be revisited and reevaluated in order to remain accredited. Since Seacrest added new grades, teachers, space, or construction with each consecutive year, we were reviewed eleven times in eleven years by the Florida Kindergarten Council, and in addition, once we had progressed to the third-grade level, by the Florida Council for Independent Schools as well. I imagine Seacrest might hold the record for being evaluated the most number of times within a decade.

Fire!

Field trips and visits from the community gave our kindergartners as well as our preschoolers a wealth of knowledge gained from direct experience, and despite the increasing liability and risks in this day and age, Seacrest has continued these trips and interactions so that students can learn first-hand how a courthouse or a farm or a bird sanctuary or a hospital is operated and managed.

Field Trips

In the earlier years, meeting safety and insurance regulations was as simple as obtaining a chauffeur's license and permission slips from parents at the beginning of the year. Now, because of insurance requirements, new laws and stringent regulations, teachers and administrators are no longer allowed to drive on field trips and there are numerous forms to be filled out by staff and parents. Due to the regulations, field trips are becoming almost a thing of the past in many schools, but Seacrest continues expeditions as an invaluable source of learning for our students.

Most of our trips ended without incident, but several remain memorable, one in particular, not because of the excursion itself, but of what we found when we returned. It was a Friday afternoon in the spring of our second year, and we were returning from a trip to an orange grove where the children had hand-picked fruit, learning how the trees were planted and cared for and how the fruit was harvested and shipped.

Driving toward home with the children singing in the back seat, I noticed the sky ahead was black with thick clouds of smoke. Naples sits at the edge of the Florida Everglades, and forest fires are fairly common in early spring before the rainy season begins. In the vast expanse of wetland grasses and marshes along Alligator Alley between Naples and Fort Lauderdale, you can sometimes see miles of charred underbrush, cypress, and scrub pines. Conservationists tell us that when the fires are caused by natural means, such as lightning strikes, the results are beneficial—the underbrush is naturally cleared and nutrients from the ash help preserve the balance of nature in these fragile wetlands.

As we approached Seacrest, I realized that this fire seemed much closer. In fact, it appeared to be located over a large area of woods startlingly close to the school, the church, and my home. As if on cue with my mounting anxiety, fire engines roared past us. Turning onto our access road, Jack stood waiting at the corner, white-faced and grim.

"Get the kids home. Get them away from the school quickly," he commanded solemnly. Beyond the buildings, I could see a solid sheet of flames being swept by winds high over the tops of the pines.

With outward calm but an inward sinking heart, I hurried my load of children into a teacher's care, rushed inside the school and began calling parents to collect their children. In less than an hour all the children were safely on their way home.

We then turned our energies to aiding the efforts to save our home, the church, and the school. Our home was nearest to the wind-driven flames. First we called the high school where Jack's and my teenagers were in class and left word for them to come home as quickly as possible.

Our little neighborhood was well out in the country. We relied on well-water. There were no fire hydrants. The firemen had already inflated a large portable pool and were filling it with water from the lake. We watched showers of sparks flying over the roof of our home. Although many houses in South Florida are built with concrete block and stucco, we had opted for a home built from rough-sawn cedar transported in from the Pacific Northwest. Our architect had designed it so that it blended into the woods with decks and glass, lending a peaceful sensation of being part of the natural environment.

Everyone, including the church staff and our teenagers and their friends, hooked up all the hoses we could gather, climbed up on the roof and aimed steady streams of water on the rooftop and the sides of the house facing the fire. In the meantime a nearby neighbor with a tractor began digging a circular trench around our five acres of woods.

At one point the fiercely driven blasts of wind mushroomed, taking on a surreal life of their own, sucking up and fanning the flames into a raging wall of fire, sending out clumps of red-hot fire balls. That's when I began thinking that I should climb down from the roof and go inside while there was still time to gather up family photos, a few clothes, my mother's handmade quilts, my best china and silver.

It's only a house . . . The only thing that matters is that we're all safe, I kept repeating to myself, like a mantra. But at the same time another part of me insistently whispered, *Yes, but it's not just a house. We put our heart and soul into every board and batten, cabinet, and cupboard.*

While my mind fought this battle and my body fought the flames, the wind miraculously died and shifted. The firemen brought the flames under control just short of the trenches, and our home was saved. Sometime in the midst of our epic ordeal, a couple from California arrived, unnoticed and unattended. They had been scheduled to conduct a presentation at the church that evening, and we had invited them to be our house guests for the weekend. We met them for the first time, blackened with soot, drenched with sweat, and trembling from fatigue and fright. Without hesitation, they swung into action, lugging pails of water to the still smoldering woods, searching for live embers and drenching them with water.

School convened the following Monday, and we were oddly comforted by the thought that the woods would pose no harm for years to come, since all that remained of the lush green forest were blackened, charred stubs. Before the following year had passed, we were pleasantly surprised when new growth emerged from the ruins, and a profusion of baby saplings and luxuriant new green native vegetation began to regenerate. The resilience of nature was nothing short of miraculous. Afterwards, when other upheavals and unexpected crises entered our lives, I remembered those green young saplings bursting into new life, and was reminded that out of crisis come new seeds with the promise of new growth.

Spaced Out

Although we have been plagued by other natural disasters, including hurricanes, tornadoes, and floods, most of our upheavals have originated because of space, or to be more accurate, by the lack of space and delayed construction.

Our plan to begin with one grade of preschoolers and then add on a grade at a time was part and parcel of the success of Seacrest. We could build the following year's curriculum based on what the existing students were learning. We could evaluate our strengths and shortcomings and improve our program with each additional grade. We could carefully select the next teachers with time to introduce them to our philosophy, goals, and expectations.

But what do you do when everything is ready for the next grade and a new batch of incoming four-year-olds, teachers, and parents are prepared but no space is available? The dilemma became our nemesis over and over. The picture of delightfully expressive children in their sensory-rich environment run by talented teachers was a fascinating contrast to the frustration of lagging construction.

With kindergarten well into its first year, we concentrated on the addition for first-grade. The parents had become attached to the school's country setting, and Mr. Sheehan had generously purchased ten acres of land adjoining the church property. Our brochure and news clippings stated in black and white for all to see that: "The permanent location and school will be established and built by the fall of 1985," in time for the new first-grade class. Spring came with no sign of construction.

Since Mr. Sheehan was a real estate developer, he had taken on the responsibilities of construction and the new mortgage, as well as the salaries and the equipment for the classrooms. The tuition during the first two years had been set at the impossibly low figure of $1500 per year. We knew that to attract people to a new school, the tuition had to be affordable for a broad spectrum of the community. We determined at the outset that Seacrest would be a school available to children from all socioeconomic groups and that those who could not afford it would be awarded scholarships or financial aid.

Needless to say, no matter how meticulously and carefully we managed our expenses, the income from tuition always fell short. Although I kept our benefactor apprised of our budget during the ten years he supported the school, he never indicated that we were out of line with our expenditures, and he willingly donated the annual shortfall between income and expenses. With all his largess, I could hardly justify my mounting frustrations with delayed construction . . . at least verbally.

It became apparent that our building would not be in place by the beginning of the school year. We had used every available space at the church, so we were ready for some creative options that came our way through "The Little Brown Trailer." This new odyssey began in the summer of 1985.

III

EMERGING

CHAPTER 11

Little Brown Trailer

Great learning can take place anywhere, any time, under any circumstances—in the middle of a desert, on a mountain top, on a deserted island, in a one-room school house, or under a tree. That was what I tried to believe as four classes of kindergartners and prekindergartners finished the year and there was no visible sign of construction for additional classrooms.

Although Jack said he loved the sounds of children, my intuition told me that our use of the church facilities was moving beyond reasonable limits. The constant noise and capers of youngsters playing and learning were surely beginning to tax the nerves of the church staff, and I imagined how grateful they would be when we finally cleared out the kids and their paints, muddy footprints, projects, programs, parents, teachers, and traffic.

The solution remained elusive. Legend has it that the land where the church and school are located was once an ancient Indian healing ground, where natives came to be cured, to rest and renew, camping beside the banks of the creek. I visualized us holding classes under chickees (huts built of cypress poles roofed with palmetto and thatch) or setting up tents—the children would no doubt be enraptured by such a novel school.

One late spring day in 1985, our founder, Lloyd Sheehan, and I sat together on a bench in the patio of the church. I was intent on conveying the urgency for construction.

"Parents keep asking me every day when the building is going to begin, and I have no answer. We have no place for our first-graders to go next fall and it's making me crazy! If just a few trees could be cleared on the Seacrest site, it would help us psychologically, if nothing else. If something doesn't happen soon, I'm afraid it's going to affect our relationships with the church, the school and my marriage," I blurted out in one long breath.

"Well, Jane," Lloyd said patiently, "Maybe you need to do something about handling your stress." And then he added, "The building will be built in its own time."

Over the next decade, during each new phase of construction, the phrase, 'in its own time' was repeated over and over in my mind, like a chant, because the newest construction project was always late. Nevertheless, my request that day must have prompted some miraculous maneuvering because early the next morning, sounds of heavy, rumbling equipment came from the woods nearby. Peering down the road, I saw a hulking, yellow bulldozer uprooting trees, slicing into the untouched wilderness, opening up patches of bald, naked ground. The Seacrest building had commenced.

I was filled with an unexpected mixture of relief and loss at the sight of the land being stripped; up until then, it had been like a private sanctuary. The signs of progress taking over the environment is a conflict for most of us who live in this southernmost tip of the gulf coast of

Progress

The First of Many Groundbreaking Ceremonies

Florida, with its small-town flavor, surrounded by uninhabited terrain, white beaches and ten thousand pristine islands dotting the blue-green sea. It is a community that has its own breed of down-to-earth millionaires and fisherman, trades people, artists, and merchants.

Those of us who are year-round residents of Naples love our summers and sneakers, cutoff jeans and T-shirts. There is an unpretentious atmosphere that belies the talent, fame, and fortune of those who live private lives, concealed behind dense screens of Banyans and palms. We all enjoy the freedom and informality of the summer's unhurried, peaceful habitat. As Naples grows larger, there is a sense of urgency in protecting the natural environment from over-development. I treasured the untouched woods surrounding my home, so it was a shock when the building actually began.

On the one hand, we needed additional classrooms soon. I whimsically wished the school would be built somewhere else so that we would not have to live and learn so close to the upheaval and noise of machinery and the ugliness of barren land, uprooted trees, piled-up rubble, and concrete blocks. But on the other hand, I was relieved it had finally begun.

Toward the end of school, we had an official ground-breaking ceremony for the construction of our new building. Each child, teacher, board member, and some of the parents took turns digging up a shovel-full of earth, affirming the attainment of a new cycle.

In the meantime, we still needed space for our first-graders, in addition to the incoming classes of prekindergartners and kindergartners. We settled on a temporary building and retained the space at the church for another year. The temporary building was actually a Little Brown Trailer, which we planted at the edge of the Seacrest property, adjoining the church acreage, so it was an easy walk to the existing classrooms. This little brown trailer had a central room, barely large enough for a dozen or so child-size bodies, a teacher, and a tutor, but with planning and imagination, we shuffled around pint-sized tables, chairs, shelves, and equipment until it all fit. On either side were two smaller rooms, and there was a bathroom off the main room. With an even larger stretch of the imagination, we envisioned a circle of petite children and a teacher sitting on the floor in one of those pocket-sized rooms.

After inspecting every square inch, Becky, the prekindergarten teacher, proposed that she give up her existing classroom to Peggy, the newest teacher and her premier class of first-graders. Becky would use this portable space for her new incoming four-year-olds.

In her typical manner, Becky presented her plan in detail, complete with concisely measured floor plans accurately drawn to scale. She concluded the space would be adequate if a screened-in back porch, a fenced-in playground, and a small covered front porch were built. We would limit the prekindergarten enrollment to one class in the morning, using the space in the afternoons as a childcare center for the children whose parents worked late in the day.

"This is the best solution for all of us," Becky said, adding two final requests. "We need an additional sink on the back porch for washing up, and we need our own commercial-sized dumpster." She was obviously planning a busy year despite the cramped quarters.

With a guarded eye to the budget, I had to deny Becky's last two requests. The existing sink in the bathroom would have to suffice, and we couldn't afford a dumpster for this temporary facility, I realistically told her. "After all," I reasoned, "this is just a temporary building, and it will be gone next year when the school is built."

In hindsight, I should have known better than to take Becky's thoughtfully crafted plans so lightly. As soon as the construction of the screened-in porch was completed, I discovered a sink resting securely in the corner of the porch, next to the back door.

Surprised and puzzled, I turned to Becky and asked, "Where on earth did this come from?"

Unperturbed, she replied, "Oh, *that*. I just decided I needed a new sink at home, so I thought my old one would do just fine out here."

Becky got her sink, and I kept my budget intact. This is just one of many such instances where the Seacrest staff gave more than a hundred percent to make the school successful and comfortable for everyone.

A new class meant new furniture and new supplies, and so that August, we once again mobilized our energies to the summer ritual of unloading, unpacking, and cutting down the newest set of furniture cartons. As Becky prepared to transport dozens of empty cartons over to the church dumpster, she broke her wrist while loading the cartons onto the back of a borrowed truck. For many weeks thereafter, she accomplished her tasks, including the opening of the new school year, with a cast on her wrist, which rendered her right hand virtually useless. Her feeble, left-handed written communications looked like faint, illegible chicken scratching. Each time I viewed Becky's struggles, my guilt mounted at having denied her the ease and convenience of her own dumpster.

Even before the injury, that summer became a comedy of errors. The next class of four-year-olds could not pass through the doors of their new space until we had passed through the initiation rites of county codes. Once the passage was declared finished by a legion of officials, a certificate of occupancy would be awarded. The procedure opened up a whole new arena of escapades as we raced toward the finish line.

Carpenters, plumbers, air-conditioning technicians, electricians, well-diggers, painters, concrete mixers, excavators, fence installers, and landscapers vied for territorial rights within the meager confines of The Little Brown Trailer. Timing is one of the most critical elements for the successful completion of remodeling. If one of the members comes in at the wrong time, the consequences can be disruptive, costly, time consuming, or even damaging as the entire flow of work is interrupted. We quickly learned the importance of sequential order in remodeling.

First, the carpenters moved in to build support beams, flooring, siding, and roofing for the back porch. No problem here, thanks to a Seacrest parent—a building contractor who offered his services to construct and supervise this portion of the project. Yet, from then on, nothing progressed without at least one major glitch.

The well was dug in the wrong place. The newly installed chain link fence had to be dismantled to allow for passage of machinery for the installation of a septic tank. No sooner were the mounds of dirt replaced, landscaped, and sod laid, when an enormous truck, straining against the confinement of limited space, backed over the new underground septic tank, crushing it along with the newly planted sod. There was nothing to do but dig up the sod and earth, remove the crushed septic tank, install a new one, cover it up, smooth it over, re-plant, and re-fence.

Meanwhile, underneath the building, a separate scenario of misfortune was being created. In a narrow crawl space, barely large enough for a thin man, electricians, plumbers, and air-conditioning technicians took turns inching their way around on their backs and bellies as they assembled a network of wires and pipes. The space below was dark, dank and cramped, and more often than not, subsequent workers would bump against, undo, or disconnect some vital element of their predecessors' efforts.

But at the end of the summer, a day finally came when the lights and electricity, air conditioning, toilets, and running water all worked—and at the same time. The grounds were fenced, and boasted playground equipment and blooming hibiscus shrubs. A gravel driveway and sidewalk offered convenient access. The back porch was covered with weatherproof carpeting generously installed by Seacrest parents, Ann and Tim Ross. Another parent, Robert Hayes, completed the landscaping and sprinkler system. These were the first of numerous projects and services these particular parents would provide over the years.

The inside rooms resembled a doll house for four-year-olds. One of the little rooms was outfitted with a circle of carpet squares, bulletin boards, and shelves. At the opposite end of the building there was a cubicle for the teacher and her accouterments plus a second-hand refrigerator for snacks. Our certificate of occupancy was mounted over the fire extinguisher, inside the front door, next to the license for operating a school. With jubilance, we displayed the proof that we had met the requirements and passed every inspection for The Little Brown Trailer.

The Store

Despite the misadventures of our summer's labor, the simple little building had been transformed. On the first day of school, when parents and children stepped inside, they were charmed by the miniature panorama of a child's world. Becky had created a richly detailed wonderland for learning, set in an imaginative and cozy little dream house. The children immediately claimed it as their own. After all, who but they had their own house, designed just for them, in scale to their own size? Becky, too, was thrilled at having a space of her own.

The children of The Little Brown Trailer advanced and grew in a lighthearted, inexhaustible fusion of expeditions, multidimensional layers of experiences, and creative masterpieces. There were Indian festivals, complete with dances, costumes, songs, instruments, and folk lore. First-hand knowledge was transmitted to the four-year-olds by a real, live medicine man, a descendant of the legendary Osceola of the Seminole tribe. The students were given Indian names, which were amazingly descriptive of their personalities. Names like Running Dear, Little Dancer, Singing Star, Wild Fox, or Smiling Eyes. Becky was named, "Big Chief" and Janine, who was Becky's tutor, (the teacher's assistant) was "Indian Helper." Everyone proudly wore long, colorful necklaces bearing their names.

There were trips around the town and the surrounding countryside to visit merchants, artists, florists, postal workers, or fishermen—depending on the theme of the week. A trip to the grocery store not only meant real lessons in math, manners, and science, but a tasty treat from the bakery as well.

Every parent contributed his or her special expertise to help enlighten the minds of the students, or to donate their services to the school. Bonny and Norman Dery, parents who were optometrists, came each year to check all the students' eyes. The children of dentists, nurses, carpenters, aerobics instructors, horticulturists, and others swelled with pride when their own mothers or fathers were chosen as the celebrity of the day. The children held performances, including a memorable circus, in which each boy and girl became a clown, tightrope walker, lion tamer, or trapeze artist. Some performances and celebrations were shared with the other classes of Seacrest. The traditional Halloween parade and Thanksgiving feast surpassed that of the previous two years.

The First Course in Conflict Resolution

It is perhaps a commentary on the state of adulthood to note that the first major conflict at Seacrest happened not among the impetuous capriciousness of the children, but among the parents. That year's Christmas/Hanukkah performance for all the classes were produced and directed by the parents of the kindergartners and first-graders. The theme centered around customs and costumes from other countries and cultures. Midway through the planning stages, the parents of the older classes of children found themselves embroiled in a debate about whose children should play particular roles. Emotions escalated into heated arguments as tempers flared and accusations flew back and forth, while the teachers, the children and I stood in the middle, trying to remain neutral mediators. The title of the program provided an amusing and ironic twist to the clash: "Peace Around the World."

The parents must have kept their emotions in check at home, because their children seemed unaffected by the disputes and debates. The conflict was settled by the children themselves when they voiced their own preferences about which character they wanted to be.

In my memory this was the first full-blown conflict among the pioneers of Seacrest. Although I was surprised at the time, I later realized, as we added grades, that occasional disputes and feuds are an inevitable part of human nature. All of us are capable of collapsing into destructive, closed-minded behavior when our special interests are threatened. The situation is doubly true when our children are involved. Although we recall the incident with laughter, at the time it seemed alien to Seacrest's mission, which was to teach and practice peaceful means of settling conflicts.

Meanwhile, the children over in The Little Brown Trailer and their parents were unaware and insulated from the fracas of their older compatriots. They happily planned and rehearsed their part of the program. In the end, when everyone came together on the eve of the production, hearts were captivated and emotions were healed by the images and sounds of Santa and helpers, kings and gift-bearers, Rudolf and reindeer. Exuberant, unsynchronized voices heralded the songs of distant countries. Tiny feet stood underneath evergreen boughs while dancers guided and prompted each other to the tunes of ancient folk music.

It was the innocence of early childhood that insulated these little ones from the shock experienced by the rest of us on the day the spaceship *Challenger*, across the state at Cape Canaveral, exploded seconds after its launch. Dan, a Seacrest parent who was driving into the parking lot as it was happening, gave me the news coming over the radio. High above the building and trees, a wide ribbon of silver vapor leading to a circular puffy ball hung suspended against the brilliant blue sky, and as we watched, two tails split off from the ball, curving slowly downward in wide arks. Stunned into disbelief, minutes passed in silence. The only sound came from the notes of a bird, perched on a branch of a Mahogany tree. As with other events of collective tragedy, the vividness of the moment remains branded on our memories for all time—where we were, what we were doing, who we were with, and every graphic detail, as if captured in a slow-motion scene of a movie.

Dual Purpose for The Little Brown Trailer

As the school year progressed, The Little Brown Trailer served its dual purpose commendably, opening its doors each afternoon to the children of Seacrest whose parents worked outside the home. We initiated this After School Program, perhaps the first in our area, during the beginning stages of Seacrest.

As a working mother myself, I knew the hassles, not only to find suitable after-school care for my children, but the problems involved in transporting them from school to another location. In today's world, moms who work out of the home are in the majority, but still solutions are often difficult to find. We wanted to be of service to the parents as well as the children.

During Seacrest's first year, we concluded that it was not beneficial for the four-year-olds to be transported into a different environment after school every day, making the shift to another set of friends and supervising adults. In addition, the daily transportation became a challenge for everyone to manage. Vera Lindabury, one of our board members, volunteered to transport the children to a nearby day-care center, but we soon realized that it would be better to keep the children in their familiar group for the afternoon hours.

It was actually Peggy, one of the Seacrest parents, who volunteered to supervise all the children who needed after-school care in her back yard after school. She organized games and activities for the small group of friends. When Peggy took the position as the first-grade teacher for Seacrest, the arrangement became impractical. Thus,

The Little Brown Trailer became a convenient and happy place for the After School Program.

The tutors each took turns supervising the children in the After School Program. This sequence worked well until Brenda, one of the tutors, became pregnant. It was the first pregnancy of a Seacrest staff member. As her time for delivery drew near, we all took turns trying to relieve Brenda from the afternoon heat on the After School playground. Brenda's pregnancy became the focal point for the entire Seacrest population, including the students. None of us knew then that hers was the beginning of a long, continuous line of expectant mothers among the young married Seacrest staff members. From then on, there seemed to be a steady stream of ceremonies for brides and babies, even including a couple of hastily arranged weddings performed by my husband, Jack.

Yet Another Role for the Trailer

We planned to remove the trailer when the new building was complete and ready for occupancy in 1986, but we had formed an attachment to it, and we recognized its potential, so we decided to keep it around. It sits there to this day, and has served many purposes over the years, including space for the teen programs from the church, giving us an opportunity to repay a small portion of the kindness extended to us in the early years.

But in a more immediate and unusual turn of events, The Little Brown Trailer metamorphosed into a honeymoon cottage for Fran and Andy Stein.

Fran joined the Seacrest staff as a tutor assistant to the kindergarten teachers. As we discovered both her musical talent and her natural ability with children, she evolved into our first music teacher. Fran had an easy, calm manner, a perpetual smile, and a natural gift for relating to children. She often sat on the floor in a circle among her students with her guitar and an amazing array of children's songs.

Her ability to draw music out of children is a rare and seldom seen gift. I have known scores of technically talented musicians with degrees and years of experience. But in her early twenties and without a degree, Fran possessed something more. Through her inspired leadership, the children's voices seemed to emanate from the tips of their toes, rising through their hearts, and out into the air like brilliant, bright beams of sounds. Quarter notes, rests, and half notes became second nature to the children through the rhythm of dance. Math and

Connecting to the Music with Fran

literature, drama and movement blended together through the gift of Fran's music. Whether teaching the older students to play recorders and guitars, or younger ones triangles and tambourines, Fran kept the children in tune and on the beat and connected them to the music within themselves and each other.

Andy moved to Naples in loving pursuit of Fran. Yellow roses began to arrive at Seacrest on a regular basis. Fran's frequent blushes and secret smiles could hardly keep the truth from our seasoned eyes, and she finally succumbed to probing inquisitions, admitting that they were engaged.

Andy was a naturalist who loved the mountains. Fran was attuned to sea and sand and warm winters. They managed to work out an agreement to suit both their lifestyles. Following their wedding ceremony, held high atop the Rocky Mountains where Andy worked as a park ranger in the summers, they compromised by living in Naples throughout the school year, departing for Colorado for the summer months.

The arrangement worked well for all of us. Fran, Andy, and Charlie, their small shaggy black Peekapoo dog, set up housekeeping in The Little Brown Trailer, hooking up a stove and kitchen sink. Fran taught music during the school day and guitar lessons to Seacrest students after school. Andy agreed to work as our custodian, maintenance person, and security guard. In his spare moments, he wrote wonderfully descriptive poetry about the mountains in Colorado.

Fran and Andy eventually moved permanently to Colorado, where Fran finished her degree. Later, after their first child was born, she resumed teaching. Although the trailer has had many uses and guests, we will always remember their particular tenure as a romantic interlude in the history of The Little Brown Trailer.

The Permanence of the Temporal

Buildings are rarely temporary, as we soon learned. They have a way of becoming permanent. In later years, Nancy Brooks, a tutor and dance instructor, made one of the most dramatic changes, transforming the trailer into a studio for aspiring young ballet dancers. Nancy's husband replaced the screen porch with wood siding and a mirrored wall, and the carpet gave way to parquet flooring. The outside was painted white with green trim. A quaint and tastefully designed sign that read "Studio in the Pines" hung from the front porch. Although the dance studio incarnation bestowed the trailer with this official name, those of us who have been around the longest still prefer to lovingly call this humble little hut, "The Little Brown Trailer."

CHAPTER 12

1986 Unity Way

Seacrest was beginning its fourth year when we finally moved into our own, newly constructed building on Unity Way. The year was 1986, and so our new address was appropriately listed as 1986 Unity Way. I cut the wide red ribbon to the entrance as parents proudly herded their children together for the opening ceremonies of our new building. To the teachers, families, and board members the modest building symbolized a supreme accomplishment. It was a day that marked a significant event in the history of Seacrest.

The thick pine woodlands near our school deflected the sun's morning rays as I stood at the entrance, looking eastward at the faces of Seacrest students. The seven-year-olds, the seniors of our group, were entering second grade. As the original class of Seacrest, they were the worldly sophisticates, eager to lead the way into their new domain. The four-year-old newcomers peered out from behind parents' backs, wide eyed and solemn, uncertain what lay ahead. The kindergartners and first-graders gravitated toward their friends, showing off first-day-of-school outfits with their fresh faces glowing in the dewy morning light.

Following a brief message to the students, we guided them to their new classrooms. The smells of freshly painted walls and recently laid carpet filled the hallways. By the end of the day, the newness of

1986 Unity Way

the building would be seasoned by the ways of children, whose trademarks would soon be left in every corner of space: the tables would be christened with glue and leftover lunches and fingerprints would mark the height of children on doorframes.

The children were instantly comfortable in their new surroundings, mostly because we were comfortable. And that comfort was a direct result of the personal participation by most of the teachers and many of the parents in bringing the new Seacrest building from conception to reality. Everyone at Seacrest got involved, from start to finish, and so when the school opened, it was already an old friend like one's house or place of work. Teachers and parents were an integral part of the design decisions and many participated in the construction of the building and grounds.

Much is written and discussed today about the importance of establishing a sense of ownership among all the people involved in an organization. Our experience of designing, creating, and furnishing a school from the ground up lent itself to this idea as much as anything we ever did.

The joint effort of design and implementation allowed us to enjoy the talent and expertise of many people. As a result, we found ourselves with an exceptionally functional and creative school design. The initial stage of the Seacrest building consisted of seven classrooms, each measuring thirty-by-thirty feet, a small library, a multipurpose room with a little stage and storeroom, a tiny kitchen, my office, and a midget-sized front office with barely enough room for a secretary and minimal office equipment. A diminutive storeroom and janitor's closet opened off the hallway. The first playground was positioned at the north end of the building, just outside the prekindergarten and kindergarten rooms.

One of the parents, Robert Hayes, planted a young Ficus tree to shade the playground. Over time, as each new addition to the building was constructed, Robert transplanted this same Ficus, along with the playground apparatus, to different locations. This sturdy and fast-growing tree continued to spread its branches and roots, happily adjusting to wherever it landed.

The seven classrooms housed one prekindergarten class, two sections of kindergartens, two first-grades and our latest addition, one class of second-grade. The remaining classroom was used for the before and after school program.

Each classroom was equipped with its own bathroom and an additional sink near the back exits. An art island was designed at child-comfort height of thirty inches, with storage underneath. The surface was covered with a washable vinyl area so messy projects could be easily cleaned up. A large carpeted area with movable, ergonomically sound, multipurpose furniture offered a flexible floor plan and ample space for a diversity of activities and movement. Walls were filled with bulletin boards and strips of cork for displaying children's work. The blueprints were revised for additional electrical outlets, a request made by the teachers, who knew that most classrooms never have enough.

We installed full spectrum lighting, ceiling fans for each classroom, and one wall of windows. The halls opened to the outdoors. These ideas were not whimsical wishes; they were the result of my having worked in a newly constructed public school in Southwest Florida that had few windows, halls that were closed and stuffy, and harsh blue flourescent lighting. Structures like that, sealed off from the world, were supposedly designed to be energy efficient, but to me, it felt claustrophobic and stark. The classrooms were always too cold or too hot. More important, students were shut off from the natural environment. It defeated the advantages of living in Florida, where we are fortunate to have mild winters and plenty of sunny days. My definition of energy efficiency includes the option of turning off the air conditioners, opening the windows, and turning on the ceiling fans when weather permits.

Seacrest's design, more like the old-style Florida schools, with open hallways and windows, encouraged students and teachers to take advantage of the outdoors for eating, recreation, and lessons. We researched the studies about optimum colors for learning, and then each teacher selected her preference among the shades of soft, cool, or warm colors. The teachers opted for white marker boards on which they could

Ultimate in Parent Involvement

use a variety of bright colors, rather than the darker, traditional chalk boards.

Through our intercom system, classical music could be heard in the classrooms, library, and multipurpose room each morning while students prepared for the day. Underneath the skylights, green plants graced the classrooms and hallways.

Ann and Tim Ross, Seacrest parents who are interior designers, helped us select the carpet and blinds, purchasing and installing it all at their cost. Another Seacrest family built the art islands. Jack and Andy and other husbands mounted the marker and bulletin boards. All of us at one time or another wielded a paint brush. Robert Hayes, the parent who was a landscape artist, designed, donated, and installed the landscaping of native plants and trees, the sod and the mulch for the playgrounds. Frequently, Robert's six-year-old son could be seen working alongside his dad.

To my great relief, at this stage of Seacrest's development, I finally acquired a secretary. That meant I no longer had to do all my own typing, bookkeeping, filing, records, and answering the telephone. I interviewed and hired Pat during the summer, and so I was slightly astonished when she reported for work the first day and announced that she was pregnant. It did not matter. Pat was a beautiful bundle of high energy and efficiency, and her pregnancy seemed to boost her energy level even higher.

In addition to new classroom teachers and tutors, Cheryl came as our first librarian, working many months before the building was completed, designing her space, ordering all the books, materials, and furniture and putting it all together before we moved in. We hired a Spanish instructor and also a parent who took the dual role of supervising the After School Program and teaching art during the school day. The teachers had the luxury of their own tutorial assistant, and their classes were limited to fourteen children. The tutors also helped in the After School Program. Eighty students were enrolled in Seacrest in 1986. Although the cost of operations far exceeded the income from tuition and fund raisers, our benefactor, Mr. Sheehan, continued his financial backing as well as his encouraging support.

Whenever my friends from the public schools heard about our small classes and tutorial help, their eyes widened in disbelief, then narrowed into tiny slits of envy and frustration over their own overcrowded classes. I never convinced my former public school colleagues that despite the small class size and extra help, the Seacrest teachers worked longer hours and extended their labors far beyond the boundaries of a typical teaching load.

Techno Phobia and the Technical Revolution

Since its inception, Seacrest had only female teachers. There was no plot of any sort, just circumstances. But in 1986, Roy Bonnell appeared at Seacrest with an impressive portfolio of qualifications in the field of computer technology. He stood well over six feet, with a distinguished crop of prematurely gray hair and an infectious laugh. Schools were experiencing the first craze of user-friendly computer programs for children, and the race was on for the evolutionary shift to technological savvy. Roy not only brought us into the computer age, but he brought the first balance to our matriarchal staff.

Over the years, I tried, unsuccessfully, to steal away a few of my talented male friends from the local public schools and had concluded that indeed, "a good man is hard to find." The men with the necessary qualifications for an elementary program were uncertain about leaving the safety net of benefits and tenure in the public sector for the insecurities of a fledgling private school.

Roy and his wife, Karen, owned and operated a summer computer camp in North Carolina, and they agreed to rent eighteen of their Apple computers and software to Seacrest. So in addition to a new teacher, we had an instant computer lab. Within weeks, the students were communicating effortlessly in their dazzling new language of bits and bytes, commands and controls, disks and drives. The children could dismantle and reveal the inner workings of their computers, describe and illustrate the function of each component part, and reassemble it all back together. They learned the binary numeral system through planting a "Blooming Binary Garden." Different colored small plants were used to lay out a pattern that represented a code for each number and letter, consisting of zeros and ones in the binary system. For example, red flowers represented one number or letter, and yellow flowers another, with each pattern separated by mulch in the background.

The students constructed robots, designed to obey the commands of the owner with the tap of a hand-held control. Eventually, Roy and the children built a human-sized robot, christened "RTC," for "Robotic Talking Computer," which was quickly changed to "Robot Trash Can," because RTC was built from recycled materials. His head was fashioned from a bleach bottle. A blue trash can formed the body, and the arms and legs were made from aluminum dryer-vent tubing. An old blue baseball cap, garden gloves, and tennis shoes completed the outfit.

Their electronic wonder could spring to life, emitting whistles and bells with flashing lights blinking on and off, and glide across the room, picking up objects. He could read stories and books that the children had written, sing songs, and perform tricks and stunts. He was the major character in a play produced by the students, entitled, "Katie and the Computer." Before children began their lessons for the day, RTC would prepare them mentally with relaxation and imagery exercises designed for success.

Seacrest City

RTC's talents were exploited again when the young students combined all their knowledge gained from field trips, geography and civics lessons, research reports, and science into creating a model of a Southwest Florida town called Seacrest City. Wires were connected from the robot to flashing lights, highlighting each building as RTC told the story of the town.

It did not take long for the teachers, tutors, and parents to realize that under Roy's tutelage, the children were alarmingly out-pacing them in technical skills. They entreated Roy to teach an adult computer class so they could catch up. I remained in the Dark Ages of typewriters and longhand as both students and teachers passed me by. Claiming lack of time as my alibi, I stayed in the background of anything to do with computers. I effectively set up an internal resistance to anything that was remotely related to electronics. Anytime I came within three feet of a copy machine, movie projector, or computer, it seemed instantly to shut down and refuse to function. After a while, everyone on the staff made certain that I stayed at a distance from the electronic devices, which suited me just fine.

Whenever a student would ask me for help on a computer, I immediately called on the nearest classmate to come to the rescue. When I had to access something myself, I would painfully make my way through the mystery of icons and commands to retrieve the information I needed. These infrequent attempts were done in secret, when no one else was around, usually on weekends. So ingrained was my techno-

RTC

phobic reputation that when someone caught me at the keyboard, she would burst forth with an exclamation of surprise.

"Jane! What are you doing?" as if I were trespassing on forbidden territory.

Meanwhile, at home, my teenage children and husband had become computer whizzes. I wrote my entire doctoral dissertation in longhand, convinced that my brain worked solely through the medium of a number two pencil and a yellow legal pad, while Jack and my son, Kevin, transferred many hundreds of handwritten pages and revisions into the computer.

My resistance weakened as my responsibilities at Seacrest diminished, and I finally purchased a 486-IBM clone that was supposed to do practically everything—once you knew how to unlock its secrets. Much to my surprise, I soon found myself approaching an addictive fascination with all the possibilities waiting to be discovered and applied. Though the breakthrough for me occurred a decade later than for nearly everyone I know, it serves as a useful reminder that it is never too late to learn—and that is a philosophy entrenched at Seacrest as well.

While adults may sometimes be put off-balance by children's rapid and increasing knowledge, at Seacrest we are determined to be sure that no one feels threatened when the students display greater knowledge than their teachers and parents. We are willing to lift the limits of yesterday's preconceived restrictions about how and what children can learn. If educators hope to maintain even a snail's pace on the information speedway, a no-limits approach to learning is especially applicable to children and technology.

Children today view computers as a natural part of their lives; they possess no fears or apprehensions when presented with a keyboard and a mouse. The Internet, CD ROMs, modems, and programming come as naturally to them as learning to talk or walk. They usually ignore long, detailed instructions, and simply turn on the switch and figure it out for themselves, consulting with a partner when they need help.

I am glad, finally, to be part of the computer generation. My appreciation for technology continues to grow as I see what can be accomplished. For instance, just think about the way children, or for that matter, people in general learn. A computer is a tool that demands much of our senses and concentration. It waits for a personal command to follow orders. Its function is to take you into a position of power, aimed at a specific target. It gives you clues along the way with immediate and personal feedback to help you decide if you are on the right trail or if you need to take a different path. It captures and absorbs your mind and keeps your attention focused on the goal. You can go fast or slow, back up and repeat, stop or go ahead. And all the while, you are in charge of your own learning.

The current developments in technology hold breathtaking possibilities. New information, images, and sound are being brought to our fingertips on an incomprehensible planetary scale.

Our children, more than at any time in history, will need to be equipped with new ways to utilize information. More than ever before, they will need to hold a deep sense of moral responsibility for using the new possibilities for a healthier, wiser, more humane planet.

Building a Robot

CHAPTER 13

Inside Scenes

Richard leans into his teacher's side and she drapes one arm around his shoulder, as if to remind him that he is favored. Diane Miller is the only teacher who has gained total trust and wholehearted love of this first-grader. Up until that year, Richard's teachers have been stymied by his antics. He is not what you would call a cooperative student, and he rarely participates in the group projects or completes his assignments. Diane's unwavering determination that every student will be successful is boosted by a velvety-soft serene manner, underscored by youthful fashion-model beauty, and waist-length blond hair. Melting like putty under the spell of Diane's charm, Richard suddenly becomes infused with ambition to master whatever task is asked of him.

Diane also understands Richard's need for structure and order and for his own space. In the summer, before the 1986 school year began, Diane's father, a retired school administrator from New York, constructed a loft in the corner of her classroom, painting it to match the soft peach color Diane selected for the walls. The loft is used for reading and for small groups to plan projects or dramatizations or book reports. Sometimes it is used as a bribe, and Richard loves nothing better than to climb up the steps to the loft and work, elevated above the others.

Every detail of the room is organized for order, convenience, comfort, and beauty, extending to Diane's daily dress. She wears high heels and a different outfit to school every day. Brain-based learning techniques are incorporated into her curriculum, including the use of positive affirmations, relaxation exercises, and varied repetition. Taped classical music plays softy in the background of the children's lessons.

On this Monday morning, Richard tells the class about nesting sea turtles—where they nest and how they have to be protected. Following his lead, the others in his class share their stories and information about wild animals and birds in Florida. Next door, Peggy, the other first-grade teacher, steers her class down the hall, out the front entrance and into the back seats of vans, waiting to drive to the Nature Conservancy's Rookery Bay, where the class will experience the sights and sounds of the twelve thousand acre estuary for exotic birds, ospreys, eagles, manatees, and bottle-nosed porpoises.

Peggy is the scientist among us, and her classes are immersed in experiments and discoveries in the classroom, on the beach, at the Big Cypress National Preserve, Corkscrew Sanctuary, or right outside the back door of Seacrest. Turning her classroom into a laboratory, most everything is subject to scientific study, to be poked and probed, researched, and classified. After a few initial surprises, I am accustomed to finding snakes, hamsters, tadpoles, guinea pigs, ant farms, assorted bugs and other varieties of sea, land, air, and swamp creatures crawling, floating, or flying around Peggy's classroom. When an occasional snake makes its way onto the playground from the woods beyond, we always call on Peggy to identify and decide if it is poisonous or harmless.

Dauntless Dawn

After everyone is securely fastened into their seat belts and bag lunches are stowed away, the first-graders wave jubilantly as they leave for a day of high adventure. Not ready to tackle the stack of correspondence and phone messages piled high on my desk, I wander down the hall and into Dawn's second-grade classroom. The children are standing around the art island, painting replicas of zebras, tigers, monkeys, and rhinoceroses, surrounded by grass and jungle, contained inside a large three-sided box. Off to the side of the art island there is a display of African masks, beads, primitive wooden instruments, and rattles. A large map of the "Dark Continent" hangs on the wall at child height, where bold red, green, and yellow markers have traced the routes of early explorers.

Some of the teachers tend to wander on an exciting path away from approved lesson plans—some more than others. We often push the envelope, but always with the enrichment of the students in mind. For instance, the sanctioned curriculum for second grade studies traditionally calls for a standard Community Helpers theme which centers around food, clothing, and shelter in the immediate environment. On the other hand, Dawn, our new second grade teacher, is fiercely devoted to the no-limits approach to teaching. She rarely follows the published manuals or our own Seacrest curriculum, and her unconventional approach occasionally even disturbs the other teachers, who are, in comparison to the public school system and other private schools, already considered mavericks. "Dauntless Dawn," as I call her, is in her twenties and will try anything to keep her class interested in learning. She loves adventure and the unexpected. Her classes are never boring.

Dawn also loves to travel. Because she studied and lived abroad during her college years, she has friends everywhere. Spanish, French, geography, and foreign cultures are her favorite subjects. She is the first in line to give up her seat on an over-booked plane; the prospect of a free trip somewhere is infinitely more alluring to her than being on time to a holiday celebration or conference.

So, ignoring the standard fare in social studies, Dawn has her second-graders immersed in the interior wilds of deepest Africa, following the first explorers and traders along the Congo/Zaire and Nile into the land of parched deserts, steamy jungles, and majestic mountains. The children forage through newspapers and travel magazines for current happenings, comparing cultures and searching out obscure countries on maps and globes.

Later in the year, the geography, history and culture of Florida will be explored along with New York, Spain, California, or wherever else Dawn's intrigues happen to land. The children dance and sing their way into Spanish, French, or math.

There may be some gaps in the second-graders' mastery of the approved curriculum. But they are imbued with the belief that learning is exciting and the world is filled with adventure.

Center Time

It is "Center Time" in kindergarten. Corners of the classroom, tables, and shelves are organized for practicing the academics and

Going Shopping

applying the concepts of kindergarten. Each center is prepared for a specific purpose. Individuals or small groups either select or are assigned to a center equipped with a carefully designed tool for learning. Manipulatives, games, puzzles, blocks, computers, listening devices, books, art materials, and various other articles are targeted to engage the attention of the five year-old minds and bodies.

Over in the Housekeeping Center, five-year-old Cindy is dressed in a long, flowered skirt, high heels, a string of pearls and dangling earrings, topped with a black, curly wig. She coos and sings to her baby as she meticulously dresses and wraps her in a pink, fringed shawl, laying her gently in the stroller. Tossing her fur stole around her shoulders with a flip, checking her lipstick in the mirror, and pulling her purse over her shoulder, Cindy strolls the baby to the store, staggering in her high heels.

In the adjoining corner of the classroom, Chris, the grocer, stands inside the window of the bright green and yellow store, waiting to serve his customer. A wide navy and red striped tie is looped askew around his neck over a T-shirt. A straw hat sits loosely on his head, covering his ears and eyebrows. Chris greets his customer politely. Cindy requests the items on her list: milk, hot dogs and buns, ice cream and apples. As the grocer gathers the items, he adds up the cost of the groceries, writes out the total and hands the bill to Cindy. Fishing the bills out of her purse, Cindy carefully counts out a hand-full of dollars and shoves them through the window in exchange for the groceries, which she piles on top of the baby.

"Okay, now you owe me some change," reminds Cindy, whereupon Chris scrabbles through a pile of money and counts out three ones and two quarters.

"Here's three dollars and fifty cents for your change," says Chris. With an exchange of thanks, Cindy strolls her carriage, baby, and groceries back home.

Through my teacher's mind I summed up a few of the concepts that were being practiced by the scenario: adding, subtracting, counting with money, good manners, family care (even accounting for the minor slip of the placement of the groceries), and verbal expression. In the other centers, small groups and pairs are engaged in activities involving fractions, counting, geometric shapes, adding and subtracting groups of numbers. One child is measuring the sprouting seeds and recording the findings on a graph. Another is dividing a deck of cards into four stacks, with three cards in each stack.

You can discover a remarkable amount of information about a child in "Center Time," by just listening in on conversations and observing. Social development, emotional strength, verbal ability, academic understanding, and attitudes all surface. I was particularly fascinated one day when I watched Andrea and Martha playing "school." Andrea was a college professor, instructing Martha, the student. Taking on both the mannerisms of her teacher and her mother, Andrea skillfully guided her student through an art project. She praised, encouraged, demonstrated, and questioned.

"Oh, that's going to be fantastic!" she exclaimed. "Now here are all your materials. I'll leave you alone so you can work by yourself, but I'll be right over here if you need me."

A few minutes later Andrea returned and praised her pupil again, offering a bit of instruction in the use of her materials.

"Here's one way you may want to try. Can you think of another? Great! You're really getting the hang of it now. Oh, and here's a wet towel for the cleanup. While you finish up, I'll be right over there to fix you a nice snack."

The phrases, mannerisms, and techniques coming from Andrea were a near-perfect replica of her teacher, as she internalized the values of independence, positive guidance, and encouragement.

Tracker and Other Animals

Across the hall, an intern from the Nature Conservancy has come to visit Becky's prekindergartners, carrying two large wire cages.

The four-year-olds sit cross-legged in a circle on the floor, waiting to see what will emerge from the cages. A scurrying sound comes from one, as two masked eyes peer out at the children, prompting squeals of laughter. The leader, a young woman dressed in khaki shirt and shorts, opens the cage door and gently lifts a raccoon onto the floor, holding it securely with both hands. She discusses the features, habitats, and diet of the animal, and through a series of interactive questions, the group learns about the habits, family life, and safety of raccoons.

The second cage contains an armadillo, and a similar demonstration and talk follows. Every child is allowed to relate a story about a previous experience, some of which have nothing remotely to do with armadillos, raccoons, or other animals. Nevertheless, the intern listens politely to each, giving an appropriate but positive response.

Seacrest teachers and students are great fans of these close encounters with wild animals, and while most are exciting, one memorable visitor stretched the limits of excitement.

Naples is home to a famous naturalist and panther expert, Jim McMullen, who spent a lengthy amount of time in the Florida Everglades, tracking the endangered Florida panther.

In his book, *Cry of the Panther*, Jim describes with spellbinding detail his relentless but compassionate stalking of a panther in the Everglades. The book reveals how he dedicates his body, mind, and soul to his mission to search out, protect, and save the endangered panther from extinction. It is a journey reminiscent perhaps of his combat experiences from the jungles of Vietnam, which become eerily merged with the Florida swamps as Jim finds himself becoming both the hunter and the hunted.

Following this incredible, often life-threatening expedition, Jim exits the Everglades with a panther cub cradled in his arms. Naming the female cub Tracker, Jim raises her on a ranch. The two make frequent visits back to the cub's natural habitat in the swamps. Part of the time, Tracker lives in a natural setting with Phil Fisher and Natalie Guess , Seacrest parents, well known for their paintings and batiks of Florida wild life.

Our adventurous experience with Jim and Tracker begins when they arrive at Seacrest early in the day. When Jim opens the back end of the truck, two blazing yellow eyes stare at me with a steady, mesmerizing gaze that seems to bore right through me and out the other side. Tracker is sitting quietly on her haunches, watching. I am struck by her size, the swishing tail, the rippling muscles underneath the reddish brown fur, the large paws, and imposing features of her face and ears. But it is her eyes that draw my attention. The wary, watchful eyes follow my every move, and I am grateful that Tracker's cage seems secure and sturdy.

The early-childhood classes are the first to be introduced to Tracker, and I sit on the edge of my seat as the four-year-olds take their places on the floor a few feet from Tracker's cage. As Jim tells the story of the Florida panther, Tracker paces back and forth in her confined space, taking in every wiggle and murmur of the children.

I hold my breath as Jim opens the cage door and Tracker steps out. The exit happens immediately following Jim's convincing lecture that a Florida panther is a wild animal, and we must remember that it could attack. He is clear that this possibility includes Tracker, even though she has been raised in captivity. Jim attaches a long, thick rope leash to Tracker and leads her around the front of the room, stroking and talking to her all the while.

Jim next invites the children to pet Tracker, one by one, giving specific instructions about exactly what part of the body they can stroke. He tells the children where they should stand so that Tracker can see them at all times, adding an additional warning not to make any sudden moves or loud noises.

My attention shifts to two four-year-olds, John and Danny, who are known for anything but standing still and silent in one place, wondering if I should position myself between them and Tracker.

After three-fourths of the children move through the line to place tentative strokes along the thick furry back, a deep, low growl emerges from Tracker's throat. Her ears stand straight up and her tail moves into a different rhythm. Although the rest of her body remains perfectly still, one can sense a shift of energy. In the next moment, Jim calmly announces that Tracker is tired and restless now, and within seconds he guides her into her cage and secures the door.

During the lunch period, Jim remains close to Tracker, keeping her calm with soothing conversation, while the children form tiers of circles around Tracker's cage to get a closer look. The two visitors spend most of the day at Seacrest, with repeat performances in the afternoon for the older classes.

Despite my fascination with this wild and magnificent feline, I am relieved at the end of the day when she is transported back into the truck. After this first-hand visit, I reread *Cry of the Panther* with new insight, realizing just how connected Tracker and Jim are, as if they were at once masters of each other, in a mutual bond of deep respect.

CHAPTER 14

Revisions and Resolutions

Forming a PTO

Although I was determined that Seacrest would not be operated through the traditional top-down style of management, with its stratified layers of authority and hierarchy, we found it necessary in 1986 to create a Parent Teacher Organization (PTO). I wanted to avoid the "us against them" mentality so often seen in most institutional organizations, and I hoped our PTO would be different from some I had experienced in earlier years. Before the decision, parents, board members, children, the teaching staff and I had melded together much like an extended family. We accomplished tasks through a loosely organized and informal structure that worked well for a small group.

Still, as we grew, it became clear that we needed to initiate a more systematic approach. A parent requested that we elect a board of officers to run the Parent Teachers Organization, and we discussed the merits of a more formalized plan for conducting the growing number of events in the rapidly expanding school.

The parent who made the request was elected president of the PTO, along with her choices for vice president, secretary, and treasurer. They organized the parents and teachers into committees, drafted a list of rules and bylaws, and opened their own bank account. I sat in on the board meetings as they planned programs and fund-raising events, intervening only when their proposals crossed over into areas that were outside their responsibility, such as staff salaries, the budget, or decisions about personnel.

During the time of transformation, I did some soul searching about what it meant to be a leader, and more precisely, about how to define my personal vision as a leader. I wrote out these goals as a guide to myself:

◆ To protect the Seacrest philosophy, its goals and vision.

◆ To be persistent in what I believe, and to be willing to defend its mission.

◆ To find the best teachers possible, who are committed to continuous improvement.

◆ To inspire people to perform above their abilities.

◆ To create the best school that can be imagined.

◆ To pursue the development of Seacrest as a self-renewing school

◆ To be free to try new ideas.

◆ To be a listener and a gatherer of others' ideas and to learn from them. To credit others with successes and take the blame for mistakes.

◆ To encourage teamwork among the members of Seacrest.

◆ To be willing to remove obstacles to success and to be willing to say no when needed.

◆ To communicate with unconditional regard and respect to all people.

For the most part, the new structure proved to be advantageous. Although the PTO scheduled monthly meetings for parents and teachers, hardly anyone showed up unless the kids were performing. The situation was especially embarrassing if I had brought in a speaker from outside. On the other hand, the special events planned by the PTO were huge successes.

The Halloween Carnival transformed the multipurpose room into a haunted house of fortune tellers, skeletons, ghost stories, and games. For the Holiday Bazaar, parents created everything from delicious pastries to handmade quilts. The Seacrest Cub Scouts and their leader scoured the woods for palm fronds, turning them into replicas of

Rudolf's antlers, nose and face. Other hot-selling items were miniature note cards designed and printed by Seacrest students. We sold out of most of the antlers and cards as fast as they were made, even before the day of the bazaar.

It seemed the more we directed our energies and attention to the children and their activities, the happier we all were. Perhaps this was the key to maintaining a balanced perspective as we continued to grow and expand.

Unwelcome Visitors

While Florida's moderate climate allowed us to use hallways as display areas for students' art and science creations, open architecture had its drawbacks. The airy hallways became a runway for small nocturnal creatures during the night.

Most often, when I arrived at seven each morning to unlock the classrooms, I would find the droppings of squirrels, raccoons, or mystery animals on the concrete floor of the halls. Sometimes, it looked as if the squirrels had been on a rampage, diving, tearing and overturning carefully arranged displays of children's projects. There were also times when my huge dog, Guido, would have a romp through the halls. It was not long before we decided to put an end to these nocturnal wanderings by installing a black metal gate at the front entrance and chain-link gates at the side entries. Our decision came none too soon. An experience shortly after the gate installation confirmed that our decision was a beneficial one.

One morning, as the sun's first rays were rising above the piney woods, I approached the entrance to Seacrest and was startled to see the outline of a human figure, stretched out across the front entrance to the school. Shards of broken glass were strewn around the gate and the entrance.

The impact of coming upon such an unlikely scene prompted an adrenaline rush, followed by an instinctive primal call for action. Instantly, I closed in to determine if the body was alive, dead, injured, or drunk, and to remove it before the imminent arrival of the children. A hasty inspection confirmed that the male figure was breathing, sound asleep, barefooted, and clothed in grimy, scruffy, and torn shirt, and jeans. Without thinking, I charged forward.

"Wake up!" I called, with a nudge on his shoulder. "What are you doing here? This is a school, and you have no business here! You have to get up and get out of here— *now!*"

His swollen eyelids struggled to open, and the bedraggled stranger shakily attempted to sit up.

"Where did all this broken glass come from?" I questioned.

The man mumbled, denying any knowledge of the glass or how it happened to be there. I responded with the firmest directive I could muster to get himself up and off the property so that I could clean up the glass. The bedraggled stranger pulled himself to a semi-upright position and drifted off down the road, barefooted and tattered.

Hurriedly, I unlocked the gate, telephoned the sheriff, grabbed a broom out of the janitor's closet and swept up the pieces of glass. I finished clearing off the sidewalk just seconds before the first car arrived. Smoothing my hair into place, I must have managed to look composed because neither the student nor parent who arrived so early seemed to notice anything amiss. I smiled that everyday kind of smile, as if it were just another beautiful morning at Seacrest. Shortly thereafter, we contracted the services of a security guard.

National Pride

Another addition to Seacrest that year was a flagpole and American flag, donated and erected by a Seacrest family. The gift spawned a new ritual. Each Friday morning we gathered around the flag pole for a short celebration of the week's events and a patriotic song, concluding the ceremony with the raising of the flag and the Pledge of Allegiance.

On the first Friday morning of our flag-raising ceremony, the sun had burned away the dawn's fog, blotting my vision as I looked up to the top of the flag pole. At its base, a ring of students stood respectfully waiting to begin. The kindergartners led the ceremony by raising the flag and reciting the Pledge of Allegiance, substituting a few words here and there, as five-year-olds are prone to do. Five years later, a kindergarten student wrote down her own phonetically spelled version of the Pledge of Allegiance, with an illustration of the Seacrest children gathered around the flagpole with hands placed on hearts and two children raising the flag. The carefully constructed printing and picture remain in our scrapbook today as a treasured visual image of one child's passage into literary acquisition:

> I pleg a legise to the flag of the Unide Stasse of Amarka
> and to the re publk for wich it stads onw nashe und a God
> in Uveizb for livrd and gust and for all
> An*dee Naccarato, Kindergarten Class of 1991*

Traffic Control

Often, as I have mentioned, my energies were directed toward a wide array of concerns that seemed far removed from academics, but which nevertheless were an integral part of operating a school. Problems with traffic and safety ranked high on the list of time and energy-consuming frustrations, and traffic control definitely comes under the purview of an educational institution.

As the school grew and the ingress and egress of our little community became more congested, we saw the need for developing a parking plan. One hair-raising episode propelled us into action. A six-year-old student, tired of waiting in the car for his mom to return from the school building, turned the keys in the ignition, shifted the gears in the car and drove off into the nearby woods, finally rolling to a gentle stop. Such are the complexities that come with growth.

Even though we developed all sorts of parking rules, mishaps were not uncommon. Once, a young mother came to retrieve her older child while leaving her two-year-old in the car—with the keys in the ignition. Upon returning, she found that the younger sibling had locked the doors with the windows up and was happily galloping to and fro across the front seat.

The mother enlisted our help. First, we tried to cajole him into pulling up the lock, pantomiming directive gestures. These antics only prompted gales of delighted laughter from little brother, who loved the fact that he had a whole flock of people gathered just to entertain him with their funny faces and flapping arms.

Before we resorted to dialing 911, Roy, our science and computer specialist, came to the rescue. Using a broom handle, he attached a makeshift hook on the end, inserted it through the back window of the van, snaked it to the front window and clicked open the lock.

Traffic was usually brought to a standstill by ceremonies such as flag-raising, fire drills, Halloween parades or Walk-a-thons. Well-established traditions at Seacrest only made the matter worse after we moved into our new building.

As parents drove up to drop off their children, I provided the service of opening the car door; assisting each child in gathering up his or her book bag, lunch, and other assorted items; helping the child out of the car; offering a hasty greeting to the parent; and closing the door as the next car drove up. While we were still in our rented space at the church, long before the school was built, the daily ritual became a wonderful tool for communication with the parents. It was a time when parents could convey important little details about their children. Perhaps Jimmy had run a temperature the night before, or Betsy had come home crying over an incident on the playground. The exchange offered me the opportunity to pass on messages and reminders of current happenings, to answer questions, or to jog memories of overdue tuition payments.

Once we were in our new building, it became increasingly difficult to retain a fraction of the former personal touch while keeping the inflow of cars moving. As parents know, there are times when children cannot be hurried, no matter what the circumstances. There always seemed to be a few sleepy ones who had not yet pulled on their socks and shoes, which could easily result in stalled traffic.

At one point, I decided that we would have to forego the morning ritual, and the children would have to let themselves out of the cars. It was a bad decision, one which parents were not willing to accept. The problem was happily resolved by parents and a few staff members taking over the job themselves, along with the aid of a few older students. An assembly line was formed each morning, thus initiating an easier and more efficient method of opening car doors, helping children out, and keeping the traffic moving.

New Babies

As Seacrest grew, my own understanding ripened into the realization that our school was emerging into a microcosm of life itself. We were a small community of people who shared the same challenges, struggles, and joys as those in a larger society. For me, a new birth never failed to evoke a time for celebration. The event was a moment in time when the mundane gave way to the miracle of new life, bringing with it all the pure, innocent beauty of a new creation, where present, past, and future merged with regeneration and renewal.

Just as in the community at large, we witnessed the cycles of life at Seacrest. Newborn babies were always a time of sharing joy, and with a school of young teachers and parents, there was a steady flow of baby brothers and sisters being paraded through the school. I often attended to my duties with a baby cradled on my shoulder.

My role as surrogate grandmother to new babies provided me with a deep source of satisfaction and a sense of being a part of the continuum of generations. With such a close-knit community, I observed every step of the infants' progress; I saw the first wide, toothless smiles, little hands grasping toys, the first teetering steps, and infant coos and gurgles transcending into words with meaning. In the flick of an eyelash, the newborns grew into their first prekindergarten class, striding confidently into the big world of School, led by the reassuring hand of an older sister or brother.

A year never passed without a tutor or teacher announcing her pregnancy, and it was not unusual to have several babies born in the same year. Sometimes, I wondered if I should have hired only postmenopausal women. But we managed to fill the maternity leaves of absences, celebrating each birth with elaborate baby showers.

My secretary Pat's new baby arrived near the end of the school year, and since few people were around during the summer months, Pat brought her baby girl to school each morning along with diapers, carriage, changes of clothes, and other infant necessities. Pat was the only person I ever knew who could type, answer the phone, carry on a detailed conversation, and nurse a baby, all at the same time. She never missed a beat in attending to her doubled duties.

The arrangement was satisfying to Pat and me and seemed to suit the baby. We took turns burping, rocking, and changing the infant; taking phone calls; and managing the summer's work. There were a few occasions when we would hide the infant away in the adjoining conference room for the sake of propriety, but those instances were rare.

As our little microcosm reflected that of life around us, we did not escape the tragedies that the universe deals out as a part of the cycle. Some babies were lost through miscarriages. A two-month-old died of Sudden Infant Death Syndrome one morning while two older sisters dressed for school. We felt the pain of the parents and grandparents' grief, with a loss too deep to comprehend, caught in our own helplessness at not being able to do enough.

During the times when tragedy struck, all of Seacrest banded together— parents, students and staff, to do whatever could be done and to form a staunch circle of support, like a clan conjoined by family ties. Our full-fledged support in times of crisis still holds true today, even as Seacrest has expanded and grown.

And when I hold the newborn babies, I am moved as much today as in earlier times: These are the ones who will form the next links in the Seacrest clan. They symbolize the passage of time. I look at the fifth or sixth-graders and remember carrying them around when they were a few weeks old. I picture them as adults with *their* first newborn, and I can visualize a future generation at Seacrest.

Celebrating Babies

CHAPTER 15

Retreats and Renewal

At the end of summer, the Seacrest faculty meets together for a day's retreat to set the stage for the new school year. Before Keewaydin Island was sold to developers, it was our special meeting place. Accessible only by boat, our ritual voyage to the island began when we boarded the fifty-year-old *Kokomis* for the crossing to the northern tip of Keewaydin Island, a barrier island with seven miles of white sandy beaches stretching southward along the gulf.

Although the passage takes only a few minutes, we are transported into another time as the *Kokomis* slips through the mangroves and comes to rest beside the rustic dock pilings lined with wooden benches beneath a thatched roof.

We are the only visitors. Winding our way to the beach, we see the giant, twisted branches of a sea grape and an ancient gumbo limbo tree, bearing witness to another era. Shafts of sunlight penetrate through cabbage palms and live oaks as the sea breezes diffuse the early morning mist. Although the lodge and Old Florida guest cottages are closed, an invisible staff has trimmed the hibiscus and raked the flower-bordered footpaths, so that the surrounding natural refuge holds a sense of being lovingly tended and carefully preserved.

Keewaydin has a rich and adventurous history, with archeological traces of the vanished Calusa Indians. It has been a vacation spot for some of the country's most illustrious families who came to enjoy the unpretentious charm of an unspoiled sanctuary. It is said that there was once a small private school on the island. For many decades, Keewaydin was handed down through families who understood its uniqueness and who were determined to preserve its way of life, in tune with nature.

Under the chickee beside the shore, we arrange the cane beach chairs in a circle where we review the Seacrest philosophy. Soon after, we break up to walk the beach or swim in solitude. It is a time for introspection and renewal; subsequently, individuals pair up to share ideas and personal goals.

At midday, the group reconvenes under the chickee, and our discussion is directed toward modifications and new possibilities for the school as a whole. The details of organizing, scheduling, or planning are deferred to the forthcoming days at school. This is a day to bathe our minds in the warmth of sun and sea— to combine relaxed communication and fun.

At lunchtime, the mood shifts quickly into a party mode as we polish off sandwiches, cake and cookies, draining chilled bottles of soda. After lunch, we loiter along the shore's edge as the waves roll in at high tide in the lull of the afternoon sun. Gazing lazily at the clusters of men and women engaged in quiet conversation, I wonder what unseen challenges will emerge in the new year, wistfully imagining smooth and easy days unfolding into a year of perfect harmony with no major upheavals. Such an unlikely scenario is easy to imagine in an environment protected from outside forces, where wild life, native plants, and pristine beaches appear remote from the bustling activity of the mainland.

Of course, my whimsical imaginings are pure fantasy, spawned by a day in a tranquil paradise. Inevitably, Seacrest would surely encounter its share of obstacles and new problems to solve in the year to come; yet I recognize that it is the constant flow of growth and change that provide us with opportunities for new learning. The combination of our Keewaydin retreats and the promise of new challenges ahead are both characteristics of a self-renewing school. It is what Robert Waterman writes about in his book, *The Renewal Factor*, when he describes the individuals within the organization who are inspired to look for better ways to do things, and who have the power to implement their own ideas.

I am always inspired by the openness, tenacity, and the stream of creative ideas generated by the faculty when we are in an informal, relaxed state. Meeting together periodically in a retreat setting is an important element in the concept of renewal, both for the organization and the individuals within the organization. It is a time for clearing the mind and replenishing the spirit.

The act of self-renewal takes many forms and is practiced in a variety of ways, depending on the choices and circumstances of individuals. Ideally, we can set aside periods during the week for activities that restore our energies and re-create a sense of balance. But too often, we become so immersed in daily responsibilities, the time for self-renewal becomes more and more infrequent. It is never a simple task to find and maintain the balance between work and play, tradition and innovation, or individual and collective goals. The organization succumbs to the influences of unscheduled and unexpected events. With too many conflicts competing for our time, we may begin to lose sight of the larger purpose. Being out of balance becomes the status quo.

In Stephen Covey's book, *First Things First*, he offers many ways of rethinking and reorganizing our lives so that we can reconnect to purpose and vision both for ourselves and the organization. For many, nature provides a powerful source of renewal. On finding balance, Covey writes:

> There's a sense of balance and harmony in nature. Seasons come and go with regularity. There are cycles of life, giving and receiving in a beautiful harmonious whole. Even cataclysmic events—storms, earthquakes, floods—are part of a larger harmony, a natural cycle   of growth and change. Nature is always becoming. The beauty of nature constantly unfolds in accordance with its laws.

Our days on Keewaydin Island held the sense of being at one with nature. This magical island gave our retreats the gift of being immersed in a wondrous natural hideaway—a place where we seemed to be our more authentic selves than in our real-life world. The purpose of our work became more clear as we allowed the rhythm of nature to renew our energy. For a little while, I was able to put aside the sense of urgency in completing too many tasks with too little time in the days to come.

Time to Renew

IV

NEW ADDITIONS

Chapter 16

Leaders as Learners

Lynne

Sometimes life offers you a synchronistic moment—a moment that seems to appear in a way that defies explanation. At the beginning of the 1987 school year, I experienced such a moment.

Seacrest had progressed to the third grade, and we added more prekindergarten and second-grade classes. The new teachers were hired, all of whom were experienced and talented. Two of the teachers, Jennifer and Judy, had enrolled their own children in Seacrest in earlier years and were familiar with the school, the people, program, and philosophy. The newest faculty members labored voluntarily through the summer preparing for the new classes.

Our year-old building was filled to capacity on the day it opened and, as usual, we needed space. Two portable classrooms were to house the ever-expanding Seacrest population. Once again, there were the responsibilities and accompanying challenges in construction tasks and equipment purchasing.

The "normal" events that preceded the start of school each year were of crucial importance. Demands came from all quarters: paperwork and administration, students and faculty, maintenance and landscaping.

It seemed to me that every teacher and every parent wanted personal conferences. And predictably, two staff members presented me with the year's annual notice of pregnancies, which meant an immediate search for substitutes. As if all that was not enough, I was in the midst of my work on a doctoral degree, which included lengthy seminars and the creation of a dissertation.

One Sunday morning a few days before the term began, I woke up realizing it was not humanly possible for me to do all that was required. Despite my awareness of the importance in keeping a balanced perspective, I was stuck in a black hole crammed with urgent details. Any semblance of self renewal I had gained from our day of retreat had vanished. There were not enough hours for me to complete the tasks for the school in the few remaining days before the children arrived. Depressed and exhausted, I phoned a personal friend who was a family counselor, and in a quavering voice I asked for an appointment.

"I'll be right over" was her immediate reply. Isabel "Andy" Stanley is a no-nonsense person who cuts to the core of life's challenges. She is not interested in hang-ups with your mother or self-esteem problems from being a middle child. Practicality is her method, and I had observed the remarkable and quick results of her work in helping children and families find *practical* ways to manage their lives. And I desperately needed a quick fix. Life was closing in on me.

She listened patiently as I explained my dilemma. Her answer came quickly: I needed to hire an assistant administrator, and she counseled that I needed to let go of the notion of finding the *perfect* person—a warm body would fill the bill at that moment.

The following day, dressed in jeans and T-shirt, I mulled over Andy's advice while unloading and processing boxes of furniture and instructional materials in the multipurpose room. My secretary interrupted me with a call to the office to meet a teacher applicant.

Another interruption—I decided to give the teacher at most five minutes of my time. Little did I know in my angst and frustration that serendipity lay around the corner and down the hall. Within a few minutes I found myself face to face with the person who would become my associate, my best friend, and ultimately the leader of Seacrest.

Striding into my office with a plastic smile, I put out my hand to greet Lynne Powell, ready with an apology for my faded jeans and a tight schedule.

"I hope you'll be able to come back later when things are a bit more settled so that I can spend more time with you," I told her.

She caught the implication of my message and replied with a disarming warmth that broke through my deliberate reserve.

"I'll come back at any time that's more convenient with you. One of the Seacrest parents, Ann Ross, and I are tennis partners, and she insisted that I had to stop in to meet you because she knew that I would love you and your school at first sight. It sounds like the kind of school I've been teaching in for many years in New Hampshire."

Whether it was Lynne's words, her radiant smile, or intuition from a deeper level, I felt an instantaneous connection. I wanted to know more about this stranger. Without my realizing it, we settled into a relaxed conversation, and I forgot everything else. Somewhere between Lynne's description of her experiences in the small town schools of New Hampshire and her recent move to Naples, I told her that I was looking for a second-grade substitute for an upcoming maternity leave.

She seemed more than interested. "Children at this age can learn so much more than people realize," she offered enthusiastically. Without thinking further, I not only offered Lynne the substitute position, but I also heard myself revealing my need for an administrative assistant. Aware that Lynne was listening intently, I told her everything I needed help with.

She said very little as I talked, and yet I knew in my bones that she was a person who represented more than just the "warm body" who could help me. With nothing more to go on than an intangible but compelling perception of trust, I asked Lynne if she would be interested in considering an administrative position. Her acceptance came as a natural and unremarkable outcome of our exchange. She would fill the temporary second-grade position and at the end of the six-week maternity leave, she would give administration a try.

We did not talk contract, or salary, or specific job description. Within less than two hours, I had found the exact person I needed. Or rather, she found me, or perhaps we found each other. I am always surprised as I reflect on that moment how from an ordinary meeting an extraordinary partnership was formed, as if our agreement was nothing more dramatic than making a date for lunch. Almost without noticing, we had turned a corner that would change both our lives, simply by saying "yes" to each other.

During Lynne's teaching assignment, the second-graders successfully reached the high expectations she had set for them, and I was restlessly counting the days until her inauguration as my key assistant. Since we were short of office space, we found a small desk and moved it into a corner of my office. When the day finally came for Lynne to move into my office, I was surprised at how little it bothered me to share my space. For as long as I can remember, having my own space has been a basic, almost sacred need. It probably would not have worked with anyone else.

For one thing, Lynne seemed to hold a sixth sense that knew when to disappear for a few minutes. She also became an expert at reading my body language, and she even discovered some things about me that I did not know. For example, she recognized a drop in my blood sugar level about an hour before lunch. She took to keeping a stash of peanuts in her drawer and just before eleven o'clock, she would pop a handful of nuts on my desk and give me a knowing look, regardless of whom I was with or what I was doing. It was one of many minor among the major miracles Lynne performed daily.

With all there was to be accomplished, delegating jobs to Lynne was not a problem, and she accepted whatever task I laid out. None of the hundreds of books and articles I have read about leadership, management, or shared power quite fit the description of Lynne's and my working arrangement. We never got around to sitting down and designing a job description, deciding who did what. Our work intermingled, merged, or separated into different responsibilities, depending on the circumstances.

I remember after reading Steven Covey's inspiring book, *The Seven Habits of Highly Effective People,* suggesting to Lynne that we develop a definite set of responsibilities and goals for each of us. Her response was to ask me if I was unhappy with her work, and if I was, we should adjust our way of working; Otherwise, we should continue to let our work evolve as we had. To me, this showed real insight about our partnership. Lynne and I were growing and learning, making adjustments how and when they were needed, rather than defining our work into separate categories.

Although a carefully designed plan may have been more efficient, I doubt that the end result would have worked as well for us. Our informal teamwork allowed us easy access to each other's strengths and ideas. We worked side-by-side, sharing the combined duties of director and principal. As our work evolved naturally, I continued to handle the business details, correspondence, conferences, meetings, hiring new staff, dealing with the perpetual construction, and the overall supervision of Seacrest. Lynne took on the responsibilities of admissions, curriculum planning and development, and working with individual students and teachers.

Working with the premise that two heads are better than one, our jobs frequently overlapped as we worked together on long term projects or the daily tasks of operating Seacrest. When I was stuck on a problem, Lynne was quick to provide a solution. We frequently wrote together, composing everything from updates on brochures and program planning to letters that required sensitivity and diplomacy. We solved problems over lunches and rehashed daily dilemmas over the phone in the evenings. When necessary, we could fill each other's positions, which allowed us both time off for families, vacations, and educational pursuits.

Whenever a student was in trouble, Lynne became the child's best advocate. One mid-afternoon I returned to my office, weary from a long meeting, to find Bobby sitting with his arms crossed tightly over his chest, chin held up defiantly, with his mouth set in a mulish grimace.

"No, not *again*," I thought to myself. It was the third day in a row that Bobby had been sent to our office for bad behavior. Over the course of several years, Bobby's constant disruptions, skirmishes, defiance and poorly done work had formed such a predictable yearly pattern that his teachers had pretty much exhausted their resources for "what to do with Bobby." They were ready to give up and were recommending that he be expelled.

On this afternoon, Lynne was sitting with her back to Bobby, seemingly oblivious to his "tough guy" stance. As I walked in, she turned to give me a discrete wink and continued her work. Taking her cue, I sat down at my desk without making eye contact with Bobby, shuffled through some files and began to write.

After being ignored for another few minutes, Bobby began uttering loud sighs. He shuffled his feet and tapped his fingers on the arm rest of his chair. When no response came from either Lynne or me, he cleared his throat a few times and finally spoke.

"Well, whadda ya gonna do to me *this* time?"

Turning slowly to face Bobby, Lynne asked in a hushed, calm voice,

"I would like to know what you are planning on doing for yourself. And I'd like to know if I can help you."

"Nope," came the reply. "Nobody can help me."

When Lynne asked him to explain, he said, "Cause everybody hates me. Except maybe you. The kids in my class all think I'm dumb. My teacher hates me 'cause I don't get my work done."

Holding my silence, I waited for Lynne's response.

"Well, Bobby, I know very well that you're *not* dumb. Maybe you just have to prove that to your classmates. I can help you prove it to yourself, and I can also prove to you that you can get your work done. Are you interested?"

During the next few minutes, Bobby and Lynne negotiated a step-by-step process, in which Lynne promised to help Bobby with his school work and in turn, his part of the bargain was to behave in the classroom. Every day after that, over the course of several weeks, Bobby brought in his assignments, and he and Lynne would sit together at a little table outside the office and finish his work. Lynne taught Bobby several little tricks and short cuts for his math, got him motivated enough to complete his reading assignments, and checked his spelling and writing.

Although Bobby's work improved, I would not say he turned into a sterling student overnight, either in behavior or academics. Yet, there were some sizable positive gains made under Lynne's guardianship—in Bobby's view of himself, and his general outlook on his classmates and teachers. You could see a few layers of Bobby's resistance gradually melting under Lynne's constant encouragement and careful prodding. While the rest of us had run out of patience and energy with Bobby, Lynne would not give up until he had tasted and savored the sense of success and achievement. Lynne made good on her promise to prove that Bobby was not dumb, and maybe he came a little closer to believing it himself.

Most university courses in supervision, public relations, finance, or school law tend to be theoretical with little practical relevance to the realities of school. In addition, to deal with the minute-to-minute concerns and problems that crop up with unexpected regularity, a leader must be able to inspire and communicate a shared vision— something learned most often from experience and not readily found between the pages of a textbook. Lynne's on-the-job experience prepared her for leadership better than any course one could take in educational administration.

Leslie Ann, when she was a seven-year-old student at Seacrest, wrote this poem for Lynne. The poem reflects the image of Lynne's leadership from a child's point of view.

We are the sea, you are the sun
You bring light to everyone
You care, you teach me too
So this is why I love you

Love to Dr. Lynne Powell from Leslie Ann (age 7)

Lynne

CHAPTER 17

Expanding

In 1987, Seacrest was entering its fifth year. With the addition of third-grade, we needed nine classrooms to house the ever expanding student population. After one year in our new building, we were bursting at the seams, and so we began the toilsome process of adding a wing with three new classrooms. Knowing, from the already mounting past experiences, that the addition would *not* be ready for the fall, we installed two portable classrooms, which took the better part of our time and energy over the summer months. While the new wing was under construction at the north end of the building, two new teachers, Judy Brown and Jennifer Amico, held their second-and-third-grade classes in these portables, positioned on the south end.

As the parent of three Seacrest students, Jennifer was at the forefront of major fund-raising events. She headed up many committees for curriculum writing, global and international cultural programs, or technology. Jennifer's husband, David, was president of the Parent Teachers Organization for two separate terms. Jennifer and David made sure things got done, and together they organized fund-raising activities and gathered energetic teams of people who were willing to work.

Between school and late night meetings, Jennifer carted her own children off to other after school activities. Having raised a gang of children myself, I empathized with Jennifer when her pace across the parking lot was a little slower and her greeting a little less vibrant. I knew, though, that by the time she greeted her third-graders, she would be ready to go another round, full speed ahead.

Jennifer's class soon discovered that nothing got past their teacher's awareness— as if she was equipped with a second pair of eyes in back of her curly, short hair. Under Jennifer's tutelage, the class worked hard and smart. Let me describe a typical day in Jennifer's third grade classroom.

On a Friday morning in October the breezes offer the first hints of cooler, dryer air and a promise of autumn. The ditches are filled with water from the late seasonal rains, and the earth is moist and soft beneath my feet. Jennifer's class has just returned from the playground, stamping off traces of mulch and sand on the deck of their newly erected portable classroom.

Entering her classroom, I observe the third-grade students who are well into the study of early American history. They are surrounded and immersed in hand-crafted Indian villages, globes, maps, and charts depicting the routes of ocean voyages and trails of explorers. They carry clipboards of collected Spanish words and phrases. The first stages of a relief map of the Atlantic Ocean, Europe, Africa, and America are drying on a table, waiting to be outlined and painted. One group constructs a sailboat out of wood, string, cardboard, yarn, and glue, while another group huddles together, putting the final touches on a report to be presented to the class.

Nearby, John and Tom alternately stand and sit as they pore through stacks of library books and encyclopedias, searching for information about sea life.

Listening in for a moment, I overhear Tom ask his partner, "Do you like salmon?"

Not waiting for a reply, Tom continues, "I love it! Before I cook it, I marinate it in dry wine, lemon juice, olive oil and some spices, and then let it sit in the fridge for a while and then my dad and I grill it, and it's ummmmm, dee-licious!"

Not to be outdone, John jumps in, "A good kind of fish is Strawberry Grouper and Yellow Tail Snapper. We catch 'em and eat 'em. Have you ever eaten Barracuda? We catch 'em, and if they're over five feet, you can't eat 'em. They're poisonous. I heard about this guy that ate one, and his nose started getting really weird, and it swelled up and he finally died."

Moving to another table, I watch Pete dip paper strips into starch and paste them onto a relief map. His work is interrupted by a spill.

"Ouch! I spilled starch all over my knee and it's stiffening up! Ow, my fingers are hardening. I gotta wash it off. Be back in a minute."

Along one wall, another group of third-graders prepare to plot a map with illustrations of the school areas and surrounding roads. A sign above their work reads, "Seeds of Change." Other slogans are posted around the room: "Heroic Helper" and "We Learn from Our Mistakes." Color photographs show the ships of ancient mariners. *Yachting Magazine* and poems and stories about the sea are propped on shelves along with a collection of rocks of many shapes, sizes, and textures.

Later in the day, during the science period, the third-graders will work on the inventions they have designed and built in their study of simple machines. These ingenious and bizarre contraptions are constructed with wood, string, pulleys, wheels, inclined planes, and motors. Most are designed to help with home chores. They include an automatic bed maker, an automatic dog feeder, a remote control trash collector, and a lawn sprinkler that recycles water as it sprinkles the grass.

Beyond the Basics

Inside the other portable classroom, Judy stands before a wall of orange and purple squares, triangles, circles, and rectangles mounted on blue and green burlap. The geometric shapes are duplicated in vivid colors on the white marker board. Colored rods and geometric blocks are lined up across the top of the second-graders' desks as they maneuver them into mathematical formations. Simple addition and subtraction progress into multiplication and division as Judy's lesson advances. The attributes, properties, and symbols are discussed and arranged by color, shape, and size for equal equations, fractions, and whole numbers.

With prompting from Judy, the seven-and eight-year-olds complete each segment of the lesson by writing the numerical representation of their designs on the marker board. At that point, Judy substitutes the letter X in various places on both sides of the equations. As quickly as she asks what each X stands for, every hand shoots up and most know the correct answer.

Judy does not tell the children that they are doing higher level math, including the beginning concepts of algebra. I tell this story to point out how easily children can grasp and understand concepts that are usually considered to be beyond their level. By counting, arranging, and manipulating colored geometric shapes, the second-graders apprehend patterns and relationships to higher level skills within a meaningful context.

It is easier for children than many people imagine because mathematical systems are built on structures of patterns represented by symbols, and from the time children begin stacking and arranging their first set of blocks, making patterns is an easy and natural process. I once had a statistics professor who stacked concrete objects, told stories, and created images to help his *university* students grasp the abstract principles of statistical analysis. He was doing what all good teachers do . . . making new learning understandable as well as interesting.

Never Too Young to Help

I often wish I knew more about fixing mechanical things, such as car engines or movie projectors or video recorders. Behind a door in the school office there is an electrical panel filled with mysterious (to me anyway) switches, buzzers, alarms, and lights. Every time a buzzer goes off and red lights start flashing, I am struck with terror. An administrator should know what each of these switches does, in case of any one of a number of emergencies. But it was a seven-year-old wonder who rescued me from a mechanical crisis early one morning on the first day of the 1987 school year.

It all began with a new sprinkler system—part of the improvements made by our landscape-architect-in-residence, parent Robert Hayes, when he moved the school's playground equipment to the south end of the building, beyond the two new portable classrooms. The Ficus tree that provided shade for the old playground was also transplanted to a safer spot in front of the portables. And he installed an additional sprinkler system that provided water for the Ficus tree.

Just as most of the students were to arrive, the sprinklers burst forth full blast, past the Ficus tree, mushrooming over the walkway to the new portable classrooms. Unless something was done quickly, two classes of children would begin their first day of school drenching wet. Without a clue as to the location of the turn-off valve, I dashed into the office and phoned Robert. He explained where it was and added that his son, Carl, helped install the system and knew the location of the valve. Even though Carl was only seven, I knew he could help. I quickly spotted him among the early arrivals and told him my predicament, asking if he could locate the valve.

"Sure!" he replied with total confidence.

Leading me directly to the valve, which was hidden behind clumps of grass, he expertly shut off the sprinkler. Giving Carl a quick hug and lavish words of praise and thanks, I added this seven-year-old's name to my list of people to call for rescue.

Cooperative Play

With the new playground set for action, a second male teacher agreed to come on board to teach physical education. Both a Seacrest parent and husband of Shannon, one of our kindergarten tutors, Randy Crawford was no stranger to our philosophy or to the Seacrest community. Our music teacher, Fran, Randy, and another Seacrest father often joined forces with their guitars and banjo to lead the children in memorable performances.

Randy had worked with young people in a wilderness program and was committed to the idea of cooperative play and team building. He selected competitive games that could be won only through team work. Peaceful solutions and helping each other over hurdles became a built-in part of children's daily routines. Randy's activities focused on a specific problem to be solved in order to accomplish a task, and both the problem and the task required the total participation of the whole group in a cooperative effort. Everyone became a winner, a leader, and a follower. Everyone had to help and be helped.

One morning I stood on the playground, observing a class of second-graders clumped together in a tangled heap of twisted and contorted bodies, with Randy positioned in the center. The object of this exercise was for the group to unfold themselves out of the tangle without letting go of each others' hands, or switching hand positions. As a bystander, it looked like an impossible task. But ever so slowly, moving first one way and then another, the group, moving in a snail-like fashion, crawled and climbed under, over, and between each other, gradually unfolding like a giant coil of knotted rope. With few directions from Randy, the group unfurled itself into a perfect circle, still holding hands.

The shouts, demands, and disputes of typical competitive games were in stark contrast to what was being played out before my eyes. There was no need to remind anyone about good sportsmanship or taking turns. The exercise required the total involvement and help of everyone, literally wrapped up together, engaged in a unified purpose of detangling. It was interesting to imagine the limitless possibilities of this kind of teamwork. Perhaps these little people would grow up to apply these same skills of cooperative effort in later life, and as a result become better problem solvers.

Dress Codes

At a parents' meeting in October 1987, I gained new insight into how strongly people's values are tied to emotions. I had three topics to present to parents and teachers for discussion, two of which I thought were critical questions for the future of Seacrest, and a third topic I assumed would be of only minor significance. I was wrong.

A tuition increase was my first topic, and one I thought would cause a great deal of anxiety. The yearly tuition had been impossibly low, and our benefactor's yearly contribution to cover the short falls was expanding out of proportion. On the other hand, we were determined to ensure that Seacrest would not be an elitist private school and that it was affordable to the community at large. The concern of losing any families because of money was uppermost in my mind.

I had prepared my case, collecting facts, figures and reasons, and providing visual aids including overhead transparencies and handouts. After the presentation, I asked for questions or comments, thinking there would be an onslaught of debate. There were none. No questions.

There was only one comment from a parent, who stood up and said that no one could question that because of our benefactor's generosity, we received unprecedented services for minimal cost and that parents surely recognized the fact that a tuition raise was in order. So much for topic number one.

On to number two, the weighty question of whether or not we should initiate a middle school for sixth, seventh, and eighth grade students. I was astonished to find that except for one lone dissenter, the parents gave an overwhelming sanction for a Seacrest Middle School. Indeed, the group was so enthusiastic that they forged ahead with questions about when we could build a high school.

This is too easy, I thought, grateful that it all went smoothly. I was so off guard that I went into topic number three overconfident and with too casual a posture.

The final topic for the meeting, which held the big surprise for me, was the seemingly simple discussion of whether we should consider uniforms for students. In my mind, the issue had not even the remotest import when compared to the first two issues. I raised the issue because it appeared as children grew older, they tended to dress sloppier.

The oldest boys, in third grade, appeared in class dressed in oversized T-shirts hanging down to their knees; hair cuts favored a long single, shoulder-length strand of hair hanging down their backs. The girls appeared with six inches of flourescent dangle earrings. The taller the girls grew, the shorter their shorts got until they just nudged the edges of their dimpled bottoms. Their shirts got progressively shorter and tighter, sometimes with bare tummies peaking out between rolled-up shorts and tight shirts.

Some mothers implored me to install uniforms as a dress code so that they could avoid morning squabbles over clothes with their daughters. The mothers were losing the battles. Having raised my own daughter through various stages of fashion, I was well acquainted with the hassles, and I also knew it was likely to get worse during the teenage years. To be fair, controversies over dress did not apply to all students, and many parents were still able to set the parameters for school attire.

I had no burning biases for or against uniforms, as long as we had a dress code in place for neat and appropriate clothing suitable for the South Florida climate. But an explosion occurred as soon as I raised the question of uniforms. In a flash, the parents divided themselves into two separate, near militant camps.

It was the only time I came near to losing control of a group of people—parents or children. As I looked on in disbelief, I saw faces transformed from smiling benevolence to intense, unyielding expressions. Voices were raised, and parents, normally polite and courteous, began to interrupt each other. The tension escalated and the air turned thick with dissension.

I observed the melée for a few minutes and determined that the lines were drawn with no immediate chance of consensus. I announced that we would close the discussion, thanking people for their views, and stating that I would make a final decision after considering all opinions and options.

The next day, I received several letters. One parent wrote that as much as they loved Seacrest, his child would have to leave if uniforms were required, detailing a lengthy list of reasons about how uniforms would destroy the entire philosophy of the school. Others, who were pro-uniform, outlined the benefits, giving examples of how uniforms equate with better manners and behavior, decreased competitiveness, and a more positive image for the school.

An implausible number of hours were spent pondering the 'uniform' debate. Did uniforms equate with improved behavior and better manners? If everyone dressed alike, would the students forfeit their independence and become clones of each other? Were children looked down on if they couldn't afford the trendiest (and most expensive) brand of sneakers? Did the type of clothing students wear influence learning or character or moral values?

The issue was finally settled through the establishment of a more stringent dress code. We devised a "Seacrest Outfit." It consisted of a polo shirt, available in white or the Seacrest colors of blue or green, with a little emblem of Seacrest below the collar on one side. Students could wear white, tan, or navy trousers, slacks, shorts, or skirts. These were to be worn on special occasions or whenever classes went off campus on field trips.

In retrospect, it would have been easier for everyone if I had made the "Seacrest Outfit" a daily requirement, reserving my right to override differing opinions. Several years later, as students advanced into their middle school years, some appeared in the latest trendy outfits. Heavy, dark, ankle-high combat boots with deep grooves in the soles became a badge of acceptance, with only a specific brand name deemed acceptable. These heavy, thick, hard boots worn in the ninety-degree plus heat served as firm testimony to the importance of fashion over comfort. Some of the boys appeared in baggy shorts with hem lines falling halfway between the knees and ankles, topped by ultra large, long T-shirts.

Girls who could override their parents wore combat boots too. Those who came to school with skirts or tops that were too tight or too short were sent home. At least, that was the rule. But in reality, faculty members and parents had differing definitions of what was too short, too tight, or inappropriate, making the whole issue of dress extremely complex.

Why was how a student dressed such an emotional issue? Perhaps because some parents had negative memories of uniforms from schools that required students to wear white shirts and ties or plaid skirts all through school. At the other end of the spectrum were the exhausting daily battles over dress between parents and children.

I recall a passage by John Gardner, in his book, *Self-Renewal*, written long ago.

One of the interesting findings contained in recent research is that the creative individual as a rule chooses to conform in the routine, everyday matters of life, such as speech, dress and manners . . . He reserves his independence for what really concerns him—the area in which his creative activities occur.

I think John W. Gardner had the right idea. Putting our energies into more creative activities seemed like a good idea to me. And yet, the issue of appropriate dress vs. current trends is an age-old debate. Nevertheless, I never again mentioned the dreaded word *uniform*. Other, less volatile labels were used whenever the subject of wearing apparel was discussed.

CHAPTER **18**

Finding the Right Teachers

People often asked me how I found the teachers who shared the special qualities for which I looked in putting the Seacrest goals and philosophy into action. Usually, I found that my initial impression in meeting a person face to face served me better than an impressive resume.

The people who knew me best also knew the kind of person who would be able to work successfully at Seacrest, and an informal network formed, usually by Seacrest parents, who had the most vested interest. For example, my assistant and right-hand person, Lynne Powell, was discovered by Ann Ross, the parent who, with her husband Tim, had helped us through each stage of the interior design and construction. It was Ann who insisted that Lynne come to meet with me, intuitively knowing that we would appreciate each other.

A mutual friend from Mankato, Minnesota, found Diane Drengler when we added a second prekindergarten class in 1988. Through the years, as new teachers are recommended, I hear the phrase, "That person is a *Seacrest* teacher!"—And everyone seems to know what that implies. It was clear from the beginning that Diane was the quintessential "Seacrest teacher." My only challenge in hiring Diane was in convincing parents that their four-year-olds would be just as well served and cared for with this new and unknown teacher as they would be with Becky. By that time, Becky's reputation as the first lady of early childhood education was well established. But Diane's dedication and congeniality soon put everyone's fears to rest.

During the beginning weeks of Diane's first year at Seacrest, I sometimes questioned whether or not she was real. I always arrived at school by seven to unlock and make sure everything was ready for the day. Teachers arrived at seven-thirty, and it was unheard of for anyone to appear earlier than that, especially on a Monday morning. But Diane would often be waiting in her little sports car in the parking lot when I drove up. Leaping out of her car, she would bound over to help me with my stack of books and files, her face lit up like a beam from a high voltage spotlight.

"Jane!" she would exclaim. "It's Monday! We have another wonderful week at Seacrest!"

At first, I stared at her, dumbly, thinking she was kidding, not quite sure how to respond. After a while, I realized that this was really Diane being herself, and that exuberant positive nature was undeniably genuine and absolute. It was the way she met life each and every day.

When the pace in the office escalated to the point where I was drowning in paper work, phone calls, skinned knees, and scores of people and details that demanded immediate attention, I would sneak down the hall to prekindergarten.

There, I would collapse into the peaceful and uncomplicated beauty of voices singing to a guitar, or listen to "Snuggles," the puppet, questioning and congratulating children on their latest adventures in learning. Taking a moment to rest and re-center, I was able to view the world of Seacrest through a new lens of innocence and fresh faces.

Cowgirls and Boys

Although there are a few newly hired teachers who seem to grasp the Seacrest philosophy and move right into the scheme of things, for the most part, there is a period of adjustment. Sometimes, the first year at Seacrest can be overwhelming for a teacher. For one thing, most teachers are not accustomed to having parents and visitors in their classrooms on a daily basis. They rarely have the administrators walking in and out during the day. Parents who send their children to private schools justifiably expect more of everything: More communication; higher performance from both teacher and child; better grades; exemplary discipline; safe, wholesome atmosphere; happier children.

While faculty members provide a substantial amount of time in helping new teachers, they also have high expectations, keeping a vigilant watch for signs of trouble, thus adding another source of potential stress to the newcomer. Then, there are the ongoing field trips, fund raisers, and festivals; projects and productions; permission slips, conferences, records, and reports, all of which must be planned well in advance.

Not the least of potential stress producers for the new faculty members are the expectations of the Seacrest supervisor or administrator. I fully expected every teacher to provide a multisensory, interactive, interdisciplinary program, with purposeful, successful learning for all children. In addition, I wanted students to be safe, well behaved, creative, independent, responsible, and academically motivated. Finally, I wanted them to be excited about learning.

What is so remarkable about all the expectations listed above is that so many teachers *are* able and willing to meet these prerequisites, and it is not surprising that occasionally one will leave after a year, to seek a less demanding position.

It is not my intention to depict the Seacrest teachers as perfect humans with no flaws. To the contrary, these women and men share the same frustrations, bad days, failures, and inadequacies as most other human beings. Even the eternal optimists have down days. So do those who flourish on innovation and hard work. Each individual has his or her own set of conflicting behaviors and attitudes that lean toward the darker side of human nature.

I believe the critical difference between teachers who seem to thrive at Seacrest and the ones who become disillusioned are those who are committed to their own self-growth. The principles and purposes of the Seacrest mission are embodied in their personal lives as well. They are able to forgive themselves and others for mistakes and move on, focusing on the present rather than on the past.

One pervasive characteristic that stands out in working with Seacrest teachers, either individually or collectively is the mélange of strengths contained within the group as a whole. These are all strong teachers—strong minded, strong-willed, strong in their convictions. There are no clones here. The singular differences among strong teachers can bring both blessings and burdens. When the combined strengths of faculty members are aligned in solidarity, the diversity of thought leads to an often profound exchange of ideas. On the other hand, too many conflicting opinions can cause a state of disequilibrium. According to some, that is not always a negative. For example, Tom Peters, the best-selling business author advocates the chaos theory as a powerful motivator for positive change and new opportunities.

The challenge for me as the leader of such a strong and diverse group was to listen actively to different points of view and to facilitate respect and dialogue. I also had to be conscious of my own convictions and biases—to remain open to new possibilities. Whenever a discussion became too combative during faculty meetings, I could tell at a glance when I was off -base with one, or right on track with another, simply by observing individual expressions. I learned as much about my own strengths and weaknesses from faculty meetings as from any of my other interactions.

As Seacrest developed, our faculty meetings evolved into a range of formats. Individual teachers or teams took turns organizing and leading discussions. We began holding our weekly meetings before school, when minds and energy levels were fresh, boosted by fruit, rolls, juice, and coffee.

Most of our teachers come from public schools as I did, and although their reasons for moving from public to private institutions vary, there are some common motives. They certainly do not leave the safety net of tenure, substantially higher salaries, and greater health and retirement benefits without serious thought.

The perception among many that private schools offer an easier job is, in many respects, a false assumption. Private schools do hold a wide berth in determining the makeup of students, objectives, philosophy, and values, resulting in a more homogeneous population. Administrators do not have to accept or retain students with violent behavior, and they have more autonomy and fewer restraints in hiring or replacing teachers. Some private schools are driven by test scores and stringent academic requirements, with the intent of maintaining a higher level of ability and achievement among its students. Parents are generally interested in their children's success, and they tend to be more involved with school activities and affairs.

On the other hand, private or independent schools are subject to pressures that are not usually confronted in public schools. There are no tax dollars for private schools. Independent schools such as Seacrest are not subsidized by parochial dollars.

Seacrest was fortunate in having a benefactor who gave generously during the early years of development, but that is no longer the case. Every cent has to be raised through the members of the school community. Tuition never meets the full cost of teachers' salaries, equipment, maintenance and operations, much less construction of facilities.

A significant percentage of parents depends on financial aid, and the success of an independent school is greatly determined by the amount of money raised for this purpose alone. The time, energy, and pressures invested in planning, managing, and executing all the fund-raising activities for multiple purposes extract a heavy toll on parents, board members, and school personnel.

At Seacrest, we live in a fish bowl, where every action is visible and scrutinized. Parents are quick to let you know about the slightest concern. Sometimes their anxieties are legitimate, calling for immediate attention. Parents often offer helpful and supportive suggestions in improving our program, and whenever possible, we try to follow through with requests that are reasonable. The first rule of communicating with parents is never to react defensively. We try to listen from the parent's viewpoint and come to a mutual understanding, even when concerns may seem frivolous and trivial.

Requests and suggestions from parents or teachers must be weighed against both the individual and the mission of the school. There have been times when a parent complains because we do not give first-graders enough homework or ditto sheets to fill out, or maybe we do not teach the basics in the way *they* learned. Maybe a teacher is too strict, or not strict enough, or grades too hard or too easy. Most of the time, the issues can be solved through straightforward, explicit communication.

There were times when I encouraged parents (or teachers) to seek another school that was more aligned with their values. And, of course, there were parents who took their children out of Seacrest for reasons other than the cost of tuition. Some wanted a more traditional schooling. Others wanted the convenience of public school transportation, or a less demanding schedule or work load as parents. And some left because of unresolved differences in personnel.

Although I was usually (but not always) disappointed whenever a family left, Seacrest has been fortunate through the years to have more applicants than space. Still, teachers' salaries and positions in any private school depend on keeping the enrollment up, with enough students and classrooms, while at the same time, maintaining the advantages of smaller classes in a small school setting. Such a contradiction is not confronted by teachers on so personal a level in most public schools.

After I was offered the opportunity of starting a new school, I first had to come to terms with my lifelong commitment to public education. I saw what happened to the little public school in my hometown after desegregation came to Alabama. All over the South, private schools sprung up overnight to accommodate the white children of the more affluent, limiting any chance for equity in either the public or private schools. When I took on the challenges of creating a new independent school, I wondered if I could avoid the not so subtle trap of elitism. Would it be possible for me to maintain the close connections with my public school colleagues, or would they view me as one who had abandoned the ideals of public education?

In my mind, there is a parallel between the mostly white private schools, and the predominantly poor schools filled with racial minorities. Both are marked by inequity. At Seacrest, we never have a racially balanced student body, and we are the poorer for it. While I appreciate the advantages of autonomy to explore new possibilities and build on our collective strengths, free from the external constraints of bureaucracy, the lack of diversity bothers me. And I worry about the future of public schools. More and more, the lines among public schools are drawn and driven by location and economic jurisdiction.

The most hopeful answers I have found come from Deborah Meier's pioneering work in public schools, and from her writing. In her book, *The Power of Their Ideas*, she offers practical suggestions, based on real experience:

> Creating smaller and focused educational communities, enhancing the climate of trust between families and schools, developing workable models of self-governance, increasing the heterogeneity of a school's population, and using pedagogies that respond to diverse learning styles and student interests are all

factors that current research suggests correlate with improved school outcomes.

. . . Virtually all the major educational task forces, for example, agree that dramatic changes will require removing stifling regulations that presently keep schools tied to outmoded practices, to doing things in lockstep. They agree that if we want change we'll have to put up with non-conformity and some messiness. We'll have to allow those most involved (teachers, administrators, parents) to exercise greater on-site power to put their collective wisdom into practice. Once we do all this, however, school X and school Y are going to start doing things differently.

Deborah Meier also believes as I do that nothing much is going to change for the better without excellent teachers. On two recent occasions, I heard a district superintendent and a leader of our country make speeches about improving our educational system. Both proudly announced that enormous sums of money had been allocated for the construction of bigger, better school buildings. I had the distinct impression that the new buildings would be the basis for improved education. Maybe I misconstrued the meaning of their message. I hope so. Still, I wonder what would happen if all the billions of dollars presently being earmarked for larger buildings were spent on attracting and keeping better teachers.

Several conclusions can be made from observing and participating in the process of communication among the members of the Seacrest faculty. First, teachers are active participants in making decisions. Learning is enhanced through the expression of diverse viewpoints. Respect is increased in the process of bringing opposing opinions out into the open. A wider range of choices and alternative ways of thinking are developed through open dialogue. Finally, I believe that the collaborative style of leadership and communication engenders a sense of satisfaction and ownership of faculty members, resulting in increased productivity of the organization as a whole.

CHAPTER 19

Inner Beauty, Outer Chaos

Seacrest seemed to be forever scaling the next scaffolding of construction. I began thinking of Seacrest as a two-dimensional character, with each part distinct and separate from the other. Inside the classroom, children and teachers were a synchronized blend of sound, color, rhythm, and texture as they began a new school year to create new patterns of awareness and expanded learning. The inner part was like the image of a pearl created around a grain of sand, encased within an outer shell, protected from the pounding stress and upheaval of outer turbulence.

Outside, the constant turmoil and disarray of building three new classrooms took its toll as the office staff tried to maintain a sense of order and efficiency. When Seacrest began its new school year in September 1988, we thought we were finished with the chaos and misadventures of expansion.

But the first day of school that year was full of contrary surprises. When parents drove onto Unity Way that morning, it looked as though we had reached the pinnacle of traffic tie-ups. A tangle of cars resulted in a total standstill; not one car was able to move in or out. Cars were backed up onto the highway beyond. Through cautious and patient engineering, we created an opening at the corner, and directed drivers out safely.

Returning to the office, I found that the copy machine had broken down under the flurry of last minute demands. My secretary, Pat Frank, had disappeared. I discovered her hidden in the multipurpose room, sobbing uncontrollably. She had broken down along with the copy machine, caving in under the stress. Pat was a person who liked to have everything under control and in perfect working order. She needed to have the sense of completion in her work, and when she realized the futility of the present situation, she found a private space to quietly "lose it." I sympathized. Soothing her as best I could, I encouraged her to take as long as she needed to collect herself. I headed back for the office, and steeled myself for whatever came.

The newest faculty member came in to announce her pregnancy. Through a forced smile, I congratulated her and wished her well in her new position, hoping that she could at least last until spring.

Finally, there was a peaceful lull, and it appeared that we had managed to survive the early morning eruptions. The children found their way to their new classrooms; another year had begun and all was calm—or so I thought. I was out front visiting with a parent, Linda Hayes, and holding her new baby, Brooke, when a prekindergarten tutor came flying down the hall, calling, "Jane! Come quick! Our toilet's overflowing all over the classroom!"

Linda and I each grabbed a mop and bucket from the janitor's closet and scurried down the hall. Moving into the classroom, we began mopping up water, which had flooded the bathroom and vinyl area and was seeping into the carpet and under the furniture. The four-year-olds and teachers continued their lessons, seemingly oblivious to two women dressed in white heels and first-day-of-school finery, feverishly but silently mopping up the flood.

We were beginning to make some headway when the tutor from the adjacent classroom summoned us. Their toilet, too, was overflowing. In rapid succession, others came bearing the same tale of woe. It was becoming obvious that this ominous problem was going to have consequences too severe to be easily handled by two women in high heels with mops. We promptly curtailed all toilet flushing throughout the school and thereby created a new emergency. With a school filled with elementary children, our only alternative was to escort classes in rapid succession up the road to use the facilities at the nearby church.

While plumbers labored to solve the mystery, threatening storm clouds gathered in the skies outside. The rains hit around lunchtime, just when the children were heading out to the playground. As they all scampered back into the safety of classrooms, torrential rains plummeted out of the skies. Inside the three brand-new classrooms, the ceiling tiles began to emit drips of water that quickly turned into steady streams, landing onto the heads of students. To make matters worse, a solid sheet of water poured through the dividing line of the abutment in the hall, between the new addition and the original building.

What next? I wondered as I flew from one disaster to the other, throughout what seemed to me to be an endlessly horrific day. In contrast to these catastrophic circumstances, I was fascinated each time I passed a classroom and saw serene and happy faces, as teachers and tutors calmly guided the children through a lighthearted and lively first day of school. It was as if the inner structure of Seacrest was filled with perfect health, harmony, and vitality, while the outer structure was crumbling around us.

The news from the plumbers was not good. In the process of construction, concrete had carelessly been allowed to solidify in the drains, causing the whole system to be plugged up. While the leaks on the roof were being repaired overhead, jackhammers were drilling into the concrete floor, carving out a five-foot strip down the center of the hall.

The entire process dragged on during the first week of school, and near the week's end, while I was meeting a deadline on my doctorate, Lynne held the workers hostage, laying out their orders. She informed them that enough was enough, and that they were not leaving until the drains were repaired, even if it meant working all night. Lynne stood guard over the crew until midnight, releasing them only after they had finished the job.

Despite all the turmoil in the outer structure of Seacrest, the inner core miraculously remained an uninterrupted flow of organized learning. As much as I longed for beautiful surroundings on the exterior of Seacrest, with everything operating and functioning as it should, I had to acknowledge that the inner core was what made the real difference. I only hoped that some day we would have enough space for a respite from construction.

A New School Year Begins

CHAPTER 20

Balancing the Budget

Late spring was always a difficult time for everyone. Student and faculty contracts had to be finalized for the next school year. Raises in tuition and salaries had to be balanced against the projected income and expenses, capital planning, scholarships, new equipment, and materials. Every dollar had to be measured and analyzed in gut-wrenching decisions and sleepless nights. How many students would we lose if the tuition was raised? How large an increase could we squeeze out of the budget for teachers and tutors? How much money could we raise for scholarships? Each year, my skin grew a little thicker in the spring. It was the time when I knew that no matter what I did, it was going to be met with resistance from a certain number of people.

The really great teachers can never be paid as much as they are worth, and I believed the truism applied especially to Seacrest teachers. Even though the major portion of our budget went for salaries, it was never enough. To this day, it torments me that teachers are paid much less than other professionals. What other job could possibly be more important than teaching the ones who inherit the future? After all, our children *are* the future. They represent the foundation for everything—from finances and medical care to forming a global network in building a saner, healthier planet.

Teachers are the deciding factor of a successful school, far above the institution itself. Good teaching counts for more than whatever the school administrators say or do. If parents are satisfied that their children are happy and receiving the best education possible from the best teachers, they will overlook other issues. In that respect, an independent school is like any other business. The bottom line is that parents will pay for a superior product, and the teachers are not only the producers of services, but they are the sales persons as well.

During budget planning time, I soon realized monetary issues placed me, as the leader of Seacrest, as the target for blame. It was a painful lesson for me because I put so much energy into keeping tuition low, enrollment up, and salaries as high as possible. Nevertheless, I had chosen to be the leader, and I had to take the penalties along with the rewards. I was grateful that Seacrest faculty salaries were higher than most private schools, and that Seacrest teachers received a raise each year, even in the leaner years of a major recession, when positions were being eliminated and schools being closed around the country.

Whenever anyone was upset with me—a teacher who wanted a larger raise than we could give, or a parent who complained about the burden of tuition—I tried to understand his or her side and not to take it personally. If I could not offer more money, I offered appreciation and encouragement. I knew that on the other side of any doubts they might have about me, these were men and women who invested their time, energy, and faith in Seacrest.

When the springtime agony of budget-planning was near the end, it was a relief to see the dark corners of doubt and dissonance fade away under a glow of excitement, bringing us back to realignment.

"Authors and Artists Night," a much-heralded event at Seacrest, is always held late in the spring. Each student is encouraged to display a book he or she has created, written, illustrated, and bound. Art projects throughout the year are saved to be exhibited for Authors and Artists Night. For weeks prior to the event, older children help younger ones put their stories into the computers, and assist them with spelling and sentence structure. Parents come in to lend a hand with the bookbinding, utilizing wallpaper samples, scraps of cloth, paint, marbleized paper, and collage materials to provide texture, color, design, and strength for book covers. The four-year-olds dictate their stories to their teachers. The project involves nearly everyone at Seacrest, from the librarian to the custodian. Local artists, authors, and photographers also lend expertise and support.

Authors and Artists Night

On the day of the presentation, parents, children, and faculty spend the day setting up displays, preparing food and drinks, arranging, hauling, hammering, and cleaning. For a number of years, the event was held in the multipurpose room, which was transformed into a glowing fairyland of triumphant shiny faces, slicked-down cowlicks, velveteen dresses, proud parents, and relieved teachers. Robots, computers, and video tapes relayed flashy testimonials to the age of technology. Grandfathers helped themselves to handmade versions of "scratch and sniff" books, while four-year-olds crammed mounds of finger foods into bulging cheeks. Diamonds of light electrified the air, ignited by flashbulbs aimed at budding young authors presenting their colorful books of all sizes and shapes, each with its own plot, style, and design.

The annual celebration of inventive minds, with its mix of hard work and fun has a unifying effect. The whole Seacrest community participates, and the wounds of the budget battles are quickly healed through the cooperative wonder of the children's creations.

On the morning after one of these events, Adam greeted me as usual in the hall. From the time Adam was in kindergarten, he walked beside me each day as I began my sequential procession of unlocking and opening gates and doors and turning on lights. He liked to hold the doors open for me and help me raise the flag and sweep off the front walk. There would usually be some minor preparations or rearranging to do. But after the major school-wide productions, the task of clearing and cleaning is gigantic. There were many times when I would work half the night to put everything in order for the next day.

On that day, the morning after "Authors and Artists Night," some "angel" had appeared to purge the evening's disarray. Adam and I found that every table and chair, dish and utensil, scrap of food, spilled juice, piece of equipment, plywood backdrop, book and display had been un-hung, dismantled, cleaned, and maneuvered back to its allocated place, ready for a new day's arrival of sleepy-headed heroes and heroines. Although I had my suspicions, the person or persons who shouldered the act of altruism remained anonymous—a gift of the highest order.

V

UNIQUE GIFTS

CHAPTER 21

The After School Program

Seacrest's After School Program is considerably more than a baby-sitting service where children wait for their parents to pick them up after work. From its inception, soon after the school was established, this program proved to be one of the unique features of Seacrest. Back then, I knew of no other schools in the county with an after-school program that was designed to be an extension of the school's curriculum. In fact, only in the last few years have schools begun to recognize the importance of safe, professional, well-run extended day-school programs in a society where the majority of fathers and mothers work outside the home.

Because we want the After-School Program to be a time when students can pursue their interests and expand their skills, the program gets bigger every year, both in numbers of students and types of activities. And each year, the system for checking kids in and out becomes more elaborate, mainly for safety, but also for keeping track of who goes where and for how long. Parents have to sign their children in and out and note the time. If any other person comes to fetch them, we have to know who they are, with written permission from the parents, including a description of the automobile. When in doubt, we request identification, and if there are remaining doubts, the child is not released.

Although most of the security and safety precautions are mandatory for any school, the Seacrest After School Program demands an extra set of safeguards, because of the large number of activities. You name it, we have it: dance lessons, team sports, gymnastics, swimming and tennis; drama, sewing, and art and crafts; study stations and computer stations; outdoor play for young children at one end of the building and a variety of sports for older ones at the other end; piano lessons, instrument lessons, choir groups, guitar lessons and band; Brownies, Daisies, and Cub Scouts; cooking and snacks; dozens and dozens of indoor games. Some classes are held on campus, others off campus. The off-campus classes require transportation. There are permission slips and fees, billing statements, payments, and late fees to keep track of for each participant.

For a number of years, Polly Holmes was both the coordinator of the After School Program and the physical education teacher. As far as I'm concerned, both jobs are the hardest in the school, for sheer endurance. In early fall, up until mid-October, every day is muggy, whether it rains or shines. Your shirt sticks to your back and your hair is plastered to your brow in sticky clumps. The grounds are often soggy and muddy from summer rains. Mounds of aggressive fire ants spring up overnight.

Imagine running around, coaching, and cheering the kids on, hour after sweltering hour, as classes come bounding out to the playing fields for their hour in the sun. On rainy days, the physical education teacher is faced with a test of courage—invading a teacher's classroom, disrupting her planning time, and rearranging all the furniture so that students can do their rainy-day sports.

After school, ninety or so children come charging into the multipurpose room to be signed in, organized, and grouped into outdoor, indoor, or off-campus categories. In the multipurpose room, art, drama, or dance compete for the stage. Cooking activities and snacks overflow from the kitchen to the tables in the main room, where there are groups working on the computer, doing homework or research, working puzzles, playing chess or other games.

Notwithstanding the physical, mental, and social capacities required in managing both the above programs, perhaps Polly's greatest contribution at Seacrest was the way in which she developed the attitudes of the children she taught. She never allowed them to say, "I can't," when teaching children a new skill. As children fumbled the ball, or stumbled over a new piece of equipment or stunt, she kept reminding them to repeat, "I CAN!", until they reached the first successful feat. By setting goals and achieving them with a positive mental attitude, the students were practicing some of life's most important principles— courage, perseverance, and self-confidence.

Tutors

The tutors, or teaching assistants as they are now called, not only provide the support needed to sustain the After School Program, but they assist the teachers in the regular classrooms as well. Although the teachers consider the tutors to be their "private property," the budget could not support the cost of salaries for tutors without their additional hours spent in the After School Program. Some, like Terri, Vickie, Wendy, and Lidia, have worked at Seacrest since the school was in its infancy, and they could probably outshine many seasoned teachers in overall ability and creativity. In many ways, the tutors are the glue that holds Seacrest together, and it would be a distinctly different school without this positive and unique group of people.

Viewed from the outside, the tutors are most often found working behind the scenes, quietly preparing materials and snacks, assisting small groups and individuals with lessons, and supervising classes on the playground and during lunch. They adapt themselves to the contrasting styles and expectations of teachers with surprising strength and endurance.

When I read about Mother Teresa and the inspiring way in which she serves, I think of the tutors who, without fuss or fanfare, "accomplish something extraordinary by doing something ordinary with love, one day at a time."

Office Staff

As one might expect, many of Seacrest's faculty and staff members have their children enrolled in Seacrest. What is unusual is the fact that the children were there first. In the early days, I once heard someone say that they thought Seacrest was primarily a school for teachers' children, because we had so many parents who were teachers in other schools. As the school continued to expand, a number of parents applied and obtained positions as Seacrest teachers, tutors, or office staff members.

Pam, who worked in our office for a number of years, came to Seacrest first as a parent, enrolling her four-year-old son in prekindergarten. Like so many others who remembered their school years with distaste, she was determined that her son would get a better education. Until Pam was hired to work full time in the office, she appeared at Seacrest every day to help in whatever capacity was needed. She had a no-nonsense approach to discipline with her son and a sixth sense with children. She seemed to know when they needed help outside the classroom and she would check to make sure they got to the right place at the right time, or get them lunch if they forgot theirs, or find lost sweaters.

Pam knew all the children's schedules, their parents, grandparents, and baby-sitters. She knew everyone's problems better than I did, and she often took care of other people's children if they were out of town. And in fact, Pam took care of me in much the same way as she did the children, always reminding me of appointments, gathering the materials I needed, finding lost items, or putting my car windows up if it started to rain. I think as much as anyone, Pam felt a real sense of ownership in her devotion to Seacrest.

Others, like Pat, my first secretary, and Wendy, had their babies soon after they started to work at Seacrest. There are several parents who have been at Seacrest from the beginning, in 1983. Although their children are now in high school, they have remained at Seacrest to work. Barbara and Caroline, for instance, have participated in nearly every activity the school has ever had, from substitute teaching to driving on field trips or leading fund-raisers and Cub Scouts.

As members of our office staff, they handle everything from computers to skinned knees and tours for prospective parents. The office is often jammed with kids, teachers, tutors, parents and visitors, all needing immediate attention. Meanwhile, the phone is always ringing; printers, copiers, and computers are clicking and whirring, grinding out various forms of communications by the hundreds.

With everything that goes on in the center of communication, one might expect a mass of confusion and chaos And yet, whenever I step into the office from the outside, there is an air of calm efficiency and congeniality. Children, faculty, parents, and visitors alike are always greeted with friendly professionalism. This to me is the measure of service at its best.

As the office personnel evolved over the years, I came to recognize that the level of teamwork practiced here requires a special level of expertise, encompassing a wide range of skills including specialized technical mastery and exceptional ability in personal communication. There is a high degree of autonomy combined with a team spirit. Despite the constant flow of people and deadlines to meet, there is a certain presence that resides in the office. It communicates a message of warmth and welcome, setting the tone for the school as a whole.

CHAPTER 22

Many Forms of Excellence

There is one God, does it matter
whether one drinks from a glass
or a cup?

Sree Chakravarti
"The Healer's Journey"

A group of ten heads of private schools was selected by the Florida Council of Independent Schools to visit and evaluate a school located on the east coast of Florida to determine if all the qualifications for accreditation were met. The visiting team members were hand-picked for their sensitivity to this unique endeavor, the first all black school to apply for accreditation. The school had been established ten years before with extremely limited funds under the sponsorship of a local Baptist church. Knowing that the school had a low tuition, rock bottom salaries, and a sparse supply of books or equipment, the team members prepared themselves for the worst, hoping that at least the safety standards would be met.

Driving across Florida on I-75, I mentally cleared myself of my own prejudgments and definitions of a good school. Donning the persona of the "missionary," I was ready to help this school in whatever way I could. As it happened, my good intentions were totally misplaced, because along with my team members, I would experience an inspiring accomplishment. I checked into my hotel, dressed for the evening reception in my most conservative black suit and pearl earrings, and found my way to the school through the back-street settlements of the modest neighborhood.

Generally, the first evening of an accreditation evaluation consists of a small reception with a few hors d'oeuvres where we meet with the school's board of trustees and administrators. The evaluating team's task is to put everyone at ease before moving into the school to examine and inspect every detail. On that night, we were met with glowing smiles and warm handshakes as we were ushered into the lunchroom, where tables were set with bright table cloths for the evening meal. Within a few minutes, the room was filled to capacity by faculty, parents, students, and visitors.

The founder of the school opened the ceremony with a welcome like none we had experienced. He spoke in gentle, heartfelt words of the vision and dream of bringing the school into reality, and of the years of hard work required to arrive at this historical moment. He told us that each dish for our dinner had been prepared with the greatest of care, so that we would leave satisfied and have sweet dreams this night and wake up refreshed the next morning to meet the students. He ended his introduction by telling us they would be praying all night that we would find everything in perfect order and that the school would pass every test.

A young pianist and a chorus of voices led us into a near mesmerized state with a jubilant rendition of three verses and choruses of "Onward Christian Soldiers." Then we were summoned to a long table laden with the food promised earlier to fill our spirits, minds, and bodies with sweet dreams. Memories of my Alabama roots were revived with the taste of fresh turnip greens, sweet potatoes, ripe tomatoes, green beans seasoned southern-style; pork, ribs, chicken, cornbread, pies, and my all-time favorite, homemade pound cake. *Sweet dreams were sure to come to me tonight*, I thought.

After dinner, the children sang and recited the reasons why they loved their school. A county commissioner spoke about what the school had done for families and for the community. Teachers told us about their commitment and love for their school. The founder's two grown sons, both professionals in their careers, described their father's vision in creating the school, and how he had instilled the values of education in themselves as they grew up. Parents spoke about what the school had done for their children.

I was touched by the words of one woman who said emphatically,

"You must promise not to *give* us anything and don't cut us any slack! We need to know that we earned the right to be accredited, and that you can be proud to have us in your organization. To do less is to do us and your organization a great injustice."

At the end of the ceremony, I glanced at the misty eyes of my team members, knowing they were as moved as I was. I think if we had been allowed, we would have granted immediate accreditation then and there. The chairman of our team, the head master of a prestigious private school in Palm Beach, had worked with the school for over a year, and he knew the extent of the effort that had gone into preparing for accreditation. Although he was well aware of what we were to witness in the following days, he withheld his views until we could see for ourselves.

The night's sleep, as our hosts had pledged, was peaceful and restful. When we arrived at the school on the following morning, eager young boys leaped forward to open the car doors, politely thrusting out lean brown arms to shake our hands. Beaming from ear to ear as they let us out, they raced before us to hold open the school doors. We were escorted into the halls where we were greeted by friendly welcomes as we made our way to the library.

My first impression was that everything sparkled—the students, teachers, walls, and floors all shone like mirrors reflecting pride and joy. The hallways and classrooms were lit with colorful works of art. Somehow, a particular group of dedicated people had managed with the slimmest of funds to build and maintain a new and beautiful school on less than an acre of land for 240 students from two-year-old infants through high school.

The teachers gathered into their morning ritual circle of prayer, requesting that they become instruments to help the children learn and to become good citizens of tomorrow. I stood in the circle as they prayed for healing in the community, and I felt the power and strength of aged, weathered hands holding mine.

As we settled into the task of observing each class of children and teachers, the air seemed charged and fused with love, care, and joy. I witnessed some masterful teaching. Many of the teachers had taught for thirty or forty years in the public schools and had come out of retirement to teach as a labor of love. Every child I saw was perfectly behaved, happy, and proud of his or her work. They wanted to show me their writing and their math, and they wanted me to see how well they could read. A few children wrote me little notes to tell me that they hoped I liked their school.

As I observed, probed, interviewed, and questioned, I discovered that the students were mostly from poor families, and that prior to transferring to the school, many had severe behavioral and learning problems. No one in our team witnessed any signs of children misbehaving or failing. To the contrary, we saw only well-behaved children who were eager to learn. From my own experience, I knew that children's behavior cannot be faked for very long. What we saw was for real.

Even though the methods of teaching were not those that I would ordinarily advocate or use in my own teaching or school, the message was clear that what was happening there, in that setting, was working. For instance, I saw a whole class of five-year-olds going through the alphabet by reciting a bible verse for each letter. Every one of them did it perfectly—a task I could not conceive of myself being able to do. Here it was coming from five-year-olds. The young male teacher congratulated and praised them each step of the way. Firm, loving, and safe standards had been set by all the teachers, and they expected and saw to it that every child would learn and succeed.

Throughout my trips up and down the halls, girls and boys would smile at me, look me in the eye, and shake my hand. Each time our team members returned to our meeting place, we shared the same impression that something remarkable was taking place. We all agreed that we would love to send our entire student body and staff to visit here to see just how polite kids can be and to see what can be done with little else but love, vision, and deeply held dedication.

At one point during the visit, the founder, who was also the headmaster, stopped me in the hall. He said, "There's a light radiating from you that's so fine! You must be a very good person." His simple words spoken with such sincerity had a profoundly moving effect on me, and I could only respond by replying that he was seeing his own reflection.

We came away from the school with a strong sense that the students we saw would not become victims of drugs and violence, and that they would be able to serve as models for others. We agreed that we would not only recommend the school for accreditation, but that we would be the beneficiaries by having this school in our organization.

In reflecting on the experiences of the journey, I was reminded that excellence can be found in many forms and settings. I was also left with a greater understanding of the imprint that can be cast from one person's vision when combined with purpose and selfless service.

VI

CONNECTIONS: AN INTERCONNECTED BALANCE

CHAPTER **23**

Leaders in Partnership

Breaking the Mold: Choosing an Innovative Doctoral Program

In 1986, when Seacrest was into its fourth year, I decided it was time to complete the work I had begun on a doctoral program several years earlier when I was still working in the public schools. In a meeting with the graduate dean of a Florida university, I inquired about innovative but reputable programs. He shared information about Nova University and The Union Institute, both of which offered the opportunity to study with professors from around the country who were at the vanguard of innovation. After researching more on my own, I discovered that there were few programs in educational leadership willing to break the mold and explore new territories of theories and practices.

Drawing from a national network of the most dynamic professors and leaders in education, these unconventional universities have designed prototype classes, seminars, field experiences, and learning activities that focus on the interconnection between disciplines, with more emphasis placed on putting research into practice.

Professional relevance, quality of programs, and scholarly excellence share equal importance.

Fully aware that the old guard professors from the hallowed halls of the more prestigious universities would view these relatively new doctoral programs as heresy, I nevertheless decided I had spent enough years in graduate classes that proved to be disappointing and of little value. It was time for me to shake loose from the mainstream of conventional credibility and go for something that held more promise, or at the very least, more excitement.

The group of professors and professionals assembled for my program in the Union Institute not only demanded excellence and intense commitments, but stimulated me to expand my thinking into new dimensions of learning. My major professor, Dr. Roy Fairfield, became my mentor and friend, always encouraging me to go beyond my preconceived limits.

My studies in educational leadership were directed toward styles of learning and teaching. Delving into the whole area of communication, the latest theories on brain/mind studies, and how individuals process information, I looked for patterns. I wanted to know how each teacher made the connective links to individual students. What worked and what could be improved upon? Were there some ways that worked best with all children? How did a "left brain, linear-thinking, auditory based" teacher connect to the "right-brain, abstract-thinking, visual" learner? How were organizations structured to facilitate optimum growth and participation? And finally, what were the qualities and characteristics of good leaders?

We all have known leaders who perform efficiently in a system designed in the typical top-down, authoritarian style of management. But what of the leaders who are committed to the idea of professionals working in partnership as a team?

As I studied the styles of leadership, learning, and teaching, I came to recognize that in order for a team-based approach to be successful, there must be trust in people's ability to take responsibility for doing the best job possible. I do not mean a leader who delegates power from above, but rather, one who demonstrates a true partnership of shared decision-making and the honoring of diverse opinions.

In examining the structure of collaborative organizations, I examined my own personal beliefs and values. If I truly believed in the principles of shared power, I needed to be clear in my own mind that this form of leadership produced a better learning environment. My self-examination demanded total honesty—to look at the parts of myself that questioned or doubted my ability and courage to walk the path of a broader, more unconventional way of leadership. I wondered if I had the skills needed to lead and inspire others in developing a community of learners committed to the idea of collective leadership—a concept that was, for most, an unfamiliar theory yet to be practiced.

Despite any doubts I may have felt about my abilities, my most authentic core leaned predominantly toward this way of leading, not only because I believed in the principles of collective leadership and shared power, but because it was the most natural way for me to be and act. The foundation had already been laid, and I would continue to grow and learn as we built on what we had already created at Seacrest.

Leadership through collaboration in a non-hierarchical system—rather than from a traditional authoritarian base—is currently under serious consideration as a way to manage schools. Educational leaders who advocate reform appear to agree that teachers and principals need the autonomy and freedom to build consensus, to make decisions, and to work as a team in the way that best fits that particular school.

Some school leaders are more open and suited to collaborative planning and change than others, and it is a complex issue. I must emphasize here the importance of knowing where your own personal power lies, and aligning your actions with the reality of your values and strengths.

After completing the final draft of *Inventing a School*, I attended a seminar on leadership presented by Barbara Shipka. She spoke about the integration of shared leadership with the traditional hierarchy in forming the organization into an organic whole. There are often times when the leader must be the decision-maker in order to move ahead. Certainly, collaborative leadership does not imply that everything must be decided on by everyone in the organization. Rather than thinking in terms of either hierarchy or teams, the leader must focus on the task at hand and the people involved, finding the balance between the two forms. In her book, *Leadership in a Challenging World*, Barbara Shipka makes a provocative statement:

> Hierarchy has been the primary organizing principle for getting work done in the West at least since the Roman Legions. Teams have been present throughout human history—primarily outside the Western workplace. Blending hierarchy and team is a deep and powerful change for business organizations. While there are templates about what teamwork is and how

teams "should" look, the most successful teams find their own way by tapping into the energy already present within their circles. Teams develop best when they are based on clear communal goals, the existing passions and interests of team members, and a candid understanding of their members' dissatisfactions and desires for change.

Here again, the importance of balance comes into play, along with discernment in using the best resources available in the most productive ways.

From the outset, I wanted Seacrest to be a joint venture—a place where decisions are made through dialogue and consensus, shared responsibility, and team-building. As a result, we all had to be willing to risk making mistakes and to learn from them. I grew and learned along with the faculty as we added new grades, new students, and new ideas.

Studying the literature of leadership abilities, I realized that if leaders are insecure, intent on being right, or feel threatened by giving power to others, they could not handle the uncertainties of a collaborative style of leadership. A strong sense of interdependence, humility, and patience are prerequisite qualities in building a sense of partnership. From Lynne's and my experience, we learned that if we intended to build and maintain a collaborative structure, we needed the inner strength to sustain the ambiguity of diverse opinions. We needed the ability to follow our intuition, to know when decisions should be made jointly or unilaterally. And we had to develop the ability to let go of things beyond our control.

Discovering and practicing our own personal systems in dealing with the day-to-day stresses are essential to productivity, not to mention a good night's rest. One can be certain that in any system, failure will happen. Crisis will occur. Mistakes will be made. Courage comes with the ability to hold and share the vision *in the face* of these inevitable challenges.

In trying to synthesize information into a manageable framework, I concluded that there is no way to build a collaborative style of leadership unless the members of the group are willing to share their ideas and solutions, implementing them in an environment of trust and respect.

I thought of all the times the faculty had come up with creative solutions to problems that seemed impossible. If schools are going to provide a better education for children, we need to break through old patterns, in which organizations are controlled by one autocratic, authoritarian leader, into a new paradigm that extends the boundaries of leadership to include the talents and ideas of the collective. With the rapid changes taking place in society, technological advances must be combined with a more global approach in teaching, based on all that we know about brain-based learning.

The commitment to shared leadership carries the elements of danger and risk. Educational leader, author, and consultant, Eric Jensen, believes that new growth and learning does not take place without the willingness to take the risk of moving out from one's comfort zone.

Committing oneself to lead in a collaborative manner is fraught with discomfort. From our own, sometimes painful experience, we learned that dealing with uncertainty and ambiguity *is* uncomfortable. Change, taking risks, learning from mistakes, and putting new ideas into action all require an intense faith in the people within the group. It must be recognized that there are teachers who value their autonomy and are not interested in a team approach. Tension can arise when strong teachers have different ideas and agendas, and there are times when teachers, parents, or administrators can obstruct change and collaboration.

Building unity and support among colleagues requires enormous sensitivity and the willingness to respect and honor individual styles and needs. At the same time, the leader must be a catalyst in creating a team approach and in building a supportive atmosphere. Each member of the team has a unique talent to give, and by focusing on the underlying principle that *every* teacher is a leader with a responsibility to the mission of the school as a whole, individual strategies become dynamic forces for positive growth and change.

Learning about leadership in a collaborative structure, honing in on the individual styles of teachers and students at Seacrest was the central theme of my doctoral research. My goals for both the school and my research were aimed at discovering more about how people learn and lead, teach and communicate. At the same time, I wanted to get a clear picture of Seacrest and to analyze it from every angle.

CHAPTER 24

Sorting Styles

The people, program, and projects of Seacrest proved to be rich and appropriate arenas for my doctoral research. The study's primary focus was to explore and analyze the ways in which people learn, communicate, and process information. I admittedly used the Seacrest faculty members, students, and my own teenagers as guinea pigs and stimuli to propel my dissertation into reality.

I wanted to understand as much as possible about the components of learning behavior, and I plunged headlong into an exhaustive study. I studied the numerous inventories and tests that had been developed to determine whether a person is an auditory, a visual, or kinesthetic learner. I evaluated tests that separated those who learn best through concrete sequential tasks from those who learn better through abstract random modes. Other tests yielded information about how people work—adaptive and innovative or conservative and conventional. I studied risk-takers versus security seekers, compared introverts to extroverts, discovered the differences between task-oriented and people-oriented learners, and how people reacted to structured or unstructured learning time.

I learned the techniques of Neuro Linguistic Programming from two of my professors, Dr. Clint Van Nagel, and Dr. Robert Siudzinsky.

My studies took me far afield into the work of Karl Pribram, Peter Russell, David Bohm, and Fritjof Capra— scientists and physicists on the cutting edge of brain/mind theory.

My search gave insights as to why brilliant Kathy needed an unlimited amount of time to be comfortable with her work. I began to understand why Tony needed to put things together and take them apart, and Elizabeth had to see *and* read to understand, while Jim learned best through listening. At last, I understood why my son, Steven, could only make the decision to buy a new shirt after two trips around the mall, comparing the prices and picking the threads of each stack of shirts, whereas my own decisions are often made from my first intuitive flash.

I gained a new understanding about my often painful struggle with patience, waiting for new projects to be finished—my nature calls for quick decisions and instant delivery. I usually see the whole with all its possibilities, and I want it all put into practice then and there.

Much of the information from my research told me what I already knew about myself and others at Seacrest. I had brought together an individualistic group of strong teachers. Some were perfectionists who demanded ordered detail and preplanning. Others operated best in creative clutter. There were the teachers who looked at things in black and white, and others who were comfortable with shades of gray. My own style was illustrated by a large stone, which sat on my desk, inscribed with a message for all to see: "Nothing here is written in stone." Some teachers wanted me to make all the decisions, others wanted total freedom. Some wanted a handbook of rules while others preferred to make them as needed. Seacrest contained the whole gamut: hard and soft, fast and slow, easy and tough, down-to-earth realists and lofty idealists.

Working with a diverse group of people in developing a collaborative style of leadership and teamwork was an interesting challenge. Sometimes it worked and other times I wondered if I had set a hopeless goal. Fortunately, there were significant common qualities that held us together and prevented us from splitting off in all directions.

For example, we were committed to the Seacrest philosophy, and for the most part, the teachers were motivated to do their best. They embodied the pioneer spirit for breaking new ground. They were risk-takers who believed in themselves. They cared about children and held high expectations for themselves and their students. They knew how to teach in a multisensory, interdisciplinary environment. They knew how to make learning a joyful experience and how to inspire students to expand their limits. Over the long haul, they supported each other through personal and professional crises.

Differences and conflicts were worked out through listening to each others' points of view, trying to reach a better understanding, if not consensus. There were times when the discussions became heated and we became defensive about our own issues. And sometimes I was called upon to make a decision to settle an issue. Most of the time we had enough common bonds to hold us together to move past conflicts and differences.

The collaborative decision-making process is not an easy one, and it takes time and work to build the level of trust needed, both for the process and for the people involved. Years after Seacrest had begun, site-based management and collaborative decision-making came into vogue in education and suddenly, it was the way all schools were supposed to be managed. Obviously, the process involved a difficult turnaround for the leaders and faculty who had neither the background nor the temperament for this type of organization. For those who are not committed, a collaborative style of management might be an invitation to failure.

The underlying problem in the shift to the collaborative style of management is *change* itself. While the economy and technological advances have forced people to rethink the way they do business, our educational system continues to be bound and gagged by traditional ways of thinking. Part of the problem is that when things get tough, a large segment of society can only see what used to work, when times were safer and more predictable. Rather than thinking about ways to solve today's problems and setting our minds to creating a more enlightened future, they have a mind set that says it is safer to return to the old ways.

Fragmented thinking by individuals narrows the scope of possibilities. The field of opportunity is fixed and static. Joseph Jaworsky writes about the importance of collective dialogue in making the shift to collaborative leadership:

> . . .In dialogue, you're allowing the whole that exists to become manifest. It's a deep shift in consciousness away from the notion that parts are primary. If individuals and organizations operate from the generative orientation, from possibility rather than resignation, we can create the future into which we are

living, as opposed to merely reacting to it when we get there . . . by collectively "listening" to what is wanting to emerge in the world, and then having the courage to do what is required.

Out of collective listening and thinking, important new insights occur that lead to commitment and coherent action. When everyone is a participant in the process, there is a creative flow of ideas that generates incredible new possibilities. Such creative participation is what Mihaly Csikszentmihalyi calls "being in the flow." George Leonard calls the state "entrainment"—the sense of being connected to one's own rhythm that is simultaneously interconnected to the pulse of others.

In collective thinking and collaborative leadership, the diverse styles of *all* the participants must be honored. That includes the learners and the different ways in which teachers guide them in developing shared responsibility. The divergent contrasts between teachers and learners, within and between classrooms, offer distinct illustrations: For instance, I look at the ways in which teachers expose learners to a variety of experiences, people, viewpoints, and resources. When Walter, an eminent retired physicist, comes to Seacrest to teach Joanne's fifth-graders, sparks fly. With the air fairly sizzling from Walter's enthusiasm, he makes the theories of Pythagoras, Newton, and Einstein come to life. The students cannot help but become engaged in a lively discussion about how and why things work in the world of science and mathematics. I would be surprised if Walter failed to harvest some future scientists.

Or take Karen Masell, who does not have to lecture the children in her kindergarten classes about kindness or respect or staying calm. She simply lives it, and her young charges are learning how to settle

Pure Bliss

conflicts peacefully by her example. Together, they formulate their own rules for sharing, safety, kindness, and peaceful means of settling conflicts. Everyone wants to help in Karen's room. When the older students team up to tutor their buddies in Karen's class, they too become the picture of patience and serenity. Robert Fulghum's familiar writing, *All I Really Need To Know I Learned in Kindergarten*, is a perfect description of the way Karen teaches and lives her life. Significantly, her goals for her own children, one of whom is in high school, are the same as in her kindergarten.

In another Seacrest classroom, there is Sandy Mathis, who coauthored and published a math program, which is being used nationally. Even though Sandy cannot carry a tune (which she had told me but I did not believe it until I heard her sing), she creates music and poetry and stories and butterfly gardens with her children. Sandy teaches children to use their imaginations as well as anyone I know.

During their study of sea life, each of her second-graders collected, studied and reported on different sea creatures. At the end of the study, they put on a "Sea Life Fashion Show" for parents. Designing their costumes out of paper bags and scrap materials, they cut, painted, and pasted together beads, felt, straw, and bright pieces of cloth. Hats, vests, belts, sashes, and crowns were decorated with facts and illustrations of their sea creatures. All the information they had learned was presented by the moderator as the children paraded their costumes before the audience. For the finale, they sang the songs and recited the poems they had each made up about their chosen sea creatures.

If you wanted to learn about interdependence of all life, all you would have to do is be in Caron Staples' class for a while. The classroom itself has been turned into a research laboratory for the whole universe, from outer space to herb gardens. The children gather their information from explorations to the beach, barrier islands, planetarium, local nurseries, or deep into the Everglades. Books are written and published; graphs and diagrams are developed, mounted and tracked; vegetables are harvested, cooked, and seasoned with home-grown basil, garlic, thyme, and oregano.

It was gratifying to receive a parent's letter about the ways in which Caron removes the limits on what the children can learn:

> ...Not only does she teach the children what they need to know, but she also takes their ideas and inputs them into her lesson plan. This makes our son interested in every topic . . . Mrs. Staples instills in the children that they can do most anything if

they try. The children I see in her classroom are self assured and happy.

Sometimes, creating a climate for change involves knowing what to ignore. Maybe there's a teacher who wants nothing to do with interdisciplinary teaching and, in fact, shows no sign of changing her mind. I have learned the hard way that it does not work for me to try to get that person to do something she does not believe in. What does work is to discover a teacher's special talent or skill, and encourage her to share it with others. Sometimes the act of exchanging tips and expertise can crack open resistance to other possibilities.

The above examples point to the individualistic natures of people within the system, and there are as many examples as there are people. Moving a whole group toward purposeful change can be facilitated when teachers come together to plan and conduct their own staff development, incorporating their unique styles into a unified whole.

Putting it all Together

My dilemma was in knowing what to do with all the information I had collected in writing my doctoral dissertation. The more I studied the people, programs, and projects of Seacrest, the more differences I found, and the harder it became to pull all my information together into a coherent final form. My professors had warned me about taking on too broad a topic. At that point, I understood why doctoral dissertations were limited to the study of the minutest aspect of a subject, which could be tested and analyzed under a carefully screened and controlled environment. That way, the statistics from the evidence could be revealed and contained in a nice, square box and tied with a neat bow—no loose ends hanging out.

The problem was, I had never figured out how to do that with real people, who are multiplicities of loose strings and unorganized parts. None of the people I knew fit into neat categories—at least not the teachers or students or parents of Seacrest. Maybe, I mused, the traditional research design should be left to the scientists who discover new drugs and test them on mice.

At any rate, I had come too far and worked too hard to change my study midstream. I would find a way to fit the pieces together the same way Seacrest had been built and developed—one day at a time.

Hands-On-Learning

Learning Responsibility

Imagination

CHAPTER 25

Balance Point

After gathering all the data over a two-year period, synthesizing dozens of inventories, tests, profile types, and questionnaires, how was I to make it useful? If every child, like every teacher, has a unique style of learning, how do we attend to these differences in ways that are practical and manageable for the teacher? Such were the questions that had to be addressed not only in writing my doctoral dissertation, but for the ongoing development of Seacrest as well.

While the data I had gathered were interesting and provided me with some insights, the missing link was how to pull the information together in a meaningful context, both for myself and for the faculty. In coming to wholeness, I needed to simplify. If I were to take all the information I had explored and studied, and bring it together in its simplest and purest form, how should I proceed? Could I communicate it in a word or a phrase that would somehow catch the essence of the central core?

One spring morning in 1988, all these questions were floating around unorganized in my mind. Instead of forcing myself to answer them, I put on my cutoff jeans, an old shirt, my gardening gloves, and walked outside from the back deck to pull weeds from a rock garden I had started.

The early morning sun reflected off drops of silver sparkles left from the evening's shower, outlining a perfect spider web suspended between the ferns and a young sapling. I began weeding between the coral and lavender Impatiens, making my way over to the ferns. Standing up to stretch, my eyes caught the web again. I looked at the fragile silken strands interwoven in perfect symmetry and design, and the words *interconnected balance* leaped to the forefront of my mind. Could those simple words represent the entire body of work I had investigated and analyzed?

Exploring the phrase further, I could envision each person and every part of Seacrest as being a strand of the web, interconnected and balanced, with the weaving of individual strands representing unique talents and strengths. One strand alone, unsupported and unconnected would soon weaken, break off, and be scattered into the wind. We are strengthened by the balance and symmetry of every other strand.

We teach the children of Seacrest that Southwest Florida depends on the extent to which we maintain the natural balance of the ecosystems. Plants, animals, and sea life depend on the wetlands and other ecosystems. The wetlands depend on the mangroves. Our quality of life in Southwest Florida depends on the preservation of its native environment. Just as the land and water, plants, animals, and barrier islands interact and depend on one another, the people who live here are a vital part of the interaction as well. We are a part of the web.

Rather than trying to adjust our innate ways of being in order to tap into each student's style, it seemed to me that the student would be better served if we first listened and looked for the connections that exist among us all, and then widened our level of understanding to include our *differences* as an essential part of wholeness. The diversity of individuals working together for a common cause promotes and sustains an enriched representation of symmetry.

As I searched for these answers in the classrooms, I looked for a *balanced* blend of multidimensional teaching and multisensory activities. I listened for teaching that *connected* strands of knowledge to other strands. Did the teaching and learning hold meaning and excitement for every child? I observed the way children were grouped and regrouped. I listened to the children's questions and discussions and looked at their writing and art work. I observed the way they related to what they were learning in making their own connections.

How did the teachers communicate? Did the message of the words match body language, nonverbal cues, and actions? Were the teachers being true to themselves in expressing their own talents and personalities? Were teachers continuing their learning and self-growth, or had they settled into a comfortable rut of repetition and replication?

Here, the metaphor of the spider's web holds a message of caution—to remember not to get caught within the existing boundaries, but to recognize the infinite number of opportunities beyond. The task is to continue to weave new patterns and create new alternatives.

What I looked for in a classroom was not perfection, but growth—growth in both teaching and learning, because I was never able to separate one from the other.

Sadie Bender, for example, was a seeker of growth, for herself as well as for the children she taught. In fact, I first met Sadie at a conference about learning and teaching styles. She was looking for a position in which she could delve into new ways of teaching. And I was looking for a person like Sadie for a new elementary position at Seacrest.

Teaching self-responsibility with a strong sense of service to others is high on Sadie's list. If you come into her classroom for a while and listen to the conversations of second or third-graders, you may hear the children reviewing the day's accomplishments. They use video recordings to examine their own performance, and how they work together as a group. Their self-appraisal becomes a part of the reporting system to parents.

One day, at the end of an independent work session, the class came together on the carpet for their daily discussion of the morning's work. They agreed that they had worked well in their groups and had accomplished what they had set out to do.

When Sadie asked if there was anything else they needed to discuss, one of the children raised her hand and spoke. "I think we should talk about how we can solve our problems on the playground—when somebody gets mad at somebody else and starts yelling at them."

Instantaneously, all the other hands shot up. One by one, they all revealed examples of poor behavior, and everyone had a solution.

After listening to each one, without comment, Sadie asked if the class could discover what seemed to trigger most of the problems. Jim responded first.

"Well, number one is to let everybody who wants to play soccer have a turn and don't leave anyone out just because you think they can't kick or throw as good as you, and you shouldn't hold onto the ball. Pass it to the person who's not so good, and that way they'll all get better."

"Yeah," replied Sammy, "but what if that person doesn't really want to play soccer, because he knows he's not so good at it, and maybe he doesn't want his team to lose because of him?"

Robert entered the discussion. "How's he gonna get good if he doesn't play? We need to tell him to come on and be on our team and we don't care if you miss," letting his glance slide to the person who 'missed' the most.

Then Cindy jumped in. "Well, most of the girls aren't as good as David and Jeff and Mike, and we're afraid to play because you'll tease us or get mad at us."

Jeff offered his solution for the girls. "We'll let you play most of the time and we can teach you how to get better, but I think we should be able to play some days by ourselves so you don't slow us down all the time."

Sadie listened to the exchange silently as the group continued to work out their own solutions. By listening and waiting, Sadie allowed the children to interact and connect into each others' thinking and to take the necessary steps in solving their own problems. She could have saved a lot of time by simply telling the class what they *should* do. But in doing so, she would have denied them the opportunity to assess themselves and each other, to examine their feelings and debate the issues, and to find their own answers. That was only one of the ways in which Sadie taught the children responsibility. Other ways included regularly scheduled visits to nursing homes, and sending out handmade cards for various occasions.

Jennifer, Marcia, and Sadie turned their passion for technology and computers into a weekly after-school class for teachers, tailored to fit each person's level of mastery. I am fascinated by the way in which teachers form partnerships with other teachers, and I believe it has more to do with chemistry than proximity. Team teaching is great only to the degree that the teachers are authentically compatible; this is a subjective phenomenon that cannot be predicted or forced by external circumstances.

I remembered most of my experiences with team teachers as being rich and rewarding, leading to lifelong friendships. The other side of the coin is that I remember all too well spending a couple of excruciating years with the *wrong* team teacher, an experience I would just as soon forget.

It was obvious that Jennifer and Sadie's partnership at Seacrest worked, and they bounced off each other's strengths and interests in designing dozens of strategies for the children they taught. They grouped and regrouped children for specific purposes and projects, sometimes bringing the children from both classes all together in one large group. The first part of the day was usually spent in the acquisition of basic skills in spelling and grammar, math and reading. Around midmorning, there was a shift into organized action. In less than five minutes' time, their classroom would be transformed into a construction site for inventing and building original machines. As the day unfolded, the pace ebbed and flowed in a series of active and quiet, creative and conventional and unconventional activities.

One of the more courageous adventures of this team was the annual "Read-In," when all the children from Jennifer and Sadie's classes slept overnight in the multipurpose room. On the Friday night of the sleep-over, the children arrived at school lugging sleeping bags, pillows, sack suppers and drinks, and their favorite book. Contrary to what one would imagine, it was actually a relatively calm evening, with a few games, a picnic, and book-sharing before they all settled into sleeping bags to read until lights-out time. Amazingly, they even slept a few hours as the night wore on.

Other partnerships form, either spontaneously or for specific purposes throughout the school in quite different patterns. There are teams for planning, program development, staff development, field trips, festivals and musicals, parent volunteers, cross-grade-level teams, and projects of all kinds. Then there are the friendships that form, extending to after-school hours and social gatherings.

I realized, with startling clarity, that the data, tests, and studies I had gathered for my doctoral research were not only being played out everywhere I looked; the information was beginning to converge into a multidimensional, interactive whole. The balance point that I had been looking for came from the uniqueness of individual teachers who asserted their freedom to teach and team in the ways that worked best for them and the children they taught.

My search for a balanced blend of interconnected strands of teaching and learning became progressively focused whenever I took the time to stop what I was doing and center my attention on the teachers and the children to see how it all fit together. Like sorting through the different pieces of a puzzle, they fused together to portray a panorama of a unified system of learning.

The task of completing the dissertation from my research was to simplify—something easier said than done. It involved pulling out the purest and most essential elements and variables, then putting them together into an organized model of reality. Whenever I found myself getting too overwhelmed or too tired, I tried to remember to stop long enough to look and listen and reflect. If that failed to work, I would drop everything and return to my garden. The symbolic act of clearing out weeds provided a way to clear my mind of extraneous details, so that I could sort, order, and connect the strands into a conceptual framework of patterns.

Finally, in the fall of 1988, the writing of my dissertation came to an end. When the Ph.D. degree was awarded, it seemed almost anticlimactic. Receiving the degree paled in comparison to the elation I felt when the final draft of the dissertation was completed. The real challenge, of course, was in putting what I had learned into practice at Seacrest. In the meantime, I took a deep breath, heaved a sigh of relief, and went to the beach.

We are all Partners in Learning

CHAPTER 26

The Search Continues

My interest in the studies of leadership and learning did not end with the completion of my doctorate, particularly with regard to shared decision-making and collaborative leadership. It became clear to me that good leaders come in many forms and styles. Improvement and innovation in the schools can come from leaders with forceful and dynamic styles; from nurturing supportive leaders; or from the charismatic, high energy leaders. In the February 1992 issue of *Educational Leadership*, Richard Sagor discusses some of the common elements of leaders who, on the surface, have quite different styles but who share the goal of working for improvement in the schools:

They all have the ability to bring about a transformational effect on the teachers within the system. They also are in the classrooms, they practice the art of active listening, and they view teaching as an experimental science. The faculties of these schools feel empowered to take the credit for the school's focus and success, and the teachers are motivated to voluntarily work countless hours for the intrinsic rewards that come with the freedom to be a part of collaborative planning and decision making.

As I received each issue of *Educational Leadership*, the *Phi Delta Kappan,* and various other educational journals, I continued the search for articles, books, and materials to help me in defining leaders who were interested in inclusive, collaborative ways to lead, teach, and learn. The most definitive sources came from Kenneth and Miriam Clark's books. In their 1994 publication, *Choosing to Lead*, they defined leadership as:

> ...an activity or set of activities, observable to others, that occurs in a group, organization, or institution involving a leader and followers who willingly subscribe to common purposes and work together to achieve them. A leader is a person who earns the trust of followers and thereby increases their commitment to achieve the common purposes of the group.

In the same book, the Clarks incorporate definitions of leadership from others in the field. According to David Campbell, Smith Richardson Senior Fellow of the Center for Creative Leadership, leadership includes the concept of a task to be accomplished and the availability of resources to accomplish it. And Walter F. Ulmer, Jr., past president of the Center for Creative Leadership in Greensboro, North Carolina, says, "Leadership is an activity—an influence process—in which an individual gains the trust and commitment of others and without reliance on formal position or authority moves the group to the accomplishment of one or more tasks."

Ulmer's definition, the Clarks write, implies that status as a leader is not bestowed by promotion or appointment or because one is powerful or influential. Trust and commitment cannot be bought but must be earned. The element of trust appears to be a significant factor in each of these definitions of leadership. In other words, my title as the head of Seacrest meant little or nothing unless I proved by my actions that I could be trusted and that I trusted the opinions and decisions of those with whom I worked.

Other inspiration and insight that described the kind of leadership Lynne and I were determined to develop came from a book called, *Discovering Creativity: Proceedings of the 1992 International Creativity and Innovation Networking Conference,* edited by Stanley Gryskiewicz. In the study, Robert C. Burkhart, David M. Horth, and others address the issues in leadership that occur as we attempt to meet the demands of a rapidly changing global society. The writers connect the practical application of pragmatic, analytical thinking on the one hand and holistic, intuitive thinking on the other. Including sources from others in the field, Burkhart and Horth show the contrasts between managers and transformational leaders:

> J. P. Kotter (1990) asserts that 'Good management controls complexity, effective leadership produces useful change.' The challenges posed by the current decade of change will be even more challenging in the 21st century. The change is continuous and 'even the nature of change is changing.' (Land & Jarman, 1992). The challenges are stimulating a rapid transition from an emphasis on efficient and effective management to the need for truly creative change leadership.
>   . . . Zalesnik (1992) observes: 'Where managers act to limit choices, leaders develop fresh approaches to long-standing problems and open issues to new options. To be effective, leaders must project their ideas onto images that excite people and only then develop choices that give those images substance.' This is supported by Will McWhinney (1992) who proposes that 'There is no greater leadership than that which creates meaning in the lives of the followers.'

The Center for Creative Leadership

Other than learning through on-the-job experience, the most valuable training in leadership for Lynne and me came from the Center for Creative Leadership. Seacrest is privileged to have the Clarks (quoted earlier in this chapter) as guides and leaders at Seacrest.

Dr. Kenneth Clark is past president of the Center for Creative Leadership and a distinguished leader and consultant in the fields of measurement, science, and technology, psychology, and education. Miriam Clark, an author and educational leader, was the chairperson of the Seacrest School's Board of Trustees. Because of their interest in Seacrest, they arranged for Lynne and me to attend conferences at CCL.

The Center for Creative Leadership, a nonprofit organization with centers located throughout the world, is a program designed to improve leadership skills of top level managers and CEOs from a broad spectrum of business, industry, technology, the armed forces, and education. Army generals, managers of international enterprises, and many of the top CEOs of the country's largest companies attend these conferences. As it happened, there were only two educators and few women in either Lynne's or my group. I found it refreshing to be part of a group with such diverse backgrounds and careers.

Housed in a state-of-the-art building of brick and glass overlooking the Rocky Mountains, the conferences focused on the effectiveness, performance, and skills in leadership as perceived by the leader and others in the organization. Prior to the conference, participants were required to submit to a battery of tests and questionnaires that included questions for co-workers to complete. Throughout the conference, we were given more tests. We were divided into small teams and given a series of unique problems to solve. The solutions were shared, critiqued, and evaluated by the whole group.

As we worked through mazes, blizzards, and rescues, machines were invented, global companies created, and puzzles solved with outrageously creative solutions. We discovered in our teams who were the more assertive or adaptive, innovative, facilitating, or intuitive. We exchanged feedback on each other and we critiqued our teams. We learned to trust each other and we experienced the astounding power and creativity of team work.

Throughout the conference an invisible staff of psychologists analyzed personalities, styles, skills, body language, leadership methods, and patterns of communication behind one-way mirrors. By the end of our stay, we had a comprehensive and graphic understanding of our strengths and weaknesses, frustrations and limits, skills and perceptions, and we knew our team members inside and out. The training is not for the fainthearted or insecure. But for people who are committed to self-growth, the program offers an honest and thorough interpretation and examination of skills, strengths, and weaknesses.

Of course, the real work began after the conference was over—when we had the opportunity to put into action what we had learned. For example, I learned that while I am comfortable with ambiguity, there were teachers at Seacrest who needed things spelled out in black and white terms. I needed to be much more specific when expressing my thoughts, opinions, directions, or feedback. Another thing I learned was that my impatience *shows* when I fail to communicate my ideas well—something I had to guard against. Lack of communication is one of the primary reasons for a breakdown in organizations, and, of course, educators and leaders need to communicate effectively with students, teachers, and parents. Everything we do sends out some kind of message—our body language, our words, the way we listen, and the environment—all tells a story of who we are and how we are perceived.

If we would spend more time in reflective listening than we do speaking, we would understand, trust, and respect each other more. If we could withhold judgment and give up the need to be right, we could learn still more. And if we could express our ideals and values, and at the same time, inspire others to share theirs as well, we could connect on a deeper, more honest level.

CHAPTER 27

Global Education As a Catalyst for Change

A few years after Lynne came to Seacrest, she selected Nova University for her doctoral studies. And, according to Lynne's reports, her experiences at Nova met her expectations for innovative, practical learning. Through her doctoral program, she learned from visiting professors from Harvard, Stanford, Berkeley, and Cornell— people considered to be among the brightest of the new breed of forward-thinking educators. Lynne, too, tailored her program so that her work could be directly applied to Seacrest.

Lynne decided to focus her studies on global education as the most timely theme for her doctoral work at Nova University. Her research took her far beyond the historical, geographical, and cultural aspects so often defined as global education. Her final project was a global education curriculum for Seacrest, developed and implemented with the faculty. The program is woven into nearly all aspects of the total curriculum, cutting across labels and limits of subjects and grade levels, merging the disciplines into an active, cooperative, and personalized journey for students.

Today, using the global perspective, students are guided to think about parallels between conflicts in distant countries and in Southwest Florida. They are learning to recognize how their personal conflicts are interconnected with the diverse conflicts both in the local community and across the planet. Common themes are selected to merge with academic studies at Seacrest. Community service projects are used as bridges to understand economic or ecological systems in other parts of the world.

The primary focus of the global education program is to provide students with a sense of their own identity and purpose, working from the acquisition of fundamental skills into a larger arena of telecommunications, field studies, service projects, and multidisciplinary learning. Essential links are formed between students and the global community. They explore the past and present to seek their own purpose in shaping the future. They study issues and conflicts, economics and politics, ecosystems and the arts. They connect on a personal level with their own heritage and compare it to the contrasting diversity of others. They examine their own, as well as others' prejudices and preferences, from systems of governments down to the brands of shoes they wear.

The Global Education Program, initiated by Lynne, has served as an excellent catalyst for change with a common purpose. The basic curriculum is a stepping off place for unlimited individualities within a common core, allowing teachers to use their unique talents in accommodating the special interests of children.

Seacrest media specialist, Joanne Cassio, teaches library skills, research, writing, and publishing through the use of technology. Through the Internet, Seacrest children are contacting other children throughout the world, bringing new possibilities for learning as far as the imagination can stretch.

In an interesting contrast, Lynn Shearer's fourth-graders connect up with sailors, in a program called S.A.I.L. for Kids, fashioned after the famous "BOC Challenge." The children in Lynn's class work in small groups of four to track individual sailors as they race across the Atlantic to different countries. Although sailors communicate by radar, radio, and satellite, they do not depend on technology as their main source of navigation. Rather, they use their knowledge of astronomy, ocean currents, trade winds, and weather systems to sail their small boats.

The program, *Sailing As Integrated Learning, or S.A.I.L,* is designed to teach children about geography, the environment, history, math, and the physical sciences as the children track their designated sailor's journey. The fourth-graders learn the metric system and weather instruments, grids and coordinates, and how to navigate by the stars. They learn about the interdependence between sailors and their environment, maps and globes, oceanography, life skills, nutrition, and self-reliance. When the sailors reach their port-of-call, they pass on the information about the children and cultures of other countries. A special thrill is experienced by the Seacrest fourth-graders when they receive letters from sailors.

The divergent paths of each teacher give students the advantage of understanding their world in different ways. At the same time, the tools of technology, parents, and people in the community, and points beyond add an important dimension to learning.

In recent years, two other Seacrest faculty members also completed their doctoral work. They, too, structured their studies so that they would be useful to our program. We added Caron's work in curriculum design and Jennifer's focus on technology to Lynne's work on global education to redesign the Seacrest curriculum into a highly innovative program aimed toward preparing students for the future.

Thus, the fruits of our doctoral studies were synthesized, evaluated, and transposed into workable practices. Seacrest's teachers selected (or rejected) the ideas and adapted them into their own unique ways of teaching. The final judges for success are the students themselves. Accordingly, the teachers and students are the leaders, the critics, and the purveyors of new knowledge. They are the ones who hold the true power. And this, to me, points to one of the essential ingredients of successful leadership and shared power. New systems and ideas mandated from the top simply do not work unless teachers choose to accept them and fashion them into their own creation, which in turn, is accepted and internalized by the students.

Leading and learning, then, involves an interconnected balance of trust, listening, honoring differences, and making connections through purposeful application. Shared decision making and collective thinking can be powerful motivators for new growth and positive change.

VII

LIFTING LIMITS
AND LABELS

CHAPTER 28

Primed for Success

Through the years, Seacrest has had its share of students who have been clinically diagnosed as having Attention Deficit Disorder, dyslexia, or other problems requiring specialized instruction. Although Seacrest has no programs designed for those with specific difficulties, we teach these children as long as the teachers can appropriately satisfy their requirements. Some have been able to complete successfully all their schooling at Seacrest through the eighth grade.

Sometimes the small classes, individualized attention, and multisensory learning given to all the Seacrest children can do more for those who require specific kinds of attention than the specialized programs of public schools. Occasionally, arrangements are made for Seacrest students to receive the services of specialists from the public schools. It depends on the severity of the problem, the decisions made by teachers, and the cooperative effort among child, parent, and teacher. Honest, open, and frequent communication on everyone's part is essential to the success of all children, and especially for those with special needs.

Because Seacrest has come to be known as "the school with a heart," we get many more requests for students with special needs than we can take, but among those we have been able to serve, there have been some real success stories. Part of the success lies in the fact that children are not labeled or separated, but rather, they are simply regarded as capable and responsible members of their class. The following examples are representative of the ways in which teachers meet the singular requirements of children at Seacrest.

Maria

Maria's four-year-old features looked like one of those life-sized dolls with big brown eyes, gold-rimmed glasses, and thick, shiny red hair framing a peaches and cream complexion with a few freckles sprinkled over the nose.

"Where's the playground?" she asked the day she came with her mother to inspect Seacrest.

"Would you like to go see it?" I asked.

"Yep," came the response of one who knows her own mind. "I need to know if I can find my way around and handle the equipment by myself."

"Good," I said. "I'll lead the way, and you can find out."

Maria was born with a condition known as *Lebers Congenital Amaurosis. Amaurosis*, the Latin word for blindness, does not quite reflect the true nature of Maria's vision. She is able to discern objects, and she gets around on her own once she knows the layout. The task at hand was to find out if Seacrest could provide the right kind of program and environment for this precocious little girl. If so, what adjustments would her teachers need to make for her? Could we assure her safety? Could we meet the requirements for her success, at least for her beginning school years? These were the questions I had to find out as Maria and I walked hand-in-hand through the hall and onto the playground.

When we reached the climbing apparatus, Maria let go of my hand.

"I'll try it by myself," she declared. And with that, Maria moved to the ladder and proceeded up each step. When she reached the top step, she carefully crawled onto the platform and maneuvered her way across to the slide on the other side. I am not sure if she knew I was underneath to catch her if she fell, but she came down the slide, landing on her feet, and groped her way to the next piece of equipment, which was a series of tires to climb.

After Maria had explored the climbing apparatus to her satisfaction, she wandered off to check out the rest of the playing field, with me trailing several yards behind. When she came to the metal fence at the end of the playground, she stopped, turned a hundred and eighty degrees and began tracing her steps back the way she had come. After walking for about ten yards, Maria suddenly stopped in her tracks, stood still for a moment and then sat down. Coming up beside her, I asked, "Are you okay?"

"Yes," she answered, with the smallest trace of a tremor in her voice. "The grass wanted me to rest here," she said. She has lost her bearings, I thought to myself, and this is her way of coping.

"I think the grass is a good place for me to rest too," I said, and we sat in a quiet conversation for a few minutes. I described some of the things the preschoolers did, while she in turn told me about her former preschool, a school designed for children with exceptional needs. After we walked back inside the building, we got a long cool drink from the water fountain and joined her mom in my office.

Maria announced to her mother, "This'll be okay. I'll go to *this* school." As I write these words, Maria is in the fifth grade, and none of us are sure just how she has learned to read and write. But she has. Her teachers say she reads the same books and does the same math as others in her classes. She writes her own stories as well, and participates in all the activities with other students. Next year, Maria will enter middle school, and she plans to remain at Seacrest.

Several times a week, a bus takes Maria to a public school. There she receives special instruction for the visually impaired, but most of the time Maria is at Seacrest. Her teachers make adjustments to facilitate her lessons. If she needs a certain type of lined paper, they make sure it's available. If she needs something read aloud, she gets it. If she needs additional help, she has it.

As Maria treks around the school, she often has more help than she needs. Other students surround her, trying to hold her hand as she walks down the hall or on the playground. I sometimes wonder if she's humoring them when they contend for the privilege of helping her. I have a suspicion that Maria knows the ins and outs, nooks and crannies of every square inch of the Seacrest buildings and grounds. She steps out of her car unaided in the mornings, strides through the front gate and on through the right-hand passageway divided by black iron railings, turns to the right and continues down the hall to her classroom, where she opens the door, never once faltering or bumping into anything or anyone.

The skill with which Maria manages her life is an enigma that none of us comprehend. Although she practices using a white cane on some of her treks down the hallway, we're sure she can navigate just as well without it. At some point Maria will learn Braille, but no one can predict how much she will use it. Still, we do know that Maria will find her own way to independent success. And we know that Seacrest has helped brighten her passage.

Mac

Mac has dysgraphia, which means that writing is a painfully slow process for him. His lightning-quick mind makes writing doubly painful. He retains facts and information like a thirsty sponge. Ask Mac anything about the way machines work or the ecological makeup of the Everglades and he's a walking encyclopedia. As long as he is not required to write it down.

Each year, Mac's teachers have had to learn the delicate balance between helping him to write a little more than he thought he could, and a lot more than he wanted to. At the same time, they use their intuition to know when they need to lighten up and accept a shorter written assignment.

Sometimes it would have been easier for all of us to let Mac go through school without having to write at all. But that would be giving in to a difficulty that would have left him with a real handicap for life. As it is, we do not consider Mac to be handicapped. He is good at math, a leader in sports, and an officer in the middle school student council. And in fact, he's a pretty good writer at this point.

Learning Through the Arts

It is a well-known fact that children excel and achieve in a variety of ways. In analyzing students' achievement and performance at Seacrest, we can conclude that the arts play a significant role in successful learning. Extending the curriculum through the arts increases the depth and range of knowledge and its application. While there is value in focusing on separate disciplines in isolation, the arts can be used as a means to connect the strands among history, geography, mathematics, or science.

Too many times the arts have been cut from schools by overzealous back-to-basics advocates. In the attempts to raise standards to some hypothetical benchmark, the elimination of these so-called frills is supposed to make students buckle down to "real" learning. Ignoring all the advanced research that the arts actually enhance and increase learning, the periodic waves toward conformity and fragmentary standards persist.

Ideas, perceptions, and complex thinking are advanced through the various art forms of drama, visual expression, dance, and music. More and more studies are showing that when the arts are integrated into the curriculum, students as a whole not only do better on standardized tests, but are more confident, work harder, and develop higher levels of abstract, analytical thinking.

When I observe the students at Seacrest, they are often engaged in some form of an artistic endeavor—a project, some type of performance, or creative expression. They are practicing the art of form and function. Students who combine top performance with enthusiasm, a positive attitude, kindness and respect for others, offer a gratifying measure of proof that at Seacrest our goal is being achieved. For children who, for a variety of reasons, require specialized attention, the arts can be used as a bridge in tapping into the multiple ways in which children learn.

Special attention, ongoing practice, and commitment by everyone involved are required to open the channels to children's success. It is an interesting paradox that the same premise holds true for children with specific disabilities as it does for the genius. In fact, it holds true for all children. The work developed by Howard Gardner on multiple intelligences and talents should cause us to rethink the limits and labels put on children. The related arts teachers at Seacrest often provide the motivational spark for the development of talents in music or foreign language, media and technology, or visual and performing arts.

For the student who has an exceptional talent, Seacrest provides a supportive atmosphere of encouragement and support. For instance, Danny is considered to be a child prodigy as a young violinist.

The Prodigy

Danny began learning the violin when he was six. Soon after moving to Naples from Japan, his mother found a suitable teacher of the Suzuki method. Lisa, an accomplished young violinist in the Naples

The Prodigy

Philharmonic Symphony Orchestra, took her young student in tow and rapidly advanced him through the initial variations of *Twinkle Twinkle Little Star* to more difficult pieces. Danny's daily practice periods became his mother's first priority, and regardless of whatever else was happening, mother and son sat side by side as they practiced for several hours each and every day.

Danny was in the second-grade when he made his debut on the Seacrest stage. Looking perfectly composed, he walked on stage, dressed in a navy jacket, pin-striped dress shirt and dark tie, with his miniature violin tucked under his arm. With a little nod to his mother, who accompanied him on the piano, Danny launched into Vivaldi's Concerto in A Minor. The audience was electrified by the fluid, lyrical tones produced by one so young. With a full-bodied vibrato, the small nimble fingers of his left hand accurately romped across the strings of the tiny instrument, as his bow matched the pace to produce the seemingly effortless notes. Ranging from low to high registers, trills, staccato and legato phrases, the strings were played with energy and certainty. With a long cadenza near the finale, Danny ended with a flourish.

Throughout the performance, Danny's facial expression remained impassive. At the end, he smiled, bowed deeply from the waist, and walked off the stage. Once out in the hall, he transformed into a regular second-grader, tossing his bouquet of roses up and down like a basket ball.

A year later, Danny appeared with the Naples Philharmonic Symphony as guest soloist. As the last note sounded from his performance, the audience rose for an extended standing ovation. When I asked his mother how he got to be so advanced at such an early age, she answered simply. "Practice," she said. "And good instruction from his teacher, Lisa." When I asked how long he practiced, his mother replied, "Four hours a day. Every day."

Danny is now ten years old, and has just been accepted to study at Juliard. Excluding his exceptional talent, he is a reasonably good student who plays, fools around, and behaves like your everyday young boy, filled with energy and fun.

By the time Danny's little sister was in kindergarten, she, too, was an up and coming student of the cello. From observing these and other students, I know that innate talent like this does not develop on its own. The ones who go on to higher accomplishments are taught, encouraged, and sometimes prodded by teachers and parents who put forth the time and energy for daily practice. In addition, there is often a coach, an expert in the field who works with the student, parents, and teachers. A strong team effort is required, with each of the members wholly committed in making sure that latent talent does not lie dormant and undeveloped — whether it be on the violin, the canvas, or the soccer field.

Children have a natural way of discovering their own talents. There is no need to teach them how to play or relax or to put all their attention on the things they love to do. No one has to push a child who loves tennis onto the tennis courts. With tools and encouragement from parents, teachers and coaches, children will develop skills and succeed— not just the chosen few, but all children. I would like to think that all children are given the special attention received by those with specific difficulties or to those who are termed genius.

At Seacrest we help students find their special gifts by observing what they do. What motivates them to spend hours pursuing a purpose that has meaning to them? What are they most excited about? What internal urges make them want to work hard at an activity, to do it again and again without losing interest?

Youth is a time for exploration and experimentation. It is not necessary to worry about college majors or career goals. Children have many explorations to follow before they pursue their chosen field of work. While at Seacrest, we believe their life's work is to be children. Ours is to be fully present with them; to give them the guidance and encouragement they need without smothering them with too much attention; to give them the tools they need for independence; to appreciate who and what they are at this moment; and to allow them the joy of discovering their own talents and their own uniqueness. Let them teach us about what brings them happiness and success.

Children at Risk

Even with the most difficult student—the one who has been damaged by life circumstances, the task is to discover what is most important to that child, and work from there. Consider the children with ongoing conflicts in the family; or the ones who live in extreme poverty, or with substance abuse, violence, or death of a family member. There must be ways to find something the children care about to keep them afloat. Maybe it is field hockey or learning to play chess. Maybe a student is selected to play the role of the hero in a play, or gets turned on by learning to play the guitar. Perhaps there is a particular flair for marine biology, rocketry, or photography. Help the student attach a meaningful goal to his or her special interest and reasons to pursue it. Find anything within reason that brings a sense of control and accomplishment.

For the rapidly expanding numbers of young people who wake up wondering if they will survive the day, schools are often the only relatively safe havens. Even so, we hear the alarming news that 100,000 children bring loaded guns to school each day to protect themselves.

What significant changes are taking place in some of the neighborhoods around the country where drugs and drive-by-shootings are a part of the everyday scene? Reaching the limits of endurance,

Building Confidence Through Performing on Stage

The Sound of Music

people are banding together to fight their own personal battles against gang violence, patrolling their own streets and apartment complexes in an all-out determination to take back their neighborhoods. I was intrigued by a television special that featured a program called The Jamaican/Chicano Youth Chapel in New York, created, organized, and run by teens. They administer the funds, sit on the board, and plan the programs. Meeting in a church, the group has provided a safe place for kids to congregate after school and to express themselves in their own way. Their world is portrayed through drama, dance, rap, rhythm and rock, and personal stories as they encourage kids to stop killing each other. As one teenager put it, "If I wasn't here I'd be in the streets and I'd be in trouble. I can use my talents here. I can sing and dance."

It is infinitely easier to provide a safe environment when there is a sense of community—an extended family. I believe young people are better served through smaller schools, with high visibility, where every student is known by everyone else—fellow students, teachers, administrators, and parents. The very nature of a large school tends to predetermine a lack of community and individual attention or recognition. Kids get lost in the shuffle and are all but invisible. Every young person needs to belong to a group. Street gangs are created in part by a need to belong and to have an identity. In smaller schools, teachers and administrators know if a child has a problem, or is creating a problem for others. Such personal knowledge is difficult in schools in which the student population is so large that many incidents are not seen, heard, or communicated.

While no one program can solve the complexities that confront the children at risk, the best hope for success appears to be early prevention for the very young, before patterns of failure become entrenched. Sensory-rich programs that provide tools for conflict resolution and satisfying experiences in an emotionally stable

Three-Year-Old Nursery School-A New Addition

environment are shown to produce positive results in building self-esteem, increased growth in social awareness and cognitive development.

The quality and depth of programs designed to attend to the range of needs and abilities of all children are difficult, if not impossible, to support in the current structure of large schools. Deborah Meier, who twenty years ago initiated and developed Central Park East, a small, self-governing public school in East Harlem says it best:

> Small schools mean we can get to know a student's work, the way he or she thinks. . . . It means passing them in the hall before and after we have taught them, knowing their other teachers well, seeing them in different settings and guises and thus developing a broader repertoire of ways to approach them. This close knowledge helps us demand more of them; we can be tougher without being insensitive and humiliating. It also means we know their moods and styles—whom to touch in a comforting way and whom to offer distance and space in times of stress. It means that every adult in the school feels responsible for every kid and has insights that when shared can open up a seemingly intractable situation to new possibilities.
>
> . . .In small schools the accountability we owe to parents and the public is a matter of access, not of complex governing bodies or monitoring arrangements. . . . [Leaders] know about their staff's teaching not by scanning thick computer run-offs with complex tables, but by observing in classrooms and engaging in direct conversation. And they get to know the parents.

There are times when all the resources in the world can only provide temporary support for a child who suffers a life-threatening illness. The following chapter tells how a mother and daughter experienced the ultimate test of courage, and the community's response to an appeal for help.

CHAPTER 29

Tanya

An orchid tree is in full bloom, its branches spilling over with masses of deep pink flowers. The tree stands beside the road between two wings of Seacrest, and its delicate blossoms belie its strength to withstand the frequent poundings of blustery rain storms. A bronze plaque planted at the base of the tree is inscribed with a simple tribute.

This tree
planted in
loving memory of
Tanya Lake
1990

The orchid, with its delicate strength and beauty, is a befitting symbol for Tanya, the beautiful, brilliant, and witty child who withstood the trauma of merciless surgeries, bone marrow transplants, radiation, and massive doses of experimental chemotherapy with a spirit of determination and optimism. The story of Tanya's life holds a lasting imprint in the history of Seacrest, reminding us that the effects of one person can reach far beyond the physical world.

Tanya was in the sixth grade when she died of an insidious and incurable form of cancer that grew tumors in the brain, extended into the central nervous system, and formed branches that wrapped around the inside and outside of her spinal cord.

When I met nine-year-old Tanya, the only child of a single mother, I openly stared at the beauty that radiated a presence of unusual poise for one so young. Her long, straight black hair framed a face with high cheek bones, full lips, and deep brown intelligent eyes. Her tall, graceful bearing could have belonged to a young Indian princess. One could see the striking resemblance between Tanya and her mother, Elizabeth, and there was a certain air of equality about the two of them, as if they had been fashioned from the same mold.

I began questioning Elizabeth about Tanya. What school did she go to? What were her interests? Did she like her school? During the course of our conversation, Elizabeth told me that Tanya had undergone surgery for a tumor the year before, and it was believed that the operation had been a success.

An easy friendship began to emerge as our conversation lengthened into the sharing of mutual interests. Noticing that Tanya had quietly slipped away to join her friends, I asked Elizabeth if she would like to have her daughter attend Seacrest. Her answer came with instantaneous and matter-of-fact resignation.

"Of course! Seacrest has been my dream for Tanya. There is simply no way that I could afford even part of the tuition."

Breaking my own preset rule that everyone had to pay some amount toward tuition, I immediately offered Tanya a full scholarship, adding that we were always happy to find children with high potential whose parents believed in Seacrest's philosophy. Eyes widening in disbelief, Elizabeth had to be convinced that my offer was not just idle talk, but a bonafide promise.

"When could Tanya start?"

"In September—with our brand new fifth grade class," I replied, surprised at my own spontaneity.

Tanya and her new classmates launched our fifth grade with an easygoing mix of academics and activities, accentuated with good-natured banter. Tanya became known for her colorful jokes and offbeat humor. I could never quite figure out the thoughts that lay behind the disguised mask of her ebony eyes, and I would frequently be surprised by the frankness and total honesty, once her trust overcame her natural reserve.

The kindred spirit and connection between Tanya and her teacher, Joanne Hammond, were unmistakable, as mutual respect, understanding, and admiration blossomed into a genuine love between teacher and student. For the first time in her school career, Tanya was challenged, inspired, encouraged, and tantalized to unleash and exercise her remarkable mind.

With the exception of three children who had entered the previous year in a combined class of third and fourth-graders, Joanne and her students were new to Seacrest. Perhaps the newness was part of what made the class unique. They had not yet learned to take Seacrest for granted, and most had not experienced school as a place where learning could be an exciting adventure.

Field trips, environmental studies, math problems, and scientific experiments were shared and recorded in journals and research projects. Baby chicks were hatched and tended. Local speakers came to visit and teach their specialties. Joanne created a classroom atmosphere that was peaceful and stimulating. She propelled the children to heights unknown to them, inspiring them to make leaps of mind, relating previous knowledge to broad ranges of creative ventures.

Homework and projects spilled over into slumber parties and nonstop phone conversations. Tanya's household became a paradise for animal lovers. Besides Tanya and Elizabeth, the other family members included a cocker spaniel Gypsy, Afghan hound Jezebel, brown Labrador Sara, Himalayan cat Romeo, and four Siamese cats—Gizmo, Aphrodite, Archimedes, and Nyack.

Tanya's ambition to become a marine biologist came from an intrinsic love for nature, spawned by long, sunny Saturdays spent in a small boat with her mother and friends as they explored the shallow bays and estuaries of the inland waterways. Clad in swimsuits and equipped with a picnic lunch, sun screen, and water bottles, they would sit for hours on the edges of island-forming mangroves. Long, exposed roots, almost as tall as their branches, formed twisted, bony legs that protruded downward to establish homes in the mud, becoming the start of a new mangrove forest. Snowy egrets, great blue herons, ibises, pelicans, storks, and gulls made their nests there, surrounded with an abundance of food, protected from storms and humans behind tangled, impenetrable labyrinths of roots and branches.

On other days, Tanya and Elizabeth would leave their car and set out on foot to explore the wilderness of Corkscrew Swamp Sanctuary, hoping to spot a rare woodstork nesting among the Spanish mosses or feeding between the turtles and raccoons. When the Miccosukee Indian tribe held their festival days, Tanya and Elizabeth ventured along the

Tamiami Trail, deep into the Everglades to take part in the festivities, purchasing handmade treasures of the ancient tribal culture. Although enraptured by the jewelry, weaving, beadwork, and ritual ceremonies, Tanya became upset and indignant when the alligator wrestling commenced.

When Seacrest held its annual Christmas and Hanukkah program, Tanya was selected to sing a solo. She sang "Castle on a Cloud" with a natural, pure tone, like that of a hand-crafted, primitive wooden flute. Some of the words in the song held an almost prophetic quality:

> There is a castle on a cloud
> I'd like to go there in my sleep . . .
> There is a room that's full of joy . . .
> There is a lady all in white
> Holds me and sings a lullaby . . .
> I know a place where no one cries . . .
> Not in my castle on a cloud.

The fifth grade class of 1989 had a fresh, almost pristine quality that reflected vitality, health, high energy, humor, and youth. There was no sense of the invisible and silent sickness residing beneath the surface of one of its students.

We were out on the playground on a cool, clear February day, when Lynne called my attention to Tanya.

"Jane, I'm worried about Tanya. Look at the way she's moving. Something's not right."

As we stood and watched, we could see that she was running and walking with an unnatural gait, as if she were compensating, or favoring her back, hips, and legs. As I watched silently, Lynne affirmed her concern. "Jane, you need to call Elizabeth."

Within days, Elizabeth and Tanya were in New York with the world renowned neurosurgeon, Dr. Fred Epstein and pediatric oncologist, Dr. Larry Helsen. Extensive tests confirmed malignant tumors in Tanya's brain and spinal cord. The tumors were not operable. Treatment included massive doses of radiation, high intensity chemotherapy, a bone marrow transplant, and prayers for miracles.

Between treatments, Tanya and Elizabeth returned to Naples, to be met at the airport by giggling schoolmates who were determined to keep their friend from becoming discouraged. Elizabeth's full time care of Tanya meant leaving her job as office manager of a local interior

A Seacrest Quilt Made with Loving Hands for Tanya

decorating firm. Astronomical medical expenses, plane fare to and from New York, and basic living expenses escalated with each passing day.

Seacrest, along with Tanya's grandparents, relatives, and close friends initiated a campaign for money and support. The fund-raising efforts, one of which was named "The Tanya Lake Miracle Fund," were established at two local banks to raise the $100,000 needed for experimental treatment at the medical center in New York and for living expenses. Service clubs, churches and the media, along with countless individuals joined the campaign.

Continental Airlines provided free flights for Tanya and Elizabeth back and forth from Naples to New York. Hundreds of T-shirts were designed and sold by Seacrest and church youth groups. A thousand young players in the Naples Soccer league set aside a Saturday as "Tanya Lake Day" to raise funds. They presented Tanya with a giant get-well card, a soccer ball, and jersey. A New York singer even got into the act by giving a special benefit concert. Brunches were given by local clubs.

At Seacrest, every student participated in designing and piecing together a quilt for Tanya. The teachers, parents, and students created, published, and sold a cook book. The Seacrest Brownie troop raised a hundred dollars and The Seacrest 4-H Club held a pet show to raise money. A video tape and a talent show were produced. Joe and Susan, Seacrest parents, hosted a barbecue, with a band, games, and fireworks to raise $10,000.

Hundreds of posters were distributed throughout the community with Tanya's picture and a poem that she had written earlier in the year, before her illness. The bold, black letters across the top read, *MIRACLE NEEDED*. Tanya's poem, reprinted from her own handwriting, was startlingly poignant:

> I am a miracle
> How did I get here?
> Why do I grow healthy and beautiful?
> I am a miracle.
> How do I speak?
> Why do I learn?
> Why do I exist?
> I am a miracle.
> I grow strong and live a wonderful life.
> I make the world a wonderful place.
> I am a miracle!
> By Tanya Lake

Television and radio stations and newspapers from local and surrounding communities followed the story. Lengthy articles in the newspapers included large, color photographs of Tanya, some with a full head of thick, glossy black hair, some with no hair, reflecting the results of chemotherapy, and some with wisps of newly grown hair, forming a downy, black cap. Most of the photographs included her cat, Romeo, curled up asleep in Tanya's arms.

Her own bone marrow had been extracted, preserved, and replaced after each of the chemotherapy treatments. Each time she received a bone marrow replacement, she experienced a great burst of energy, and she wanted to do everything and go everywhere. Those were the times when all of us would feel a renewed sense of hope. On one such occasion, Tanya and her doctor grabbed each other in a moment of jubilant spontaneity and danced down the hallway of the hospital, to the delight of all who happened to view the scene.

Perhaps it was the cancer that led Tanya into a conscious search for a deeper awareness of her own spiritual connection with God, hoping to find her way out of the quagmire in which fate had placed her. She asked for information about alternative methods for healing, and she began to practice visualization, prayer and meditation, directing her energy toward a higher source of support. When I was with her during this period, she appeared to carry a new depth of inner wisdom that extended beyond her years.

Although no longer able to practice gymnastics or go to parties with friends, Tanya had periods between treatments when she was well enough to come back to school, go out for an afternoon in the boat, or spend an occasional overnight with girlfriends. At school, we learned how to flush out a tiny tube that had been inserted into her jugular vein, exiting through her chest, for the purpose of injecting her medications.

Throughout the months, Elizabeth and I had nightly phone conversations, sometimes lasting for several hours, whether she and Tanya were at home or in the hospital in New York. Most of the time, the talks were upbeat and optimistic as Elizabeth relayed the day's details. Although I could hear the exhaustion in her voice, there was always something that we would laugh about. If I remarked to Elizabeth about her incredible spirit and positive attitude, she would reply, "What else is there to do, Janie?" I was in awe of her superhuman efforts and sheer dogged persistence that had enabled the two to keep on. I felt that I was the one who drew inspiration and hope from these nightly conversations.

Tanya's grandparents, aunts, uncles, and cousins kept a vigilant watch over her and Elizabeth, alerting us to specific ways we could help. Although they tried to busy themselves in fund-raising efforts and in supporting Elizabeth in her day-to-day struggle, their hardest times were the waiting and wondering.

On the twenty-first of February, Tanya and her classmates, now sixth-graders, dressed in their finest clothes, assembled in front of Seacrest to be driven across town to see a performance of "Romeo and Juliet" at the beautiful new Philharmonic Center for the Arts. Tanya appeared radiant in her pink dress, trimmed with soft ruffles and lace as she left laughing and having a good time. I did not know then that it was the last time I would see her.

At the end of February, Tanya and Elizabeth returned to New York to prepare for an experimental treatment of high intensity chemotherapy. They had gone up a few days early and visited the planetarium and the American Museum of Natural History. On the way home from a restaurant one night, they had the cab driver let them out a block from the Ronald McDonald House, where they stayed between hospital visits, so that Tanya could walk in the snow for the first time in her life. Recounting that night, Elizabeth told me that it was almost as if they were on a vacation, out on the town, exploring the sights.

The treatment began. When the call came from New York on Wednesday afternoon, March the seventh, school had just let out for the day. The students had been deposited in their parents' cars, and were headed for home, or dance lessons, or soccer games. The teachers were back in their classrooms, preparing for the next day. Our office manager, Pam, walked me into my office and handed me the phone to receive the message from Elizabeth that Tanya was gone. With the phone to my ear, I stood facing the window with my back to the door as Elizabeth and I held a wordless connection. In the next moment, I felt the warmth of two strong and gentle hands being placed on my back. My friend, Vera, had appeared unexpectedly at the precise moment she was needed, just as she had done so many times before.

The next morning Tanya's classmates, her teachers, and I gathered outdoors on the grass, under the shade of the sprawling branches of the Ficus tree. One by one, each boy and girl talked about their friend, recounting their personal experiences. We laughed at the funny things and cried at the loss. One of the children declared, "Our new middle school wing will be named The Tanya Lake Wing," and in one voice, the class instantly agreed.

The decision having been finalized, the children moved into the planning of the memorial service, what they would say, the songs they would sing, the poems they would recite. Throughout the rest of the day as I walked through the halls or out on the playground, individuals or small clusters of children of various ages would come up and throw their arms around me, burying their faces against my shirt, leaving wet blotches of tears. Then, just as suddenly, wiping eyes and noses either on their sleeves or mine, they darted off with their friends to play or learn, laughing and chatting as usual.

I learned a lot about dealing with loss that day. I had believed that the teachers and I would need to use all our resources to help the children of Seacrest through the trauma of losing a close friend. What I felt and heard throughout that day, and the days to follow, was in sharp contrast to what I had expected. Rather, *the children* helped *us* to see that there is another, more natural way of dealing with grief. They opened themselves to the full spectrum of emotions, from heart-wrenching sobs one minute to joyful abandon the next. The children were being themselves, holding nothing back, living life as it is meant to be lived, in its purest, most natural form.

A year later, Seacrest held its dedication ceremony for the opening of the new Tanya Lake Wing. People throughout the community attended: students and teachers; board members and parents; Elizabeth, her parents, and relatives. The architect, builders, engineers, and bankers came to stand in the background, along with scores of others who had privately donated their services to fund, design, and erect the building of this wing as a tribute to Tanya.

The Tanya Lake Wing stands as a lasting memorial, not only to a Seacrest student who had shown such courage, but to a community that responded with open hearts to the urgent needs of a little girl and her mother. Tanya's portrait hangs in the hallway of the wing. A live oak tree grows in the playground to the north of the wing, planted and nurtured by Elizabeth. Other trees planted by students grace the landscape around the campus in memory of Tanya, including a Tabebuia, which bursts into showers of bright yellow blossoms in the spring.

As I drive by Seacrest today, the orchid tree blooms. I hope the story of Tanya will be remembered by the students of Seacrest, the ones who knew her well, and the ones to follow. I hope she will be remembered not as a deified saint or heroine, but as a little girl who loved jokes and school and animals and friends; who inspired us all to reach out and help, in whatever way we could; and who helped us to appreciate life as a precious gift, not to be taken for granted.

Tanya

VIII

GROWING INTO MATURITY

Middle School Glimpses

CHAPTER 30

Middle School

It was early June 1992, a sultry South Florida day. An orange-colored tint cast a soft glow over the early evening skies. Purple shadows fell on the still, glassy lake beyond. Garden benches and chairs were placed around tables, covered with platters of sandwiches, bowls of fruit, raw vegetables and plates of dip, cakes and cookies. Punch was stored in coolers nearby. Everything was ready for the reception. Familiar scents of jasmine and honeysuckle mingled with newly cut grass in the hushed, still air.

Later, in the warm Florida evening, five boys and eleven girls stood in a single line outside the Unity Church, borrowed by Seacrest for another special event—another milestone marking the first Seacrest graduation ceremony for eighth grade.

The girls were poised and elegant in new, freshly pressed, crisp white dresses, shining hair carefully groomed, and faces glowing with touches of blush and lip gloss. The boys were impeccably turned out in spanking white shirts, dark ties and suits, highly polished shoes, and hair jelled into fixed position.

Inside, the aisle was lined with potted palms and wide, white satin bows. Parents waited with cameras and video recorders. The music began and one by one, the students walked down the aisle, smiling with heads held high, looking like archetypes of the model adolescent.

I watched as they moved through the ceremony of short speeches, each approaching to receive his or her gift and diploma, bestowing us with hugs and hand shakes. Could this tall and serene group of sophisticates possibly be the same children who only a couple of years ago were all arms and legs and braces, tangled in awkward, jerky movements? The same ones whose eyes were fixed permanently to the ground and who were prone to sudden emotional mood swings, self-conscious giggles, unmerciful teasing one moment and sudden tears the next?

My thoughts wandered back to the neophyte organizing stages of the first middle school. The sixth-grade was already in place, with plans underway for building a new facility for the upper grades. During the summer of 1990, we began planning for the curriculum and staff for the sixth, seventh, and eighth grades. We knew that the Seacrest Middle School would have to contain something more than the ordinary fare for this age group.

There is a widely held belief among educators that middle-schoolers are at a mental plateau. During the period when the physical and hormonal changes are taking place, teachers cannot expect exceptional gains in mental growth. We, in contrast, believed that middle-schoolers have the capacity to do infinitely more than what is ordinarily expected.

I believe boys and girls of this age are fully capable of rapid advancement in academics, and I believe it is an age when they can catch a glimmer of their true nature, to learn about who and what they are becoming. When I thought about the possibilities of a new middle school, I envisioned a setting in which these young people could begin to expand their interests and talents and to begin consciously to develop their potential.

The groundwork had been laid from the beginning for the Seacrest children to integrate their skills and knowledge with their emotional, social, and physical capacities. They had a solid foundation in learning to be independent and responsible for their actions and emotions. Technological skills had been incorporated into academic classes, in writing and research, in the sciences, art and music. Service projects had been put into motion as an outgrowth of students' vast experiences in the community. They practiced learning to solve their own problems and how to work through conflicts. They knew how to think for themselves and to work independently or in teams.

Since they had a head-start on the basics of emotional and social independence and responsibility, academics and technological savvy, I envisioned the middle school learners of Seacrest integrating their human resources with technological and scientific breakthroughs, combining them with environmental and cultural forces, the arts and humanities to form an interactive network designed to create a better world for their future. A lofty pipedream, certainly.

But I know the kids of this age. They are dreamers. They are emotional. They are bubbling wellsprings of energy waiting to explode into action. They love causes. Above all, they hate boredom. So we wanted to design a middle school without boredom. We wanted to make it the most challenging and adventurous experience of their lives.

If the young people could foresee themselves using their resources and imagination to invent a better planet, undo the messes made by their ancestors and elders, and dream solutions for a healthier world, I believed they would plunge into their work with unbounded enthusiasm. I still believe this. It is an age when cynicism and disillusion have not yet invaded their hopes and dreams. They have a tremendous reservoir of energy, primed to be channeled into advanced levels of thinking with purposeful participation. High action with purposeful intention is the key.

First though, we had to devise the kind of learning environment to make it happen. We had the perfect teachers. Terry Walker could get anyone turned on to science. He had taught science at a university in California and had been a middle school administrator in the local Collier County Public Schools. He had been a middle school principal in the American Schools in Frankfurt, Germany, and Vienna, Austria. His main love was teaching and working with middleschoolers.

Terry had been lured to Seacrest by his wife, Janie, who, a year earlier, had answered my plea to come home from Vienna to teach at Seacrest. Terry and Janie understood and appreciated the nature of the middle-schooler, and they had the knack for getting everyone hooked on learning down to a finely-tuned craft.

Bill Hammond was the English and Social Studies teacher for the middle school. Like the Walkers, Bill's wife Joanne came to Seacrest first, the year we added our fifth grade class. Bill was a fascinating mixture of high intellect and unassuming modesty and humor. He loved classical literature and nature equally. Like the typical young bearded absent-minded professor, Bill seemed unaware of his brilliance, and he held an unaffected quality bordering on innocence. I knew from his prior reputation at other private schools that Bill had the capacity to make history, literature, geography, and current social issues come to life in the minds of his students. These were the kinds of teachers who made the vision of the middle school program a reality.

Before school began in 1990, Janie, Terry, Bill, Joanne, and I went on a daylong retreat to brainstorm ideas for putting our curriculum and program into place. Early one morning, we gathered at Terry and Janie's home on the water in Bonita Springs. Wearing swim suits under T-shirts, we loaded our picnic lunches and cold drinks into the cooler and onto the Walker's boat and climbed aboard.

There is nothing so exquisite as an early morning journey through the Southwest Florida canals, heading into the channel and breaking through into the expanse of the open Gulf of Mexico. I love the feathery feel of cool, moist breezes sweeping across my face, breathing in the smells of fish and sea life. On this morning, a cloudless sky promised a day of pure, unfiltered sunshine. We explored the Gulf shores until we found a deserted stretch of beach. Securing the anchor into the sand, we unloaded our provisions and parked ourselves on beach towels, ready to unleash our collective ideas and imagination in creating the best of all possibilities for our middle-schoolers.

We had attended national conferences, listened to tapes, and studied the research on the latest programs and new structures for learning, all of which promised great success. We discussed the implications of Outcome-Based Restructuring, Total Quality Management, Cooperative Learning, the global connection, and assessment tools. We talked about "transformational outcomes," technology, alternatives to tracking and ability grouping, team teaching and classroom management. We reviewed our goals for an interactive, interdisciplinary curriculum and learning styles.

As the sun's rays turned the morning into a golden translucent heat, we took time out to swim and reflect, cooling off in the aquamarine waves. Quenching our thirst from a thermos of water and munching on apples, we began to talk about what would really work for us. We talked about what we most valued. Each person spoke of what mattered the most, stripping away layers of extraneous past experiences, cutting to the core of what we wanted our middle school to be.

Once we were able to let go of how things had always been done before, we were able to click into the present—into the space where true creative imagination flows and ideas begin to pop out as fast as one can think. In a short space of time, we had the overall framework of the program put together.

On that day we only saw the vision, but we were not able to foresee the formidable events that would unfold over the summer—the frustrations and backbreaking work ahead. I only remember the feeling of sunburned shoulders and a heady sense of anticipation and pride to be working with people as committed and talented as the Walkers and Hammonds.

Reality

It is not clear why I was so shocked that our new Tanya Lake Middle School was not completed as planned that summer. You would think that after years of building additions to the Seacrest physical plant, I would have known that construction projects were destined to be delayed. In my mind, this time was going to be different. We had blueprints, an architect and a building contractor. We had a construction loan in place, and we had money coming in from parents' pledges for the building fund. The year's enrollment was limited to the number of students we could fit into our cramped quarters. With the coming year in sight, we hired five new teachers and expanded our enrollment for five new classes of students, expecting that six new classrooms would be ready for the beginning of the new school year.

When the reality set in that there was not even the remotest possibility that the new building would be ready, my spirits sank to an all-time low. I wandered aimlessly through the existing classrooms, multipurpose room, and tiny library, trying to figure out what to do. No flashes of insight came. Not even an obscure, slender thread of an idea. I gazed around at our space, trying to think. My assistant and partner, Lynne, was on vacation in her beloved home state of New Hampshire, and I did not want to interrupt her much-deserved rest by calling to pick her brains.

Until the day came in mid-August for the faculty, Lynne, and me to meet together as a group, I had all but forgotten that my most important reservoir of problem-solvers was at hand, just for the asking. As soon as I described our current dilemma, solutions poured forth. The teachers themselves quickly decided exactly how they were going to create their own classrooms.

By the following day, the faculty had developed designs and layouts for creating five classrooms, seemingly out of nowhere. Bringing in ladders, sheets of plywood, hammers and nails, they set about constructing three classrooms and a space for art lessons in the multipurpose room. Polly, the physical education teacher and coordinator of the After School Program, had her territory squeezed back toward the stage. In a week's time, the Seacrest teachers had painted, decorated, and furnished their classrooms for the opening of school. They used colorful burlap to create bulletin boards. Once again, as in past projects, the Ross family installed remnants of free carpet.

Terry, Bill, and I met with my husband, Jack, and arranged once again to rent two classrooms from his church—this time to house our seventh and eighth-graders. By the time school started, every detail was in place, ready to welcome the new crop of Seacrest learners. The older students reveled in having their own space, out of sight from the rest of us. In the Seacrest building, the newly created classes, divided by partitions, reminded me of the long-gone era of the "Open Schools."

The Open School idea must have been invented by people who had either left teaching long before or who had never taught young children in the first place. Building schools with large open spaces rather than separate classrooms was supposed to eliminate barriers between ages, grade levels, and abilities. It was supposed to foster creativity, team teaching, and more interactive and relevant learning. Having taught in this type of building, I concluded, along with my team of teachers, that open space often translated into closed realities.

In the open classroom situation, I worried that my kids were infringing on the rights of other groups nearby. I was afraid they were too noisy or that their projects were spilling over into others' territory. Our stuff was always getting mixed up with other people's stuff. Schedules and record-keeping were a nightmare. Most of us found ourselves planning fewer creative, less noisy, less messy lessons so as not to disturb the neighboring groups. I was relieved when I was able to shift back into my own, large classroom with four walls, close the doors, and allow my students to talk out loud, move around, and spread out their materials and projects to their hearts' content.

Most of the schools of that era in the 1970s gradually added walls, recreating a personal space in which a group of individuals could communicate, move, and learn with a sense of freedom. After a time, most educators concluded that innovative approaches aimed at more creativity and interaction were more likely to be successful in one's own classroom.

Despite not having their own classrooms, the Seacrest teachers carved out their own niches for lessons in the multipurpose room. People have an amazing capacity to adjust to most environments, and the teachers made it work. Despite the sharing of space, they created a sense of privacy for each class. For one thing, the schedules were arranged so that lessons requiring concentrated silence were held at the same time. For another, when the children worked on group projects, they knew how to keep their voices pitched at a low, comfortable buzz . . . at least, some of the children, some of the time.

Classes and groups took every possible advantage of the outdoors. With notebooks and pencils in hand, children would prop their backs against the trunks of shade trees or sit at the picnic tables to write. If they were preparing for an art or writing project, their teachers sometimes began by having the children close their eyes and sense their surroundings.

On one such morning, when the skies cast a soft silver light over the still moist grass, a class sat motionless with their eyes closed and senses open to the subtle sounds of nature, feeling the hint of a breeze, catching the scent of roots mingled with leaves and grass and plants.

Opening their eyes, they gazed at their surroundings until they could sight the delicate flutter of butterfly wings and honeybees nestled into a bright purple patch of wild flowers. Overhead, a hawk circled a grove of pines. Dragonflies hovered and scattered in a ritualized dance. On the west bank of the school grounds, the yellow beaks of two white egrets were tilted upward as they picked their way elegantly through the tall grass. Chameleons warmed themselves, blending into the sea of grass.

Just as a flock of birds fluttered noisily out of a nearby branch, a tiger-striped stray cat wandered around the bend of a crooked sand path, breaking the spell of concentration. Unable to contain themselves, the children leaped up to dash toward the cat, stroking its fur and pleading, could they please bring it inside and give it some milk, because its ribs were sticking out. It was plain, they said, that the poor kitty was starving.

Some of the best writing, artistic creations, and scientific observations come from the outdoor lessons, when children are given time and space to let their minds wander freely. Attention to details is magnified and imaginations open to vast ranges of possibilities. Sometimes we think that learning to pay attention only means listening to the teacher talk. But children turning their senses to the details surrounding them is the best teacher of all.

During the construction of the new wing at the north end of the building, Seacrest teachers took the opportunity to teach the children about building, community workers, and machinery, making full use of the real life experiences surrounding them.

The outside whine of heavy machines ripping out walls mingled with the inside hum of reading and singing. Just outside classroom windows, bulldozers dug into the earth, straining through brush and trees, crushing and leveling the land. Truckloads of fill were hauled in and dumped, followed by concrete trucks to pour the concrete foundation. As with past constructions, teachers and children who had classrooms on that side of the building managed to teach and learn above the racket and jangle of motors and machines.

Finally, in mid January, the construction of the Tanya Lake Wing was finished. Moving day came. Trucks were borrowed to transport desks, tables, chairs, shelves, books, and equipment from the makeshift classes at the church and in the multipurpose room. Although the older students were excited about the move, they seemed to have mixed, bittersweet feelings at leaving their private campus at the church down the road.

In later years, after the seventh-graders had passed through the eighth-grade and graduated on into high school, they returned for a class reunion. The only thing they wanted to do was to go back to their private sanctuary on the church grounds and sit on the rocks beside the lake to reminisce about their experiences as middle-schoolers.

The opening ceremonies of the Tanya Lake Wing were a time mixed with joy and sadness for another reason too. Tanya's mother, grandparents, and relatives were there among the many who helped build the wing—bankers, architects, engineers, builders, and special friends of Tanya's. A beautiful portrait of Tanya was placed in the hallway above a gold plaque bearing her name.

Another milestone was completed. Students and teachers were under one roof again, and Seacrest settled into a harmonious routine of action and adventure. The sixth and seventh-graders went on a three-day trip to the Atlantic Ocean for a hands-on study of marine ecology through the Marine Science Under Sails Program in Key Largo. All the classes explored the swamps of the Everglades and began their own

Marine Science Under Sails

Greenpeace Club. Beach cleanups and recycling became a part of their routine. Their travels extended to the sugar cane fields and packing plants of Immokalee, where they gained some first-hand insights of Haitian, Hispanic, African American, and Caucasian migrant workers, toiling side by side. The eighth-graders served meals once a month at a homeless shelter.

Articles about the importance of including community service in the curriculums began to appear. While other schools began thinking about involving students in community service projects, Seacrest classes continued and expanded community service programs as they had from the earliest years of the school. Whenever the media reported news about older students tutoring younger ones, schools working in partnership with businesses, environmental or community projects, I was intrigued by the description of these "new" programs, because at Seacrest we had always done them. These types of programs were so much a part of the Seacrest experience that we never considered them to be out of the ordinary.

Teachers frequently track down leads to find people who can bring current global issues into the classroom. One visitor, who had helped establish the World Bank in Somalia, described in fascinating detail the deep-seated cultural roots and differences among tribes, giving us all a better understanding of the conflicts we heard about on the news. A teacher discovered that a new Seacrest parent was on the first council for the General Agreement for Trade and Tariffs (GATT); so, of course, the person was enlisted to do a series of lectures and discussions.

When I look back through the yearbooks, I see pictures of floating classrooms on the Gulf, drama productions, international fairs, groups holding discussions under the Ficus tree, oil painting on the lawn, and chicken and barbecue dinners held to raise money for trips to Washington, D.C. Janie's classes sponsored Renaissance fairs. Rick, the music teacher, collaborated with Janie to produce the Seacrest versions of Broadway shows. There were flea-market sales, camp-outs on islands, a trip to the Dry Tortugas on a chartered boat and concerts at the Philharmonic. But along with all these high profile and energy-packed activities, there was also the counterpart of everyday, uneventful study and hard work in the academic subjects.

Debbie came to Seacrest as the middle-school math teacher. She distinguished herself with her relentless goal that every student should understand, practice, and apply mathematics—from basic math to algebra and higher order thinking and problem-solving skills. It paid off. In teaching her students how to use interactive loops to connect each concept to the next, they progressed into advanced algebra. Most of the graduating eighth graders tested beyond the first year of algebra in high school and went into higher levels of algebra or geometry.

The symmetry in providing the best of traditional approaches to teaching along with the interactive experiences is an important benchmark of Seacrest and its teams of teachers. Children of all ages need discipline, sequential order, and structure to build a logical, memory-based background of basic skills. Depth and breadth of knowledge cannot be developed by discovery and field experiences alone. For every trip, dramatic production, art project or creative event, teachers balance the curriculum with lessons grounded firmly in fundamental skills.

Preparing Reports Under the Ficus Tree

Partners in Science

The Related Arts teachers play a significant role in providing the balance between creativity and the discipline of concentrated study. Between international festivals, performances, games, and art shows, the students prepare reports. They practice their musical instruments. They study and memorize for Spanish exams. They work hard to complete award-winning products in art or to win against another school's soccer team. They learn to compete and win, to study, practice, and memorize. They must participate, be challenged, and take risks.

As Seacrest grew, I became more and more convinced that the most comprehensive principles of learning take place within a structure of hard work, balanced with action-packed experiences and focused attention—all of which move toward a meaningful purpose for each learner. The principles of learning could be stated as a simple formula: *Purpose plus Attention plus Practice equal Success.*

As I watched Janie teaching geography, I noticed how she captured the students' excitement and attention with a distinctive purpose. When Bill taught something as mundane and potentially boring as participial phrases, he invariably managed to inject some ingenious way to make the lesson meaningful. I never knew what I would hear or see when I walked into a classroom at Seacrest. One day, Terry's class was dissecting a sheep's heart, another day they were figuring out the frequency of waves in relationship to length and light. As coordinator of the middle school, Terry launched and supported numerous programs and adventures that are destined to live forever in the minds of the middle-school students.

Throughout the initial stages in developing the Seacrest Middle School, there were changes in the program, the building, the students and faculty. But the constancy of purposeful intention, guided by master teachers kept us on a steady course, a course personified by high adventure, service to others, hard work, and successful outcomes.

On the evening of the first Seacrest graduation ceremony in 1992, I felt a special sense of gratefulness that Seacrest had reached such a point in its journey. Building on one grade at a time since 1983, the first class of eighth-graders had come to the end of their years at Seacrest. At the end, when the music of Scottish bagpipes signaled the class to begin its recessional, I looked into the faces of the boys and girls who would soon be entering high school. I knew they were ready and well prepared to enter the next stage of their lives. Looking at the faces of parents and teachers, I knew that they shared the same feelings of pride and admiration of a collective accomplishment.

Our gratitude was magnified by events that had transpired earlier in the year. The beginning of a crisis in January 1992, threatened the very existence of Seacrest, a crisis far greater than any we had experienced. But in the twilight of that early June evening, nothing could overshadow the beauty of our celebration—we were wrapped in the soft spell of candlelight and friendship. It was a time of closeness, of endings, and of new beginnings.

Photo Credit: PhotoWorks

CHAPTER 31

The Crisis

It struck suddenly during the holiday break, when I was in Minneapolis. I received a phone call from Naples a few minutes after one o'clock on January 2, 1992, and in an instant, the secure and well-ordered existence of Seacrest went into a tailspin. The words spoken over the phone were delivered with crisp, cool formality. The unfamiliar male voice identified himself as an attorney representing a local bank.

"I am calling to inform you that Seacrest School will be foreclosed by our bank within the next few days. I thought you should know."

Seconds ticked by in dead silence. At some point I heard my voice break through the surrealistic stillness, trying to match the tone of the caller's with formal reserve.

"Can you tell me specifically the reason for foreclosure on Seacrest?"

The attorney replied that our benefactor was behind in his payments on the Seacrest mortgage. The unexpected call was *my* first notice that anything was amiss with the financial matters of the person who had founded, funded, and built Seacrest.

The United States was in the middle of a recession. It was a time when schools, both public and private, were closed or had their funding severely cut, small businesses suffered and went out of business, and massive layoffs crippled corporate giants. Downsizing became the buzz word. In Naples, the effects were particularly devastating to many large-scale real estate developers and builders.

Word spread fast in Naples, and within minutes, I received a second call, this one from Paul, the vice president of a prestigious local bank noted for its support of charitable community projects. Paul had assisted us in financing the construction of the Tanya Lake Wing. That project had been accomplished on our own, independently of our benefactor, through the help of parents, administrators, board members, and people from the community.

Recognizing that the underlying motivation of both callers was to safeguard the security of the respective loans, the two conversations were marked by contrast, from the embedded threats of the first to the encouraging reassurance of the second.

With the confidence of one who knew the pulse of his town and its personalities, and with soft-spoken geniality, Paul instilled feelings of mutual respect to the point of absolute trust. He had visited Seacrest on several occasions, and he not only knew our founder and most of the parents, but the history of our beginnings and our progress. Paul was a tall, angular, and elegant person who looked you straight in the eyes and listened attentively to every word. He had a way of making you feel that you and your enterprise were of prime importance to the community and to him personally.

On that day, Paul had done his homework well. He knew that I had gone to Minnesota to care for my two-year-old granddaughter, Hannah Jane. He knew that my daughter, Mary Jane, had just lost a baby half way through her pregnancy and was in the hospital. His initial words were underscored with empathetic compassion as he recounted the pain of a similar experience in his family.

Without mentioning the threat of impending foreclosure by the other bank, Paul instructed me not to worry about anything concerning the Tanya Lake construction loan.

"When you return to Naples, we'll meet at your convenience to work out a new plan that will meet the needs of Seacrest. In the meantime, you are not to be concerned."

Hanging up the phone, I took Hannah Jane into her bedroom and read Dr. Seuss's *Cat in the Hat* and sang nursery songs. She finally settled in for her afternoon nap. With methodical precision, I cleared the dishes from the table and put them into the dishwasher. One by one, I picked up dolls, crayons, construction paper and puzzles, placing them into the corner of the playroom. Like a robot switched to "on" I paced across the room, retracing my steps back and forth in a mechanistic pattern. I moved to the rocking chair, sank into it, and began to rock back and forth. Finally I simply sat, still and quiet, frozen in time, focusing my awareness on shafts of afternoon sunlight piercing through frosty panes in the hushed, almost eerily silent house.

As reality began to register, my first thoughts held no sense of imminent disaster or fear. I listed my options for the future. "If the school is closed down, I'll spend more time with Jack. I'll cook wonderful nutritious meals every day. I'll sit in the sun on the beach with my friends, and I'll do all the things a minister's wife is supposed to do. I'll sleep late and read novels. I'll practice my cello every day."

At some point, shadowy, vague questions of other possibilities emerged. From a lifetime of conditioning toward responsibility and the belief that with hard work I could do anything, I stood up, moving with deliberate strides toward the kitchen and picked up the phone to call our founder and benefactor, Mr. Sheehan. He confirmed what I had been told by the attorney. He was shocked that I was notified in such an abrupt way, and his voice held a subdued quality that I had not heard before.

He was a man who had developed a number of landmarks and projects in Naples. In earlier times the builders of Naples might have been able to strike a deal with bank presidents over a cup of coffee, a handshake, and trust. But times had changed, and money was tight.

Some people must have wondered how it happened that I had no knowledge about the state of the mortgage on the Seacrest land and buildings. But the way our partnership had formed from the beginning never adhered to orthodox "business" procedures. There was a mutual understanding that my role was to create the Sheehan's vision of a new school and to bring it into reality. Theirs was to provide the resources.

Mr. Sheehan was a visionary who was willing to put all his trust in me, allowing me the freedom to develop Seacrest, hire the teachers, establish the budget, and run the school. As the founder and sole financial backer, he held a protective attitude about Seacrest. There was a sense of the traditional, perhaps even of old-fashioned values that implied that I need not concern myself with the cost of land or buildings.

In ten years of funding and building Seacrest, Mr. Sheehan always accepted the budgets and expenses I presented to him. His only question, asked in every meeting, was whether the philosophy of Seacrest was being followed by the teachers and taught to the students. At the end of each meeting, Mr. Sheehan would restate his ideals, hopes, and dreams for the children of Seacrest.

On the day we spoke, he seemed stunned by the disclosure that his efforts at negotiating the payments for the mortgage had failed. He offered none of the words of wisdom or encouragement that I had come to expect and depend on whenever I needed an extra boost. We suddenly switched roles, and it was I who spoke to him, using his own words, reminding him of all the lessons I had learned from him about perseverance, courage, faith, and irrepressible optimism—about moving on through obstacles.

Hanging up the phone, the truth of our position crystallized. Seacrest School was on its own. More questions flashed in rapid succession. After having been sheltered and taken care of for nearly ten years, the time had come to be independent. Had we become so spoiled by our guardian that we were too soft or too incompetent to manage our own responsibilities?

After all, we had access to hundreds of talented and skillful men and women with a full spectrum of resources. There were parents who were attorneys and bankers, real estate developers, engineers and physicians, stock brokers, business managers, contractors and merchants, artists and writers, teachers, designers, pilots and blue print technicians —each one holding an abiding love for Seacrest and high expectations for their sons and daughters. Each step and stage of Seacrest had been built on the strength and combined forces of its parents and staff, giving their time and expertise in a thousand different ways whenever and however it was needed.

More phone calls came. Jerry Shellabarger, the school board member with the most expertise in finance, described his constant communication and attempts to come to a reasonable agreement with the bankers over the past few days. Other board members called in rapid succession, each with ideas and hopes for negotiations and settlement.

The day after my flight home to Naples, I met with Mr. Sheehan to determine exactly how much we owed to the bank for the mortgage and whether there were additional debts to other companies. The total amount of our indebtedness came to $740,000—a sum that was so far beyond our means that it might as well have been $740 million. In addition, the month's pay checks to teachers, tutors and staff members were due in three weeks, with no hope of any more help from our benefactor. There was not enough time, even if we were able through some miracle to forestall foreclosure.

That night I worked for several hours composing, writing, and rewriting a letter to the Seacrest parents, outlining the basic details of our newly acquired state of independence, ending with an announcement of a follow-up meeting for the full disclosure of our status. But before I could send out the letter, I had to accomplish one of my life's most difficult tasks: I had to tell the teachers.

At 3:15 on the following day, the faculty, Lynne, and I sat together in a classroom as I spelled out the details of our position. I had no guarantee that January's pay checks would be forthcoming. I had no answers or insight for the future of Seacrest, or how we would find the money to survive even if foreclosure could be postponed.

For the first time in the history of Seacrest faculty meetings, no one said anything. Faces typically filled with the full range of expressions, from high passion and laughter to pained grimaces or blank boredom now stared back at me like images of granite. These were the faces of men and women who had poured their minds, bodies, and spirits into a creation that was theirs: their work; their energy; their livelihood.

With my chest, throat, and eyes aching from the sheer force of containing my emotions, I continued. "For the remainder of the afternoon and evening, I want you to fully acknowledge your fears and give full rein to tears, anger, rage, frustration, or whatever you may be feeling— to let it all out."

I suggested that after they allowed themselves to experience their own emotions, I hoped they would then be able to get a good night's sleep and to prepare themselves mentally for the days ahead. Their instructions were firmly stated for the coming morning's task.

"You will greet every parent and child with absolute and total assurance, exuding confidence and optimism from every pore. There must be no doubt in any child's mind or parents' mind that Seacrest is the only school for them," I said, mustering my own air of confidence.

I reminded the teachers that it was nothing more than what they had already been doing up to this point, and that they were all master communicators. "You simply need to keep on—without missing a beat. Giving in or giving up is not an option. The only thing that can bring us down is fear. We are simply going to move forward."

At the close of the meeting I was astonished to find checks for five, ten, and fifty dollars being pressed into my hands from men and women who had just been told there was a possibility of no month's pay and no promise of a future at Seacrest.

During the days and weeks to follow, I quickly became an apprentice to a half-dozen men and women who were willing to move into my kitchen to teach me finances. I was surrounded by cups of coffee, yellow legal pads, number two pencils, and piles of boxes jammed with the history of Seacrest's financial records. Oddly enough, it was an exciting time for me because I think I have a gene that demands new learning, even in the face of danger. I thrill to the excitement of change, of exploring new knowledge, new possibilities, and new territories.

Even as a small child, I remember reaching up from my stool to the top shelves of the bookcases next to the fireplace, lifting down the thickest books containing the dusty yellowed pages of Homer, Plato, and Socrates. Not that I understood any of the obscure tiny print. Rather, I think the fascination of the unknown was what motivated me to examine unintelligible and unpronounceable words and sentences, like a detective looking for clues to a mysterious secret.

One of the first to come as a guiding force for Seacrest during the crisis was Frank Gazzola, a certified public accountant from Minnesota, who patiently laid out the past, present, and possibilities for the future financial structure of Seacrest. As an outside consultant, Frank had agreed to travel to Naples where he closeted himself for three days in Mr. Sheehan's office to examine the Seacrest financial records. Declaring the records to be in good order, he met with local accountants, enlisting their services. Payment schedules were set up and letters were drafted to our creditors. Together, we piled several carloads of file boxes filled with ten years' records and hauled them over to a spare bedroom in my house until we could find enough space at Seacrest.

Steve, our newly enlisted insurance agent, outlined the inner workings and politics of the insurance industry. Steve spoke in a thick Boston accent, frequently peppered with his own colorful stories and examples. With astonishing forbearance, he slowly taught me the rules of the game while I took notes. At regular intervals, he would pause to test my learning with short quizzes. Concerned that his sometimes salty phrases might offend the sensitive ears of a school marm who was also a minister's wife, Steve often stopped to backtrack and rephrase his words in a more conservative style.

After I had filled three legal pads with notes, Steve announced that at that point I knew more about insurance than 90 percent of the public, to which I replied, "If that's true, it's pretty appalling."

Through subsequent months, I called on Steve numerous times for advice, and on each occasion he would ask, "Do you have your pad and pencil ready?"—And we would launch into yet another lesson.

Seacrest parents who were attorneys offered their help. These young men and women had earned their place as leaders in the community, juggling babies, families, meals, and car-pooling around courtrooms and cases, late meetings, and early dawn schedules. Jane, John, Kathleen, Tom, and Ed marched me through the maze of legalese, teaching me that nothing is sacrosanct or taken for granted in the world of lawyers. Practical or seemingly simple solutions do not exist in the gray maze of legal maneuvering. Thankful to be able to turn over any and all legal business to the expertise of the talented group, I complied with whatever they advised me to do, affixing my signature and the Seacrest seal to lengthy, sometimes impossibly obscure documents.

Local accountants and the vice president and the president of our "friendly bank" joined forces with our board members and attorneys to speak at our parent-teacher meeting on the evening of January 27. Together, we told the story of our sudden leap into independence, highlighted by details of the data and debt, where we were, and where we needed to go.

As I closed the meeting, putting forth the challenge ahead, I looked out on the sea of faces of Seacrest parents, and felt myself break into a spontaneous smile. In that instant I recognized that we had already crossed over a precipice to new terrain. And I knew without a shadow of a doubt that Seacrest would survive, sustain, and flourish. I knew also that others in the audience felt this same electrifying energy of knowing. Individual faces, drawn taut and grim, reflecting fear, helplessness, and doubt at the beginning of the meeting now appeared to be illuminated with inspiration, resolve, and strength. Even though nothing had changed on the outside, there had been a shift to a collective breakthrough in which everything seemed possible.

The collective shift was described poignantly in a letter I received the following day from one of the parents.

> So transfixed was I on the black and white of the actual deficit and difficulty, and the incredible parallel of the Sheehans' success and philosophy to our own, that I became totally immersed in what pen and ink portray the situation to be. . . .pretty dreadful.
>
> It wasn't until you returned to the group as the last speaker that I felt a whole different sensation throughout my entire body. Your words, Jane, those spirit filled messages of determination, steadfastness, and recognition of the incredible gifts the Sheehans gave to every child who has attended Seacrest, hit me like nothing else has for far too long.

Today is indeed a new day. . . .Seacrest will not only survive—Seacrest will thrive. . . . above any pen and ink odds. It is indeed the human spirit that resides above all. You reminded us of the potential power that each of us have in working together for a common cause.

Looking back, I believe it was the precise moment that Seacrest moved from an autonomous state, with one benefactor and one leader, into a state of interdependence with a shared vision and a communal responsibility. A new evolutionary stage had begun, born in crisis and sustained through the faith, strength, and power of many.

At the end of the historical meeting, Jack and I went home to celebrate quietly another milestone of January 27— our wedding anniversary. Jack gave me a gold pendant, designed and handcrafted by a local Italian artisan. Chinese characters were engraved on the pendant; they said: "Crisis equals danger and opportunity."

The symbol continued to be a touchstone for me throughout the turbulent weeks and months to follow.

One Day at a Time

Within the next few days, every parent who was able and willing made a monetary donation, and by the end of the week, we had enough funds to issue the full paychecks to faculty and staff members. One giant milestone had been accomplished.

We wrote letters to every vendor and supplier, asking for a workable payment plan. Most of our suppliers were companies we had dealt with over a span of five to ten years, people with whom we had established a mutual trust. Except for one new company, all others not only agreed to our terms, but a number of them forgave bills altogether. Another hurdle accomplished.

The teachers and students came up with dozens of ingenious ideas for saving and recycling materials and supplies. Amazingly, the cost of many of our regular monthly supplies was cut in half—from paper towels and duplicating paper to tempera paints and construction paper.

Parents, grandparents, teachers, and students coalesced toward a common purpose like an army riveting its attention on one target: Save Seacrest! I broke far out of my normal comfort zone and found courage to invite total strangers to lunch and ask them for money for Seacrest.

One Japanese couple who were Seacrest parents came to my office on my request. When I asked them for a ten-thousand dollar donation, they immediately replied, "Yes, certainly!" and later apologized profusely for taking a week to hand me their check. Their spirit of generosity extended to gifts of state-of-the-art computers and printers, and they eventually became participants in the Seacrest Land Trust.

Another parent, whose child was on scholarship, brought me a check each week for ten dollars, saying that she had decided to give her weekly church tithe to Seacrest. Letters and cards of support poured in. One such letter read in part:

> During the past months, our business has been seriously affected by the recession, and we are in danger of losing everything, even our home. We had decided that we had no choice but to take our son. . . .out of Seacrest and put him into public school. After your meeting, my husband and I talked for many hours into the night and we both agreed that Seacrest is a place like none other, and that we must remain there whatever the sacrifice.
>
> We have absolute faith that our school will come through this time in fine shape. We know too, that if we keep that same kind of faith and determination, our business will recover as well. Please accept our check for $100 as a small token of our love and appreciation.

Everyone wanted to help. Everyone had great—and different— ideas about what we should do and how we should do it. Advice came from all sides, angles, and opposite ends. Parents who were attorneys and financial experts accompanied me to meetings with presidents of local banks. A financial task force was formed. New board members were added. Letters and copies of letters, FAXes and phone calls flowed to and from my office and home, extending throughout the community, state, and beyond.

A reporter from the *Naples Daily News* came to interview us. Written with exceptional sensitivity and clarity, the story transmitted our newly gained independence; the headline read,

"RIDING A NEW WAVE, SEACREST SCHOOL MOVES FORWARD TO INDEPENDENCE."

We reached an easy and harmonious agreement with our "friendly bankers" for the Seacrest Tanya Lake construction loan. Simultaneously, the other bank continued its intractable press for repayment of the past due notes. Although I have come to understand the precise and impersonal manner that some feel is necessary in the corporate financial world, my feelings at the time were not so generous. It was all new to me, and I took the meetings very personally. It seemed that one of the bank's employees derived satisfaction from the number of insults he could squeeze into an hour's meeting as he delivered his ultimatums.

In the first meeting with this person, I cringed with a slow burn creeping up to the very roots of my hair. Several hours afterward, I got angry. Not at him, but at myself. I thought, Jane, you are really naive, and it is time to wake up to the real world. Did you really believe that this person would care two hoots about your little school, or the circumstances behind our dilemma? His job is to collect the debt, nothing more, nothing less.

In subsequent meetings I learned to detach myself from any sort of emotional response, and finally came to view the person with respectful indifference as a necessary cog in the machinery. Over time, I recognized that my level of tolerance had increased, and that the words and actions of others had nothing to do with my own internal response.

During the first few weeks of the crisis, we employed a business officer. Whereas before, Mr. Sheehan's staff paid the bills and managed the budget and bookkeeping, we now had the full responsibility. In the interim, Tanya's mother, Elizabeth Lake, volunteered to donate her services as a bookkeeper until we could find and hire a business officer. Pat Handwerk, the Seacrest parent of a budding tennis champion finally came to our rescue with her MBA degree from Wharton and her entrepreneurial mind. Short in stature and long in energy and self-assurance, Pat agreed to withdraw from her relative life of ease to plunge into the task of balancing the budget.

With tenacious spunk, she assumed full ownership of bills, purchase orders and paychecks. The Seacrest building and grounds came under her watchful domain, and everything from light bulbs to leaky faucets was quickly replaced or repaired at the lowest cost. Equally at home with a wrench or a line-item-analysis, Pat had our school running at top efficiency within weeks. It hummed along like a well-oiled machine.

238

Our Business Officer Wears Many Hats

February, March, and April blended together in a nonstop whirlwind of meetings and memorandums. Board members met several times each week during those months. Most of my eighteen hour days had little to do with students, teachers, or academics. There were days when I never walked through the halls of Seacrest, and when I did, I would get a few good-natured ribs from teachers because I would be dressed in my black suit—a sure signal that I was on my way to another business meeting.

Lynne took charge of most school affairs, which once again proved that with good people an organization can continue to run successfully for a time without the leader standing watch. Although each teacher had become a leader in his or her own right, I could not have managed without Lynne's gifted capacity and willingness to handle most of the administrative details. Nor could I have managed without having her as my sounding board and confidante in our late evening talks.

Vera Lindabury, one of our board members, supported us with her quiet wisdom and encouragement. Being with Vera was to be cared for in a safe shelter—a nonjudgmental, trusted space, warmed by a blanket of unconditional acceptance, where you could be yourself and voice whatever was on your mind. We would walk the beach in a rhythmic pattern, barefooted, feeling the powdery, bleached sand between our toes, shoulders warmed by sunlight, making our way to Clam Pass. There, we would rest on the banks and sit in silence beside the aquamarine waters, allowing the sun and sea and sand to clear and cleanse our minds and replenish our energy.

And there were others, like Les and Berniece, Bill and Teddy, Seacrest parents who formed an unaccredited and unofficial system of personal support, seeing what needed to be done and doing it, quietly and anonymously. They repaired and donated computers, helped with bookkeeping, replaced athletic equipment, supervised children in the mornings, repaired lockers, drove on field trips, and planned programs and picnics for students.

Spring came and Seacrest was still alive and well, although we had not reached a settlement with the bank. On the other hand, the bank had not foreclosed. We were well aware that we would have to move out of the impasse before school ended for the summer.

Our attorneys met with our board and a decision was made to secure the services of an outside, impartial attorney. The consensus was that there was one person in town who was considered to be the best. We made an appointment and went to call on Sam.

Sam had the calm and confident air of one who has no need for pomp or fanfare. His blue eyes reflected a discrete twinkle as he listened to our story. As he began to question and probe, I saw why he had gained the unqualified respect from his colleagues and clients. Living and practicing law in Naples for a number of years, he obviously knew the town, the people in it, and the currents of change.

Proceeding to mark out our guidelines, we found Sam's knowledge about our founder and about human nature in general keenly perceptive and accurate. In his own words, Sam reminded us that there are always people who will take all they can get and then blame and attack the donor when the going gets rough. He cautioned us not to allow the Seacrest community to fall into such a trap. Our job was to protect our founder's legacy as well as the school, and to maintain our integrity in all our dealings.

Getting down to business, Sam agreed to help us set up a land trust, in which parents would loan the school the money to cover the mortgage, to be paid back in 1996. Furthermore, he agreed to represent Seacrest in all future discussions and negotiations with the bankers, and to meet with the Seacrest parents to answer questions and explain the terms. Sam ended the meeting with the astounding news that he would be *donating* these services to Seacrest.

From then on, throughout the summer and early fall, Sam worked toward a final agreement with the bank and participants in the land trust. Our task of finding the people to put up the money for the trust turned into a challenge of epic proportions. Two Seacrest parents, Pierre and David, took on the responsibility of initiating and developing the trust. Almost at once, over a dozen Seacrest parents agreed to loans of five to twenty thousand dollars, without questioning whether their money would be repaid. Others were much more cautious, agreeing finally to a loan after researching and questioning every angle and probability. One by one, others consented to subscribe to the land trust as we crept forward to the final tally.

One morning some friends of mine stopped to chat, a husband and wife who had no connection with the school. During the course of our conversation, they casually inquired as to how things were going at Seacrest. I gave them a full account of what had transpired since January. At the end of my story, they both asked, "How much would you like from us? Would you like an outright donation, or should we put the money in the land trust and donate it later?"

As it turned out, the bankers who had threatened foreclosure eventually became our partners in the Seacrest Land Trust. To their everlasting credit, they finally abandoned their threatening notices and instead, joined forces with the people who were working to save Seacrest.

Money can bring out the best or worst in people, and I gained a new respect for the power it holds. Until the crisis, I had never seen people rally together with such determination. I had never come face to face with the sudden possibility of losing everything we had worked for. And I had not known until then how much strength can be generated from people working together toward a common cause.

Thus, the winter of 1992 held the best of times and the worst of times, rising and falling from conquest to near catastrophe, inching forward, sliding backward, at times with hair-raising turns. During that period Seacrest received two of its highest tributes.

At the end of that fateful January, Bill Martin Jr., an author of children's books and living legend came to spend the day at Seacrest. Bill was a pioneer in transposing children's books into an art form, blending music and the rhythm of language with story telling and great works of art. Universally beloved and revered, Bill has the uncanny ability to cast a magic spell over tens of thousands, delighting listeners with his own brand of stories and poems, chants and music. What child has not memorized the words, rhythm, and pictures of *Brown Bear, Brown Bear, What do You See?* or thrilled to the terror of his *Ghost-Eye Tree?*

Driving to the airport the following morning, Bill told me that of all the schools he had visited over six decades, Seacrest had a unique quality. When I asked him to explain, he answered simply that it was because of the love that he felt throughout the entire school.

Later in the winter, another internationally known speaker and author came to conduct a workshop for the Seacrest teachers and parents. I first met Eric Jensen when I attended his conference in San Diego in the mid 1980s. One of the rare educators to present the latest learning theories by integrating them into his own model, he infuses participants with an extraordinary array of tools to open and expand the potential of learners. In addition to conducting conferences for teachers throughout the world, Eric also established summer camps for teenagers and college students, called Super Camp, in which young people are empowered to break out of their own limits and discover for themselves how much more they can learn and do.

A few weeks after Eric left, Seacrest became the recipient of the 1992 Model School of America Award from "Turning Point for Teachers," an innovative, international educational organization founded by Eric Jensen.

These two endorsements helped to reaffirm our belief in Seacrest and helped us stay on the path to recovery.

On November 2, 1992, the final documents of the Seacrest Land Trust were signed by forty-one people. Together, we had passed through to the other side. It would be several years before the final debt would be repaid, with each year bringing its own set of new challenges to be met and overcome. But the crisis of 1992 was over. We had accomplished our mission through the courage, conviction, and generosity of scores of people who believed in the philosophy and goals of Seacrest. And we had done it by simply going on, one day at a time, doing what had to be done.

Reflecting back over all the events of that time, we began to view the circumstances in a different light and to see how crisis can serve. In a well-timed series of synchronistic events, the crisis symbolized the need for change and growth into our next stage. We had all become so accustomed to our benefactor's unsparing benevolence that it took a powerful jolt to yank us out of our complacency and into action. It took the stark reality of coming face-to-face with the possibility of losing everything to bring us together with a task as urgent and primary as keeping a roof over our heads.

Our quantum leap into interdependent responsibility is what George Land and Beth Jarman wrote about in their book, *Breakpoint and Beyond*, where they describe how a sudden and unpredictable change can mean either the decline and fall of an organization, or it can mean the renewal and the reinventing of a healthier, more stable enterprise. If the organization survives, it does so out of the combination and ingenuity of many who are willing to work together toward a common goal, with each person using his or her own specialized skill or talent to contribute to the whole. Ultimately, the crisis served as a wake-up call for us to put into practice what we believed to be true, and to put the principles of the Seacrest philosophy to the test.

Seacrest stood stronger and wiser than before. To all outward appearances, one would not have noticed any distinct changes in the day-to-day lives of the children and adults at Seacrest, either before, during, or after the crisis of 1992. No teachers had been cut or programs eliminated. Our first class of eighth-graders graduated that June. Our children remained secure and our families intact.

Contemplating the events of the year, I looked back at the gains and losses, some of which were deep and lasting and personal—the loss of my daughter's unborn baby and that summer, the death of my twin brother. In September, Hurricane Andrew carved out its destructive path from the east coast of Florida, cutting a swath through the Everglades, driving relentlessly on across Marco Island and Naples, into our own neighborhood, tearing off roofs and screens, uprooting trees and power lines, leaving them strewn helter-skelter like piles of match sticks.

And finally, I missed the familiar steadfast, optimistic presence of Lloyd and Norma Sheehan, the founders and benefactors who had given Seacrest its first ten years of life. Later in the year, after the Sheehans had retired from the board, the school held a ceremony to honor them, naming the original building *Sheehan Hall*.

But no fanfare or celebrations heralded the signing of the final documents of the land trust and the end of the crisis. The day slipped by in its usual fashion, like any other day. Seventh-graders were doing an experiment with flasks filled with a murky greenish fluid. Huddled in clusters, eighth-graders worked out an algebra problem at the marker board. Another student made a valiant attempt at mopping up a giant puddle of royal blue paint, spilled from a jar in the art class.

Prospective parents were guided by Lynne through the halls and classrooms. Computers clicked in muted accents. Four-year-olds padded softly up the hall, on their way to hear a story in the library. Children sang. Rhythm instruments tapped and clanged. The smell of popcorn wafted from a classroom where children snuggled against soft cushions, their feet tucked underneath as they lost themselves in their favorite book of the moment against a backdrop of Pachelbel's *Canon in D*.

The echoes of an extraordinary year faded into the distance, supplanted by the exquisite beauty of the images, sounds, and smells of what was an ordinary, peaceful Seacrest day.

Technology/Media Lab

Creativity in Motion

IX

WINDS OF CHANGE

What a Wonderful World!

CHAPTER 32

Mim

In October 1992, the Year of the Crisis, the winds of change swept Seacrest onto a new course, charting a passage to safety, steered by one who was well seasoned by experience, who loved a good challenge, and who was fearless in the face of rough seas. Miriam "Mim" Clark took the helm as chairperson of the Seacrest Board of Trustees and breathed new life into our small group of tired and weather-beaten trustees, transforming our unsettled agendas into instant order.

I first met Mim when I was a member of the music education committee for the Philharmonic Center for the Arts, an exciting new cultural center in Naples. As chair of this committee, Mim led with a combination of brilliance, experience, and wisdom. I was intrigued by the ease with which she listened and questioned, gathered information, and guided. She knew how to inspire and how to gain consensus and active participation from each member. She quickly honed in on individual interests or talents and dealt out assignments accordingly. Mim had mastered the art of directing a fast-paced meeting, moving through the agenda without getting bogged down in unrelated spin-offs. At the same time, she was always able to generate a flow of ideas. I would come home from these meetings inspired—and surprised at the length and breadth of a task I had so willingly volunteered to complete.

Mim's husband, Kenneth, attended the music committee meetings, and little by little, I discovered the background of the remarkable couple. Mim had been an associate dean at the University of Rochester and actively involved with most facets of education. She had led numerous boards and committees within a wide range of community groups, education and the arts. Later, I learned that Mim and Kenneth were not only coauthors of books about educational leadership, but they were considered among the top authorities of leadership training in business and high-level government. And they lived right in Naples.

Kenneth gained prominence as a leader and author in such diverse fields as science, psychology, technology, and higher education. As one of the driving forces behind the Center for Creative Leadership, Kenneth was instrumental in establishing international centers and networks designed to train the top CEOs of giant corporations, army generals, and world leaders to face more successfully the contemporary challenges of change and global crisis. He was consultant to the White House, the Office of Science and Technology, the Central Intelligence Agency, the National Science Foundation, the National Institutes of Health, the Veteran's Administration, the Army, and the Navy. And the listing is just a sample of Kenneth's achievements.

I invited Mim and Kenneth to visit Seacrest, and after a tour of the classrooms, keenly observing the children in action, they expressed enthusiasm about the school and its unique programs. Seacrest had sparked a resonant chord with their own philosophy of education. My respect for the Clarks continued to peak as I discovered that their personal and professional relationships included my most revered educational gurus. These were educators and philosophers whose books I had read and reread, underlining passages and turning down corners of pages— people like David Campbell and John Gardner, who had helped shape my philosophy and inspired much of my work.

One evening in late October, Mim and Kenneth, Jack and I had dinner at a small, cozy Italian restaurant, ideal for quiet conversations. Throughout the meal, I described the events and the status of The Crisis of 1992—the sudden loss of our benefactor, the debt, and everything that transpired through the year. I expressed our urgent need to find a strong and experienced leader for the board of trustees—one who understood the responsibilities of a well-run school board, (including those things that are *not* the responsibilities of board members).

Then came the time for me to ask the big question.

work at hand. Mim knew that real change could not be dictated from the top. For changes to be effective and lasting, there had to be a willingness from the groups within Seacrest. Mim mobilized small groups of people into teams. As individuals presented their ideas, she put them to work in carrying out their own proposals.

Empowering people even further, Mim added representatives to the board, from the Parent Teacher Organization, the faculty, the administrative staff, and key people in the community. Students were invited to board meetings to share their views, describe their activities, and to get a first hand view of how their school was governed.

Mim's belief in shared power and joint decision-making was an important part of the process. Although people tend to pay lip-service to the idea, putting it into practice is another matter. Once Mim had formed a team with its own mission, it was expected that the members would proceed on their own.

Another important attribute in bringing about positive change is a commitment to follow-through. Many times, people will agree to do something, only to find themselves over their heads or overwhelmed with the work of bringing goals into reality. Mim had a wonderful way of keeping us going with gentle nudges. Through a friendly phone call, a note or letter, or a meeting, she kept in touch with us and our progress.

Finally, Mim served as a role model for us with her energy and enthusiasm, dependability and persistence. We felt we had to succeed, not only for Seacrest, but for her as well.

Although the changes took long hours of hard work, Seacrest was lucky in that we did not have to fight the status quo. We had Mim as a master producer of change. We had board members who were not fixed in old ways. Most of all, we didn't have to wade through multiple layers of bureaucracy. We had the freedom to act.

The process took an enormous amount of time, energy, focus, and perseverance. I have often wondered what motivations prompted Mim and Kenneth to extend themselves so fully to Seacrest. I knew part of the answer lay in their belief that Seacrest held a better vision of education, with the potential of breaking new ground as a model for others. But their commitment went deeper. Perhaps they loved the challenge of The Crisis and of understanding the nature of change and knowing how to bring Seacrest into a new and healthier structure.

Perhaps it had to do with an innate drive and a passion to make things better for the larger purpose in which they believed. Seacrest had created the vision and had grown out of its infancy. The next stage was at hand, and with crisis as the catalyst, Mim and Kenneth were the beacons to lead our vessel to firm ground. With a new hull, rebuilt for the future, the passengers within could continue to grow and learn and evolve.

In their book, *Choosing to Lead*, the Clarks wrote:

> As conditions change, leaders have an obligation to initiate actions that ensure adaptation to new circumstances . . . Many sacrifice personal advantage because they have a compulsion to get things moving. Great leaders inspire their followers to believe, to expend more effort, and to accomplish great things that otherwise would not get done.

The passage is an apt description of the Clarks themselves: with Kenneth as a source of great wisdom, Mim as a pathfinder in leading us through a remarkable time of transition. She taught us to rethink our ideas and reframe our attitudes. She taught us to find the courage to stand for what we valued. And she taught us to pool our resources in providing a more solid foundation for the future of Seacrest.

CHAPTER 33

Everyday Rituals

One of the most revealing ways of discovering the inherent nature of a school is to know its rituals. One can gain the fundamental elements of the culture and customs, attitudes and values by the everyday rituals that evolve into traditions.

People often ask me to tell them about Seacrest. "How is it different from other schools? What do the teachers do and what do you teach the students?"

I usually answer their questions by telling them about the teachers first. About how information in the brochures fail to describe accurately what they do every day. I tell them that it does not matter how eloquently the school is described, nothing works unless you have the teachers who can make it happen.

Occasionally, I may boast a bit about the students. About Seacrest's former student, Katherine, making a perfect score on her SATs and winning a scholarship to Harvard. Or about Seacrest's undefeated Scholar Bowl team. Or pointing to how Seacrest won all the competitions at the Collier County Law Fair and mentioning the standing ovation the Seacrest Mini-Minstrels received at the national "America Sings" event in Orlando. I will tell visitors that Seacrest ranked in the ninety-ninth percentile on the national achievement tests in public and private schools of its size for the past several years; but only if they ask, because I believe there are other, more important indicators of success than what these tests show.

If they ask about parent involvement, I will describe some of the major functions of the Parent Teacher Organization, such as Grandparents' Day, Muffins for Mom, Donuts for Dad, Breakfast with Santa, the Seacrest Auction, the Walkathon, Golf Outings, Book Fairs, and the ways in which they help in the classroom.

The truth is, my words are barely skimming the surface of what goes on at Seacrest every day. None of my descriptions capture the real essence of what makes Seacrest special. You have to be there, in the classrooms or media center, on the playgrounds, or in the gardens. You have to see what is being discussed, researched, constructed, tested, and tasted in the classrooms, on the stage, in the art, science, and music labs. You have to listen in on parents' planning sessions or staff meetings or kids' conversations. You need to hear the music, watch the performances, listen to discussions, read the children's stories, and follow the classes on field trips. You need to experience the everyday rituals and the larger celebrations.

So when people ask me about Seacrest, I invite them to visit, because that's the only way they can really know. We never announce visitors to teachers, first of all, because people come to visit every day, and secondly because we believe people, especially prospective parents, have the right to see an honest picture of what goes on. Therefore, *I* never know what we will see when I take visitors on a tour of Seacrest. The children, teachers, and tutors barely notice the visitors, and are never interrupted with introductions or questions.

You might be amazed, as I often am, by what you see. It would not be unusual if you happened to visit on a day when Seacrest was celebrating one of its many rituals. For several autumns, an authentic Seminole tepee was erected outdoors on the south side of the main

Our Parents, always involved, always appreciated!

The Seminoles Come to Seacrest

building. A visitor that day would have seen a class of children sitting in a circle, inside the tepee. They listen to stories told by a Native American from the Seminole tribe, of past and present life in the Everglades. They tell of the early traders, the alligators, bears, and panthers; of rituals and sacred ceremonies; of building their chickee huts from palm fronds and canoes from cypress trees; of carving out a life in tune with nature.

On a stage inside the school, two women from the tribe show hand-carved tools and cooking utensils, beaded belts, headdresses, and necklaces, woven baskets and brightly colored, intricately designed hand-stitched dresses, shirts, and skirts.

If you visit on "Sharing Day" you would witness a simpler, but no less important ritual, especially to the younger ones. Here again, you never know what a child might bring to Seacrest to show and tell to the class. They bring everything from high-tech toys to newborn baby brothers or sisters, cocoons, lizards, snakes, or new puppies. Pogo, the

Pogo, the Seacrest Resident Pony

257

"Seacrest Pony," owned by the Ross family, appears on a regular basis to help celebrate special outdoor occasions.

The most astonishing treasure I ever witnessed for Sharing Day came from two brothers, whose mother had died the previous summer. The elder brother, a second-grader, greeted me one morning carrying a small sealed square package.

"Guess what I brought for Sharing Day," he asked, proudly holding the package before my eyes.

"Must be something pretty special," I acknowledged.

"Yep," he answered. "It's my Mom's ashes."

Speechless, I looked at the child's father. He told me that his son had begged and pleaded, finally convincing his father that it was something he needed to do. Not sure how the teachers would react, I told the child I would put the box on my desk for safekeeping until it was time for sharing. At half-past nine, I went into the class to initiate the discussion. We talked about the death of loved ones and different forms of burials and memorials.

Interestingly, none of the children showed any signs that the conversation was anything out of the ordinary. They all had lost grandparents, aunts, uncles, or pets, and they all had a story to tell about burials, funerals, and ashes scattered at sea or beneath a special tree.

The experience was an important sharing for all of us. The boy whose mother had died was able to tell his story. The children responded by connecting into their own experiences and sharing their stories. For me, it was a time of unexpected insights into the minds of children. Their stories need to be told, written down, re-enacted, painted or drawn— the memories revealed in ways of their choosing.

Seacrest becomes an extended family through its small rituals and large celebrations. Parents become best friends during the planning of big events. During the years when Patty and David took turns as president of the PTO, they each widened their circle of friends from North Naples to Marco Island, especially when it came time to plan our largest fund-raiser, the Seacrest Auction. Held once a year, the benefit raises money for scholarships and it grows to bigger and better dimensions each year. Soon after the auction is over, preparations for planning the next year's auction begin. In the fall, teams swing into high gear. The theme for the event is decided, reservations for a ballroom are secured at a local hotel, and publicity and marketing tools are designed.

In earlier years, Betty and Ann were usually in charge of decorations for the theme, spending weeks designing, painting, sewing, carving, and constructing layouts and backdrops. That was before Bob and Beverly Walbridge joined the faculty as Artists-in-Residence, and courageously agreed to take on the heroic and demanding task.

There are around twenty Seacrest parents who have steadfastly worked the auction every year. Although more recent parents have stepped in to lead the auction to greater heights, most of the loyal twenty still continue to toil through weeks and late nights of preparations. On the Friday evening before the auction, teams of parents lug in truckloads of items to display, handcrafted table decorations, dozens of palms and green plants, and giant backdrops depicting the theme for the event. They work most of the night, arriving back at dawn on Saturday, working right up to the minute when the ceremonies begin, escaping just long enough for a quick shower and change into formal attire.

The parents are all artists at what they do. Pieces of plywood, canvasses, cardboard, and bolts of fabric are cut, carved, sculpted, and painted into a masquerade ball, a tropical isle, a town from the old west, or an African safari. I come to help with some of the mundane tasks like unloading materials, refilling coffee pots, or bringing in sandwiches. Observing the artists at work from a distance, it seems impossible that they will pull it all together in time. But they always do.

These are the same people who year after year put together costumes for kids and paint backdrops for musicals. They organize golf outings and lug lemonade for the children during the Walkathon. They are the ones who run the book fairs and family picnics. They drive on field trips and arrange roller skating and pizza parties. They make exotic dishes for the International Festival. They create bazaars and carnivals.

I have known these twenty or so parents longer than I have known most of the Seacrest teachers. They were there when Seacrest was in its infancy. And they know me better than most. They have witnessed my mistakes and frustrations; nevertheless, their support remains constant. We know each others' private sides . . . our losses and victories, our flaws and virtues. We built the school together.

When new parents come, they are enthusiastically initiated into the rituals of Seacrest by our group of seasoned parents. They imbue the new ones with the importance of the rituals and before long, the new ones catch the spirit, recognizing the importance of celebrating the events that will be imprinted on their children's memory forever.

The dozens of activities that are repeated over time emerge into the rituals that form the character of Seacrest—the special flavor of who and what we are. A ritual can be as simple as midmorning snack or the Friday morning ceremony around the flagpole. Or the way we celebrate holidays, or grandparents, or new babies. Rituals are formed from the daily events that give meaning to the lives of the children and the people who serve the children.

Forty years from now when people recall their childhood days at Seacrest, they will remember the excursions into the community and distant cities, or the explorations of the Southwest Florida waters. They will remember their performances and festivals, projects and inventions, and the friends they made.

Parents will remember the playgrounds they designed and built; the fund-raisers they ran and the family picnics. They will look back at the stories, pictures, and research reports, each one marking the passages of their children.

Many of the rituals of Seacrest are characterized by the various forms of artistic expression. The arts unite the intellect with the senses to communicate through multiple channels, providing children the opportunity to dig beneath the surface of textbooks, to dissect and analyze the motives, customs, culture, causes, and effects of the times.

Most rituals are born from the intrinsic urge to identify with each other, to create a sense of community and belonging. They mold a communion with the past and build bridges through time. When visitors come, they will know the essential nature of Seacrest, not by what we tell them, but from the fullness of what they sense.

The lyrics and music of the "Seacrest Song" were composed, produced and recorded for Seacrest by my daughter Mary Jane and her husband, Pat. Although the song became a tradition for special ceremonies, it was the early childhood classes who claimed it as their own, integrating it into their regular rituals. Some of the sixth-graders considered the "Seacrest Song" too mushy for their worldly tastes. But when all the younger ones sing their lungs out to this song they know by heart, their parents all get teary-eyed and so do I.

Seacrest

You can sail the deep blue ocean in a ship made out of dreams.
You can climb to the top of a mountain, no matter how high it seems.
You can write a song so beautiful for everyone to sing.
Just use your imagination, you can do anything!

If you be the best that you can be,
Shine your light for the world to see.
Oh, Seacrest is a magical journey,
If you be the best that you can be, the best that you can be.

You can make a difference, if you just believe you can.
Then you'll set a good example, for every woman, child and man.
You can help to save our planet, save the water, save the trees.
You're a person strong and loving, full of possibilities.

If you just be the best that you can be,
Shine your light for the world to see.
Oh, Seacrest is a magical journey.
Just be the best that you can be, the best that you can be.

© Seacrest School. Words and Music by Mary Jane Alm and Pat Frederick

Love in Action

CHAPTER 34

Letting Go

In the spring of 1993, I summoned the board of trustees to hold an unannounced and unscheduled meeting on a Saturday morning. With an attempt to suppress my palpable sense of elation, I announced my resignation as head administrator of Seacrest.

Thoughts of when and how I could leave Seacrest had been uppermost in my mind for several years. Not only did I need a change, but I was convinced that Seacrest needed new direction with more vitality and energy than I had to give.

The answer finally came on a Friday morning as I stepped barefooted out on my deck. Still half asleep, sipping a cup of coffee and breathing in the freshness of the still, cool silence of predawn, my thoughts had gradually come into focus. The school year was nearing the end. Our five-year accreditation review was over, culminated by months of preparation by all the members of Seacrest. Mulling over the response from the visiting accrediting team, a sense of satisfaction settled over my body, bringing with it an unfamiliar state of non-urgency. Images began to form in a nonlinear, timeless space where details merged with wholeness.

In the sacredness of a new dawn, all my work at Seacrest appeared with an immediate clarity of vision. Its inception, the year of planning, the beginning years of Seacrest, the building and development, the teachers and parents. The children. Birth and growth. Goals and attainments. Death, grief, celebration, and victory. Crisis and perseverance. Completion.

As quietly as the whisper of a breeze brushing over my face, I knew with absolute certainty that my work at Seacrest was completed. There had been a beginning and a middle, and the end of my personal contribution was at hand. Seacrest had been conceived, birthed, nursed, tended, and protected from infancy to adolescent. Like the butterfly, Seacrest had progressed from the egg stage in which ideas are born, to the larva stage of creation. It had grown within a cocoon state, protected while the new creation was being developed. The final stage of transformation was at hand, ready to share its creation to the larger world of reality.

On that early predawn morning, Seacrest had revealed its secret: we had entered the next stage, signaling the call for the next leader to come in.

Euphoria exploded my half-slumbering state into instant alertness. Quickly showering, dressing, and eating a bit of breakfast, I grabbed my purse and books and dashed to school. Lynne would be the first to share my news. Lynne was the one who had listened patiently in the privacy of my kitchen to my sometimes desperate call for escape and my psyche's need for change. And Lynne was the one I counted on to become the next leader of Seacrest. She was as prepared to lead as I was to leave and the timing was perfect.

The board members agreed to honor my request to resign the post of school head, requesting that I stay on in an interim position during the transfer of leadership to Lynne, offering me the option of creating my own job, setting my own hours. Although thrilled to be able finally to let go of administrative duties, in my heart of hearts, I had some misgivings about staying on, despite the degree of freedom so generously offered. It seldom, if ever, works for the former leader to stay. Nevertheless, I agreed to remain at Seacrest for a time, primarily because Lynne and I had worked together for so many years.

The day after I moved out of my office, clearing my desk and walls of my personality, Lynne moved in, immediately establishing her own unique symbols. My primitive musical instruments, masks, and vividly animated pictures were replaced with tastefully traditional emblems of New England. I was not able to rest until I unloaded and put away all the traces of my former office. Fully expecting that after investing all my time, energy, heart, and soul into Seacrest for so many years, I would at some point feel the pangs of loss. But it never happened. Thus far, the only feelings are those of relief and appreciation for Lynne and the others who continue the work of Seacrest.

That June, Jack and I seized our new found freedom to take a carefree trip to Europe. When we returned, we could see the face of Seacrest changing. Within a short space of time, a new middle school facility was erected, including art, music, and science labs. The technology lab was upgraded, revamped and enlarged, in preparation for all students, including the youngest kindergartners, to go 'on line' with Internet.

When school began the following fall, my new position was confusing to us all, probably more so for me than anyone. Avoiding the administrative offices, I went about my selected tasks, tiptoeing through the school in a peripatetic state of uncertainty, anxious that no one would mistake my presence for being anything other than a positive support.

My duties included orienting the new teachers to Seacrest and assisting them through the process of completing the requirements for Florida certification. In addition, I was able to observe in the classrooms without interruptions or having to dash out to the next appointment. Taking in all the activities of the children and experiencing the incredible originality of each teacher brought a renewed sense of appreciation. And yet, I felt as if my presence was superfluous. Although the feedback I gave them was positive and specific, these were seasoned teachers who were well aware of what they were doing without my telling them. What I really needed to do was to make my exit as gracefully as possible and create my own space for something new.

Meanwhile, juxtaposed against my tired and frayed mind, Lynne had taken on the leadership of Seacrest with aplomb and positive action. A resurgence of new energy flowed from Lynne throughout the school community.

With Mim's guidance and a supportive board of trustees, Lynne and her teams adopted new rules, driven by logic and the principles of good business. *Accomplishment* was the goal. The dynamics of change were aimed toward successful results. The former freewheeling 'invent and create as you go' style that characterized the beginning stages of Seacrest gave way to a paragon of efficiency and excellence. Our tireless Mim never faltered until the debt from The Crisis of '92 was paid and the school secured on a solid financial base.

As the student population grew to 350, plans for new buildings were underway. The effects of expanded growth included results that were visible, measurable, and brilliantly executed. School-wide test scores soared. Students won local, state, and national awards within a broad spectrum of academic achievement, artistic talent, and athletic performance. In the annual Collier County Law Fair, Seacrest students racked up awards in all areas: expository and creative writing, multimedia, video, debate, and posters. Each year the number of students who qualified for the Duke University Talent Search Program increased. Numerous art contests were entered and won; works were shown in local banks, malls, and airports. For two consecutive years, Seacrest students took top honors in the all county Scholarbowl contest and the Environmental Education Consortium. Advancing into regional, state, and national competitions, Seacrest students were awarded honors in the highly creative Odyssey of the Mind Program, the Peace Education Foundation and gymnastics competitions. One eleven-year-old Seacrest fifth-grader represented the United States in a European sailing competition, qualifying as one of ten U.S. students in the nine to fifteen-year-old division.

The Seacrest tradition for direct experience and hands-on science, technology, and the arts escalated and expanded as middle-school learners went on-line via live satellite to speak and work with scientists in Hawaii and Russia.

Service to others was not forgotten. Still more meals were served to the homeless, more gardens planted, tended, and harvested; beaches were cleaned, new trees planted, nursing homes visited. Boxes were filled with aid to the families of Collier County's migrant farm workers. A dozen suitcases were packed with relief supplies for Bosnian children.

When Seacrest's Traci was diagnosed with Leukemia, young classmates gathered together, surrounding Traci with powerful bands of support, as if to proclaim that this one will not succumb, and nothing less than total healing will be acceptable.

Seacrest has preserved its rituals and its legacy as The School With a Heart. In coming of age, Seacrest has taken on a life of its own, as a living, breathing organism. Its insistence on creating whole minds and bodies with unlimited inner resources endures.

The importance of the new results-driven stage cannot be overemphasized. The time was right for moving into the larger arena of competitions and external rewards. With a new face lift, Seacrest was ready to take its position as the vanguard of learning. New goals and rules were created with clearly defined criteria to provide the kind of clarity needed as the school continued to expand and evolve. But as every new goal is mapped out for future plans, Lynne and her teams of administrators, board members and faculty return again and again to ask the central questions: What is the ultimate goal of education? What does Seacrest stand for, and *how* is its mission accomplished?

Through all the stages of Seacrest, we remember to pause and reflect and question. We remember to stay open to positive change and new ideas. We honor the talents and abilities of others, recognizing the importance of shared ideas and actions.

Once Lynne became the leader, I was able to stand on the periphery of Seacrest as the observer. I watched the metamorphosis of both the school and Lynne unfolding into a bolder, stronger prototype. From the outside looking in, I observed Lynne's inherent leadership abilities galvanize into self-confidence along with her talent for making decisions with skillful diplomacy. On the days when she is caught in the undertow of too much to do in too little time, Lynne speaks longingly of earlier, simpler times when her work was easier and less complex. I remind her that today's work is what she is called to do, and no one else can do it better.

Every leader carries his or her unique energy into the organization. When the time is right for change, the new leader comes in, bringing balance and new perspectives. When leaders are able to keep in tune with their own rhythm, they can stay in touch with the pulse of the organization, knowing when to let go, leaving space for the new cycle to begin.

My hope is that the story of Seacrest will serve as an invitation to others to share their stories, not as a remedy for all the ills of education or society, but as examples of breaking through old boundaries for positive change. I want to know the stories of hope, of taking risks to create new possibilities. Your stories can form an interconnected network to inspire others to put their dream into motion in re-creating a future that values imagination and new ideas. What remains to be discovered are the ways in which we can shed our biases and fear of change to include a larger world of tolerance and respect. Perhaps the best way to do this is through the simple act of listening without prejudgement. Viewed together, the ideas and stories of others present us with a rich reservoir of experiences from which to learn and grow.

Leaving Seacrest for me meant coming home to rest a while; to walk the beach and plant new seeds; to travel to new places and renew old friendships. Writing down the story of Seacrest was both a solitary experience and a way to reflect on the journey.

The words of a former Seacrest student say it for me. Sandra was fifteen when she went away for high school. By the time she graduated from eighth-grade, Sandra had spent almost as many years at Seacrest as I had, entering as a four-year-old in the infant stages of a new school. When Sandra returned home, her mom said the first thing she wanted to do was to go back and visit Seacrest. Afterwards, she said to her mom, "It takes getting away and looking back to really realize just how special Seacrest is." Those are my sentiments, exactly.

EPILOGUE

My most valued lessons have come from students, teachers, parents, and others who shared the journey of Seacrest. Here, I return them back to you as gifts, with the hope that you will pass them on to others.

To Students:

Always look for new learning and exciting adventures. Be curious about the world around you. Be an explorer. Use your imagination and your intuition along with your intellect. Discover your talents and your unique purpose. Doing what you love will give you clues.

Like the Olympic medalists, stick with your dream when you feel like quitting.

When everything goes wrong, go play, and then start again. Face your fears, take the risks to do the things you never thought you could. Honor your mistakes and let them be your teachers.

Find the people who can help you. Help someone every day. Have fun and play hard. Take good care of your mind, body, and spirit. Look inside for your own answers.

May you protect and nourish your planet.
May you respect others and always forgive.
May you remember your roots and always come home again.
Remember to call your mother.
Be kind.

To Parents:

Read books on parenting, then put them aside and do what works for you and your children. Trust your instincts. Have the courage to say no and follow through. Say yes as often as you can.

Teach your sons to express their feelings. Teach them how to cook. Teach your daughters how to pump their own gas and fix the plumbing—(things I never learned to do, but there is still time).

Plant a garden together. Tell your children stories about their grandparents. Tell them about your childhood adventures, including some (but not all) of the things you were not supposed to do. Make up songs.

Give them chores to do—every day. Give them plenty of time to play outdoors on their own. Give them all the independence they can handle. Let them clean up their own messes.

Let them do their homework and projects on their own. Let them make mistakes, and let them know yours. Try as hard as you can not to overprotect or rescue them from life's inevitable hardships. (A tough one!) Help your children's teachers in ways that you enjoy.

May you always remember you are your children's most important teacher.
May you be gentle with yourself, especially when they turn twelve-years-old.
Above all, may you teach your children kindness and respect.

To the Office Staff:

Your job description includes, but is not limited to the following: Extra pairs of ears, eyes, and feet to do all that you do; mechanical skills for keeping all machines up and running; ability to retain sanity when machines break down at the same time.

You remember to smile while communicating with ten or more people simultaneously. You remain calm with phones ringing; new parents waiting; children needing ice packs and Band-Aids; teachers wanting twenty pages copied; administrators expecting three-hundred letters to be distributed to classrooms; and lunches ready to be delivered.

You manage to keep track of administrators' appointments, knowing who comes next and why; rescuing administrators from long-winded conferences and salespersons; making administrators stop for lunch, even if there's no time for yours.

You have developed extrasensory perception in dealing with diverse personalities, knowing the importance of keeping personal information confidential.

In summary, even though it may feel as if you are the keepers of the zoo, in fact, you are the control center of communication. You are the guardians of the school.

May you carry your role as the gatekeeper of communication with pride, poise and composure. May you cherish your sense of humor as your most valuable ally.
May your computer never crash and may the copy machines run smoothly for a full month without breaking down.

To Custodians:

A good custodian is hard to find. A great one is irreplaceable. Of everyone in the school, you are the ones for whom there are no substitutes. Every day, you put your heart and soul, mind and body in bringing order out of chaos.

You take pride in your work, because you know this school belongs to you as much as to anyone. You make our lives easier and our work-spaces beautiful, healthy, and comfortable.

May your back remain as strong as your heart is big. May the pipes never leak and the power never fail. May the children never spill another jar of red paint.

To Teaching Assistants:

Know that you are the ones who make the journey smooth for everyone around you. You make ordinary tasks become extraordinary works of art. Your smiles and praise and extra attention make all the difference in a child's well-being.

Find the joy in selfless service. Believe in yourself. Tell the teachers how you feel. Learn from each other. You are masters at your work. Know that you are appreciated (in the classrooms, on the playground in sweltering heat, and *most* especially during lunch and in the After School Program). Remember to take good care of yourselves and each other.

May your days never rise above seventy-five degrees. May your new babies sleep through the night. May you finish your teaching degree, have your own class, and Teaching Assistant.

To Members of the Board:

You are the ones who preserve and strengthen the mission of the school. You guard and protect the responsibilities and freedom of the leaders and teachers. You empower them to act without fear of reprisal, setting the tone for collaborative participation.

You know and uphold the delicate balance between careful management and new opportunities. You assume your tasks with single-minded purpose. Your integrity and wisdom inspire mutual trust. You are the leader of leaders.

May those you serve reflect the trust and faith you place in them. May your successors follow the example you have shown. May your budget always balance and each new building be completed on schedule.

To Leaders:

The school and all that it represents are a reflection of who you are and what you believe. One only has to step into the hall to know that yours is a school with a difference. Your devotion radiates from the walls and reverberates with the laughter of children. It is reflected from the stories and poems, paintings, and projects.

Your love and energy is manifested into unlimited opportunities, in media, technology, scientific journeys, masterful productions. You have opened the way for new spaces and new dreams to be created. You lead with warmth and empathy, grace and wisdom. You know how to bring your vision into reality and your insight into others is a rare gift.

May your work continue to bring satisfaction. May your heart be strong and your burdens light. May each day bring you new inspiration, new dreams and possibilities. May you see the beauty in your work reflected in the ones you guide. May you be protected and sheltered, refreshed and renewed. Knowing your work is never finished, take time to play. (Come to my kitchen for lunch and ice tea.)

To Teachers:

You are the ones who make it happen. Like the gardener, you cultivate young minds and sow the seeds of new learning. You tend the growth with care and celebrate the harvest. You know the joy of loving other people's children and caring for them as if they were your own. You know how to inspire, encourage and heal.

Your classroom is a portrait of you and your teaching. The images you and your children create tell a powerful story of your character, your style, your personality. You each in your own way have framed a space for learning that reveals your strengths, your talents, your goals.

You know the wisdom of balance in your teaching. You recognize the differences in the way children learn and you use that knowledge to tap into the multiple channels of learning. You help your students find their own way and look for their own answers.

While educators continue to invent new systems of learning, new tools and techniques, you already know and practice many of the same ideas in your own natural setting, with no fanfare, modifying them in ways that work for you and your children.

You are not fooled into believing that any one tool, technique, or system is the answer to education. *You* are the ones who make the difference. It is your unique energy and your intuitive insight that know the way to the minds and hearts of the children you teach.

Appreciate the differences among each of you. Share your gifts and learn from each other. Remember the message inscribed on the rock that sat on my desk: *Nothing Here is Written in Stone*, and always remain open to the excitement of new learning and self-growth. Your students will absorb your excitement and it will serve them well throughout their lives.

The magical teacher is the one who knows the artistry of making connections. You are the makers of magic. You catch the dreams and bring them into reality, weaving a tapestry of wholeness and beauty.

May you always cherish the work you have created.
There is no other work of greater value.
May you honor the time you need for renewal.
May you walk in balance and harmony with others
in the rhythm of your own soul.

Photo Credit: Penny Taylor Photography

ENDNOTES

Chapter 1

1. Deborah W. Meier. (Excerpt from *Nation.*) "Drop the False Image of Education's Golden Past." *Utne Reader,* (January-February 1994), pp. 80-82.

Chapter 5

1. John H. Wood. "Restructuring Education: Designing Tomorrow's Workplace." Featured Essays from *Learning Organizations: Developing Cultures for Tomorrow's Workplace.* edited by Sarita Chawla and John Renesch. (Portland: Productivity Press, 1995), p. 404.

Chapter 9

1. Betts Richter and Alice Jacobsen, *Something Special Within.* (Sonoma, Calif.: DeVorss & Co., and Be All Books, 1978 and 1982).

Chapter 13

1. James P. McMullen, *Cry of the Panther.* (New York: McGraw-Hill, by arrangement with Pineapple Press, Inc., 1985).

Chapter 15

1. Robert H. Waterman, Jr., *The Renewal Factor.* (New York: Bantam Books, 1988).
2. Stephen R. Covey, *First Things First.* (New York: Simon & Schuster, 1994).

Chapter 16

1. Steven R. Covey, *The Seven Habits of Highly Effective People.* (New York: Simon and Schuster, 1989).

Chapter 17

1. John W. Gardner, *Self-Renewal, The Individual and the Innovative Society,* p.37. (New York: Harper & Row, 1965. Revised edition, W. W. Norton & Co, 1981).

Chapter 18

1. Tom Peters, *Embracing Chaos: How to Shake Things Up and Make Things Happen.* Six audio tapes. (Niles, Ill.: Nightingale-Conant Corporation).
2. Deborah Meier, *The Power of Their Ideas.* (Boston: Beacon Press, 1995), pp, 103,104.

Chapter 23

1. Roy Fairfield, *Person-Centered Graduate Education.* (Buffalo, N.Y.: Prometheus Books, 1977).
2. Barbara Shipka, *Leadership in a Changing World.* (Boston: Butterworth-Heinemann, 1997), pp. 127, 128.
3. Eric Jensen, *Super-Teaching.* (San Diego: The Brain Store, revised edition, 1998).

Chapter 24

1. Clint Van Nagel, Robert Siudzinski, Edward J. Reese, Mary Ann Reese, *Megateaching and Learning : Neuro Linguistic Programming Applied to Education, Volume I.* (Indian Rock Beach, Fla.: Southern Institute Press, Inc., 1985).
2. Karl Pribram, *Languages of the Brain.* (Englewood Cliffs, N.J.: Prentice-Hall, 1971).

3. Peter Russell, *The Brain Book.* (New York: E. P. Dutton, 1979).

4. David Bohm, *Wholeness and the Implicate Order.* (Boston: Routledge & Kegan, 1980).

5. Fritjof Capra, *The Turning Point: Science, Society, and the Rising Culture.* (New York: Simon and Schuster, 1982).

6. Joseph Jaworski, *Synchronicity: The Inner Path of Leadership.* (San Francisco: Berrett-Koehler Publishers, 1996), pp. 116; 182.

7. Mihaly Csikszentmihalyi, *The Evolving Self: A Psychology for the Third Millennium.* (New York: HarperCollins, 1993).

8. George Leonard, *The Silent Pulse.* (New York: Bantam Books, 1981).

9. Robert L. Fulghum, *All I Really Need to Know I Learned in Kindergarten.* (New York: Ivy Books, Published by Ballantine Books, 1988).

Chapter 26

1. Richard D. Sagor, "Three Principals Who Make a Difference," (in *Educational Leadership 49,* February 1992). pp. 13-18.

2. Kenneth E. Clark, and Miriam B. Clark, *Choosing to Lead.* (Charlotte, N. C.: Leadership Press Ltd., 1994), p.31.

3. ——Clark and Clark, *Choosing to Lead.* (Charlotte, N. C.: Leadership Press, Ltd., 1994), p. 22.

4. Robert C. Burkhart and David M. Horth, "Discovering the Unseen Leader." *Discovering Creativity: Proceedings of the 1992 International Creativity and Innovation Networking Conference,* edited by Stanley S. Gryskiewicz. (Greensboro, N. C.: Center for Creative Leadership, 1993), p.128.

5. J. P. Kotter, "What Leaders Really Do." *Harvard Business Review.* (May-June 1990), pp. 103-111.

6. George Land and Beth Jarman, *Breakpoint and Beyond.* (New York: HarperCollins, 1992.

7. A. Zalesnik, "Managers and Leaders: Are They Different?" *Harvard Business Review,* (May-June 1992), pp. 126-135.

8. Will McWhinney, *Paths of Change: Strategic Choices for Organizations and Society.* (Newbury Park, Calif: Sage, 1992).

9. Kenneth E. Clark, and Miriam B. Clark, *Measures of Leadership.* (West Orange, N. J.: Leadership Library of America, 1990).

Chapter 28

1. Howard Gardner, *Frames of Mind: The Theory of Multiple Intelligences.* (New York: Basic Books, 1983).

2. Deborah Meier, *The Power of Their Ideas: Lessons for America from a small School in Harlem.* (Boston: Beacon Press, 1995). pp. 111,112.

Chapter 31

1. Bill Martin, Jr., *Brown Bear, Brown Bear, What Do You See?.* (New York: Holt, Rinehart & Winston, 1967, Henry Holt & Company, 1983).

2. ___ *Ghost Eye Tree.* (New York: Henry Holt & Co., 1985).

3. Eric Jensen. For a complete listing of books, tapes, videos or information write The Brain Store, 4202 Sorrento Valley Road, Suite B, San Diego, CA 92121. Fax: 619-792-2858. E-mail: jlcbrain@connectnet.com.

4. George Land and Beth Jarman, *Breakpoint and Beyond, Mastering the Future Today.* (New York: HarperCollins, 1992).

Chapter 32

1. Kenneth E. Clark, and Miriam B. Clark, *Choosing to Lead.* (Charlotte, NC: Leadership Press Ltd., 1994), p.22.

BIBLIOGRAPHY

Armstrong, Thomas. *Multiple Intelligences in the Classroom.* Alexandria, Va.: Association of Supervision and Curriculum Development, (ASCD), 1994.

Armstrong, Thomas. "A Holistic Approach to Attention Deficit Disorder." *Educational Leadership*, 53 (February 1996), pp. 34-36.

Association of Supervision and Curriculum Development. *Challenges and Achievements of American Education, The 1993 ASCD Yearbook.* Alexandria, Va.: ASCD, 1993.

Bandler, Richard. *Using Your Brain for a Change.* Moab, Utah: Real People Press, 1985.

Bohm, David. *Wholeness and the Implicate Order.* Boston: Routledge and Kegan, 1980.

Buckalew, M. Walker. *High-Energy Teaching - Lifelong Personal and Professional Growth: A Plan you Can Live With.* Wilmington: Independent School Management, Inc., (ISM), 1993.

Burkhart, Robert C., and David M. Horth. "Discovering the Unseen Leader." *Discovering Creativity, Proceedings of the 1992 International Creativity and Innovation Networking Conference,* Stanley S. Gryskiewicz, ed. Greensboro, N.C.: Center for Creative Leadership, 1993, pp. 127-138.

Caine, Renate N., and Geoffrey Caine. *Making Connections: Teaching and the Human Brain.* Menlo Park, Calif.: Addison-Wesley, 1994.

Caine, Renate N., and Geoffrey Caine. *Education on the Edge of Possibility.* Alexandria, Va.: ASCD, 1997.

Capra, Fritjof. *The Turning Point: Science, Society, and the Rising Culture.* New York: Simon and Schuster, 1988.

Capra, Fritjof. *The Web of Life.* New York: Anchor Books/Doubleday, 1996.

Chawla, Sarita, and John Renesch, eds. *Learning Organizations: Developing Cultures for Tomorrow's Workplace.* Portland: Productivity Press, 1995.

Clark, Kenneth E., and Miriam B. Clark. *Choosing to Lead.* Charlotte, N.C.: Leadership Press Ltd, 1994.

Clark, Kenneth E., and Miriam B. Clark. *Measures of Leadership.* West Orange, N.J.: Leadership Library of America, 1990.

Clark, Miriam B., and Frank H. Freeman. *Leadership Education 1990, A Source Book.* Greensboro, N.C.: Center for Creative Leadership, 1990.

Covey, Stephen R. *The Seven Habits of Highly Effective People.* New York: Simon and Schuster, 1989.

Covey, Stephen R. *First Things First.* New York: Simon & Schuster, 1994.

Cowen, Emory L., ed., and Dirk A. Hightower. *School-Based Prevention for Children at Risk.* Washington, D.C.: American Psychological Association, 1996.

Csikszentmihalyi, Mihaly. *Flow: The Psychology of Optimal Experience.* New York: Harper Perennial, 1990.

Csikszentmihalyi, Mihaly. *The Evolving Self: A Psychology for the Third Millennium.* New York: HarperCollins, 1993.

Drucker, Peter F., Esther Dyson, Charles Handy, Paul Saffo, and Peter M. Senge. "Looking Ahead: Implications of the Present." *Harvard Business Review,* (September-October 1997), pp.18-32.

Ellis, Arthur K., and Jeffrey T. Fouts. *Research on Educational Innovations.* Larchmont, N.Y.: 1997.

Erickson, H. Lynn. *Stirring the Head, Heart, and Soul: Redefining Curriculum and Instruction.* Thousand Oaks, Calif.: Corwin Press, 1995.

Fairfield, Roy. *Person-Centered Graduate Education.* Buffalo: Prometheus Books, 1977.

Fowler, Charles. "Strong Arts, Strong Schools." *Educational Leadership,* 52, (November 1994), pp. 4-9.

Fulghum, Robert. *All I Really Need to Know I Learned in Kindergarten.* New York: Ivy Books, Published by Ballantine Books, 1986.

Gardner, Howard. *Frames of Mind: The Theory of Multiple Intelligences.* New York: Basic Books, 1983.

Gardner, Howard. *The Mind's New Science.* New York: Basic Books, 1987.

Gardner, Howard. *The Unschooled Mind: How Children Think and How Schools Should Teach.* New York: Basic Books, 1991.

Gardner, Howard. *Multiple Intelligences: The Theory in Practice.* New York: Basic Books, 1993.

Gardner, John W. *Self-Renewal: The Individual and the Innovative Society,* rev. ed. New York: W. W. Norton & Company, 1981.

Gates, Bill H. *The Road Ahead.* New York: Viking, 1995.

Goleman, Daniel. *Emotional Intelligence.* New York: Bantam Books, 1995.

Greenspan, Stanley I. *Playground Politics.* Reading: Addison Wesley, 1993.

Greenspan, Stanley I. *The Growth of the Mind.* Reading: Addison Wesley, 1997.

Gregory, Richard L. *The Oxford Companion to the Mind.* New York: Oxford University Press, 1987.

Gross, Ronald. *Peak Learning.* New York: Jeremy P. Tarcher/Putnam, 1991.

Gryskiewicz, Stanley S., ed.. *Discovering Creativity: Proceedings of the 1992 International Creativity and Innovation Networking Conference.* Greensboro, N.C.:Center for Creative Leadership, 1993.

Harman, Willis W., and Howard Rheingold. *Higher Creativity.* Los Angeles: Jeremy P. Tarcher, 1984.

Jaworski, Joseph. *Synchronicity: The Inner Path of Leadership.* San Francisco: Berrett-Koehler, 1996.

Jensen, Eric P. *The Learning Brain.* San Diego: The Brain Store,1994.

Jensen, Eric P. *Brain-Based Learning and Teaching.* San Diego: The Brain Store, 1995.

Jensen, Eric P. *Super-Teaching*, rev. ed. San Diego: The Brain Store, 1998.

Jensen, Eric P. *Teaching With the Brain in Mind.* Alexandria, Va.: ASCD, 1998.

Joyce, Bruce, James Wolf, and Emily Calhoun. *The Self-Renewing School.* Alexandria, Va.: ASCD, 1993.

Keefe, James W., and John M. Jenkins. *Instruction and the Learning Environment.* Larchmont, N.Y.: Eye On Education, 1997.

Kohn, Alfie. *Beyond Discipline*: *From Compliance to Community.* Alexandria, Va.: ASCD, 1996.

Kotter, John P. "What Leaders Really Do." *Harvard Business Review,* (May - June 1990), pp. 103-111.

Land, George, and Beth Jarman. *Breakpoint and Beyond: Mastering the Future—Today.* New York: HarperCollins, 1992.

Leonard, George B. *The Transformation: A Guide to the Inevitable Changes in Humankind.* Los Angeles: Jeremy P. Tarcher, 1972.

Leonard, George B. *The Silent Pulse.* New York: Bantam Books, 1981.

Leonard, George B. *Mastery: The Keys to Success and Long-Term Fulfillment.* New York: Plume/Penguin Books, 1992.

Martin, Bill. Jr. *Brown Bear, Brown Bear, What Do You See?.* New York: Holt, Rinehart & Winston, and Henry Holt & Company, 1983.

Martin, Bill, Jr. *Ghost Eye Tree.* New York: Henry Holt & Company, 1985.

Marzano, Robert J. *A Different Kind of Classroom: Teaching with Dimensions of Learning.* Alexandria, Va.: ASCD, 1992.

McMullen, James P. *Cry of the Panther: Quest of a Species.* New York: McGraw-Hill, 1984.

Means, Barbara, and Kerry Olson. "The Link Between Technology and Authentic Learning." *Educational Leadership,* 51, (April 1994), pp. 15-18.

Meier, Deborah W., Excerpt from *The Nation,* (September 21, 1992). "Drop the False Image of Education's Golden Past." *Utne Reader,* (January-February 1994), pp.80-82.

Meier, Deborah W. *The Power of Their Ideas: Lessons for America from a Small School in Harlem.* Boston: Beacon Press, 1995.

Meier, Deborah W. "How Our Schools Could Be." *Phi Delta Kappan,* 76, (January 1995), pp. 369-373.

Meier, Deborah W. "The Big Benefits of Smallness." *Educational Leadership,* 54, (September 1996), pp. 12-15.

Meier, Deborah W. "Can the Odds Be Changed?". *Phi Delta Kappan,* 79, (January 1998), pp.358-362.

Pelletier, Kenneth R. *Sound Mind, Sound Body: A new Model for Lifelong Health.* New York: Simon and Schuster, 1994.

Peters, Thomas J. *Embracing Chaos: How to Shake Things Up and Make Things Happen.* Taped Series. Niles, Ill.: Nightingale-Conant.

Peters, Thomas J., and Robert H. Waterman, Jr. *In Search of Excellence.* New York: Warner Books, 1982.

Pribram, Karl. *Languages of the Brain.* Englewood Cliffs: Prentice-Hall, 1971.

Prigogine, Ilya, and Isabelle Stengers. *Order Out of Chaos: Man's New Dialogue With Nature.* New York: Bantam Books, 1984.

Richter, Bette, and Alice Jacobsen. *Something Special Within.* Sonoma, Calif.: DeVorss and Be All Books, 1982.

Russell, Peter. *The Brain Book.* New York: E. P. Dutton, 1979.

Russell, Peter. *The Creative Manager.* San Francisco: Jossey-Bass, 1992.

Russell, Peter. *The Global Brain Awakens: Our Next Evolutionary Leap.* Palo Alto, Calif.: Global Brain, Inc., 1995.

Sagor, Richard D. "Three Principals Who Make a Difference." *Educational Leadership,* 49, (February 1992), pp. 13-18.

Schmoker, Mike. *Results: The Key to Continuous School Improvement.* Alexandria, Va.: ASCD, 1996.

Senge, Peter M. *The Fifth Discipline.* New York: Doubleday, 1990.

Shipka, Barbara J. *Leadership in a Challenging World: A Sacred Journey.* Boston: Butterworth-Heinemann, 1997.

Smith, Wilma F., and Richard L. Andrews. *Instructional Leadership: How Principals Make a Difference.* Alexandria, Va.: ASCD, 1989.

Van Nagel, Clint, Robert Siudzinski, Edward J. Reese, and Mary Ann Reese. *Megateaching and Learning: Neuro Linguistic Programming Applied to Education, Volume 1.* Indian Rock Beach, Fla.: Southern Institute Press, 1985.

Waterman, Robert H., Jr. *The Renewal Factor.* New York: Bantam Books, 1987.

Wood, John H. "Restructuring Education: Designing Tomorrow's Workplace." Featured Essay from *Learning Organizations.* Sarita Chawla and John Renesch, eds. Portland: Productivity Press, 1995, pp. 402-415.

INDEX